Sir J. Reynolds. O. Pelton.

MRS. SIDDONS.

AS THE TRAGIC MUSE

THE

POETICAL WORKS

OF

WILLIAM SHAKSPEARE;

WITH

NOTES

ILLUSTRATIVE AND EXPLANATORY;

TOGETHER WITH A

SUPPLEMENTARY NOTICE TO THE ROMAN PLAYS.

BOSTON:
PHILLIPS, SAMPSON, AND COMPANY.
1851.

CONTENTS.

1*

VENUS AND ADONIS.

"Vilia miretur vulgus, mihi flavus Apollo
Poculo Castalia plena ministret aqua."
Ovid.

TO THE

RIGHT HONORABLE HENRY WRIOTHESLY,

EARL OF SOUTHAMPTON, AND BARON OF TITCHFIELD.

RIGHT HONORABLE,

I KNOW not how I shall offend in dedicating my unpolished lines to your Lordship, nor how the world will censure me for choosing so strong a prop to support so weak a burthen: only if your honor seem but pleased, I account myself highly praised, and vow to take advantage of all idle hours till I have honored you with some graver labor. But if the first heir of my invention prove deformed, I shall be sorry it had so noble a godfather, and never after ear[1] so barren a land, for fear it yield me still so bad a harvest. I leave it to your honorable survey, and your honor[2] to your heart's content; which I wish may always answer your own wish, and the world's hopeful expectation.

Your Honor's in all duty,

WILLIAM SHAKSPEARE.

[1] *Ear*, plough.

[2] *Honor*. As a duke is now styled "your grace," so "your honor" was formerly the usual mode of address to noblemen in general.

VENUS AND ADONIS.

EVEN as the sun with purple-colored face
Had ta'en his last leave of the weeping morn,
Rose-cheeked Adonis[1] hied him to the chase;
Hunting he loved, but love he laughed to scorn;
  Sick-thoughted Venus makes amain unto him,
  And like a bold-faced suitor, 'gins to woo him.

"Thrice fairer than myself," thus she began,
"The field's chief flower, sweet above compare,
Stain to all nymphs, more lovely than a man,
More white and red than doves or roses are;
  Nature that made thee, with herself at strife,
  Saith that the world hath ending with thy life.

1 The poem of "Hero and Leander," although Marlowe's portion of it was not published till 1598, was probably well known in the poetical circles. The following lines are in the first sestyad:—

"The men of wealthy Sestos every year,
For his sake whom their goddess held so dear,
Rose-cheeked Adonis, kept a solemn feast."

"Vouchsafe, thou wonder, to alight thy steed,
And rein his proud head to the saddle-bow;
If thou wilt deign this favor, for thy meed
A thousand honey-secrets shalt thou know:
  Here come and sit, where never serpent hisses,
  And being set I'll smother thee with kisses;

"And yet not cloy thy lips with loathed satiety,
But rather famish them amid their plenty,
Making them red and pale with fresh variety,
Ten kisses short as one, one long as twenty:
  A summer's day will seem an hour but short,
  Being wasted in such time-beguiling sport."

With this she seizeth on his sweating palm,
The precedent of pith and livelihood,
And, trembling in her passion, calls it balm,
Earth's sovereign salve to do a goddess good:
  Being so enraged, desire doth lend her force,
  Courageously to pluck him from his horse.

Over one arm the lusty courser's rein,
Under her other was the tender boy,
Who blushed and pouted in a dull disdain,
With leaden appetite, unapt to toy;
  She red and hot as coals of glowing fire,
  He red for shame, but frosty in desire.

The studded bridle on a ragged bough
Nimbly she fastens; (O, how quick is love!)
The steed is stalled up, and even now
To tie the rider she begins to prove:
  Backward she pushed him, as she would be thrust,
  And governed him in strength, though not in lust.

So soon was she along, as he was down,
Each leaning on their elbows and their hips:
Now doth she stroke his cheek, now doth he frown,
And 'gins to chide, but soon she stops his lips;
  And kissing speaks, with lustful language broken,
  "If thou wilt chide, thy lips shall never open."

He burns with bashful shame; she with her tears
Doth quench the maiden burning of his cheeks:
Then with her windy sighs, and golden hairs,
To fan and blow them dry again she seeks:
  He saith she is immodest, blames her 'miss;[1]
  What follows more, she murders with a kiss.

Even as an empty eagle, sharp by fast,
Tires[2] with her beak on feathers, flesh, and bone,
Shaking her wings, devouring all in haste,
Till either gorge be stuffed, or prey be gone;
  Even so she kissed his brow, his cheek, his chin,
  And where she ends she doth anew begin.

Forced to content,[3] but never to obey,
Panting he lies, and breatheth in her face;

[1] '*Miss*, amiss, fault. So in Sonnet CLI.: —

"Love is too young to know what conscience is;
Yet who knows not conscience is born of love?
Then, gentle cheater, urge not *my amiss*,
Lest guilty of my faults thy sweet self prove."

[2] *Tires*, tears, preys. The image is to be found without variation in Henry VI. Part III. Act I. Sc. I.: —

"Revenged may she be on that hateful duke;
Whose haughty spirit, winged with desire,
Will cost my crown, and, *like an empty eagle*,
Tire on the flesh of me and of my son."

[3] *Content*, acquiescence.

She feedeth on the steam, as on a prey,
And calls it heavenly moisture, air of grace,
  Wishing her cheeks were gardens full of flowers,
  So they were dewed with such distilling showers.

Look how a bird lies tangled in a net;
So fastened in her arms Adonis lies;
Pure shame and awed resistance made him fret,
Which bred more beauty in his angry eyes:
  Rain added to a river that is rank,[1]
  Perforce will force it overflow the bank.

Still she entreats, and prettily entreats,
For to a pretty ear she tunes her tale;
Still is he sullen, still he lowers and frets,
'Twixt crimson shame, and anger ashy pale;
  Being red, she loves him best; and being white,
  Her best is bettered with a more delight.

Look how he can, she cannot choose but love;
And by her fair immortal hand she swears
From his soft bosom never to remove,
Till he take truce with her contending tears,
  Which long have rained, making her cheeks all
      wet;
  And one sweet kiss shall pay this countless debt.

Upon this promise did he raise his chin,
Like a di-dapper[2] peering through a wave,

[1] *Rank*, full. Rank is often used to express excess or violence generally; and rankness is applied to a flood, in King John, Act V. Sc. IV.:—

"And like a bated and retired flood,
Leaving our *rankness* and irregular course."

[2] *Di-dapper*. This is generally printed *dive-dapper*, without any

Who, being looked on, ducks as quickly in;
So offers he to give what she did crave;
  But when her lips were ready for his pay,
  He winks, and turns his lips another way.

Never did passenger in summer's heat
More thirst for drink, than she for this good turn:
Her help she sees, but help she cannot get;
She bathes in water, yet her fire must burn;
  "O, pity," 'gan she cry, "flint-hearted boy!
  'Tis but a kiss I beg; why art thou coy?

"I have been wooed, as I entreat thee now,
Even by the stern and direful god of war,
Whose sinewy neck in battle ne'er did bow,
Who conquers where he comes, in every jar;
  Yet hath he been my captive and my slave,
  And begged for that which thou unasked shalt have.

"Over my altars hath he hung his lance,
His battered shield, his uncontrolled crest,
And for my sake hath learned to sport and dance,
To toy, to wanton, dally, smile, and jest;
  Scorning his churlish drum, and ensign red,
  Making my arms his field, his tent my bed.

"Thus he that overruled I overswayed,
Leading him prisoner in a red-rose chain:

authority. One of the familiar names of the dab-chick is di-dapper; and this was the old poetical name. Beaumont and Fletcher, in "The Woman Hater," have a comparison of the mutability of fortune with this nimble water-bird: "The misery of man may fitly be compared to a di-dapper, who, when she is under water past our sight, and indeed can seem no more to us, rises again, shakes but herself, and is the same she was."

Strong-tempered steel his stronger strength obeyed,
Yet was he servile to my coy disdain.
  O, be not proud, nor brag not of thy might,
  For mastering her that foiled the god of fight!

"Touch but my lips with those fair lips of thine,
(Though mine be not so fair, yet are they red,)
The kiss shall be thine own as well as mine: —
What seest thou in the ground? hold up thy
    head;
  Look in mine eyeballs, there thy beauty lies:
  Then why not lips on lips, since eyes in eyes?

"Art thou ashamed to kiss? then wink again,
And I will wink, so shall the day seem night:
Love keeps his revels where there are but twain;
Be bold to play, our sport is not in sight:
  These blue-veined violets whereon we lean
  Never can blab, nor know not what we mean.

"The tender spring upon thy tempting lip
Shows thee unripe; yet mayst thou well be tasted;
Make use of time, let not advantage slip;
Beauty within itself should not be wasted:
  Fair flowers that are not gathered in their prime
  Rot and consume themselves in little time.

"Were I hard-favored, foul, or wrinkled-old,
Ill-nurtured, crooked, churlish, harsh in voice,
O'er-worn, despised, rheumatic, and cold,
Thick-sighted, barren, lean, and lacking juice,
  Then mightst thou pause, for then I were not for
    thee;
  But having no defects, why dost abhor me?

" Thou canst not see one wrinkle in my brow;
Mine eyes are gray,[1] and bright, and quick in turning;
My beauty as the spring doth yearly grow,
My flesh is soft and plump, my marrow burning;
  My smooth moist hand, were it with thy hand felt,
  Would in thy palm dissolve, or seem to melt.

" Bid me discourse, I will enchant thine ear,
Or, like a fairy, trip upon the green,
Or, like a nymph, with long dishevelled hair,
Dance on the sands, and yet no footing seen:
  Love is a spirit all compact of fire,
  Not gross to sink, but light, and will aspire.

" Witness this primrose bank whereon I lie;
These forceless flowers like sturdy trees support me;
Two strengthless doves will draw me through the sky,
From morn to night, even where I list to sport me:
  Is love so light, sweet boy, and may it be
  That thou shouldst think it heavy unto thee?

' Is thine own heart to thine own face affected?
Can thy right hand seize love upon thy left?
Then woo thyself, be of thyself rejected,
Steal thine own freedom, and complain on theft.
  Narcissus so himself himself forsook,
  And died to kiss his shadow in the brook.

" Torches are made to light, jewels to wear,
Dainties to taste, fresh beauty for the use,

[1] *Gray* is said to be here used as *blue*. We have subsequently —

" Her two *blue* windows faintly she upheaveth."

But the eye-*lids* are the " blue windows."

Herbs for their smell, and sappy plants to bear;
Things growing to themselves are growth's abuse;
  Seeds spring from seeds, and beauty breedeth beauty;
  Thou wast begot, — to get it is thy duty.

"Upon the earth's increase why shouldst thou feed,
Unless the earth with thy increase be fed?
By law of Nature thou art bound to breed,
That thine may live, when thou thyself art dead
  And so in spite of death thou dost survive,
  In that thy likeness still is left alive."

By this the love-sick queen began to sweat,
For, where they lay, the shadow had forsook them,
And Titan, 'tired[1] in the midday heat,
With burning eye did hotly overlook them;
  Wishing Adonis had his team to guide,
  So he were like him, and by Venus' side.

And now Adonis, with a lazy spright,
And with a heavy, dark, disliking eye,
His lowering brows o'erwhelming his fair sight,
Like misty vapors when they blot the sky,
  Souring his cheeks, cries, "Fie, no more of love!
  The sun doth burn my face; I must remove."

"Ah me," quoth Venus, "young, and so unkind!
What bare excuses mak'st thou to begone!
I'll sigh celestial breath, whose gentle wind
Shall cool the heat of this descending sun;
  I'll make a shadow for thee of my hairs;
  If they burn too, I'll quench them with my tears.

[1] '*Tired*, attired.

"The sun that shines from heaven shines but warm,
And lo, I lie between that sun and thee;
The heat I have from thence doth little harm,
Thine eye darts forth the fire that burneth me;
And were I not immortal, life were done,
Between this heavenly and earthly sun.

"Art thou obdurate, flinty, hard as steel,
Nay, more than flint, for stone at rain relenteth?
Art thou a woman's son, and canst not feel
What 'tis to love? how want of love tormenteth?
O, had thy mother borne so hard a mind,
She had not brought forth thee, but died unkind.[1]

"What am I, that thou shouldst contemn[2] me this?
Or what great danger dwells upon my suit?
What were thy lips the worse for one poor kiss?
Speak, fair; but speak fair words, or else be mute:
Give me one kiss, I'll give it thee again,
And one for interest, if thou wilt have twain.

"Fie, lifeless picture, cold and senseless stone,
Well-painted idol, image dull and dead,
Statue contenting but the eye alone,
Thing like a man, but of no woman bred;
Thou art no man, though of a man's complexion,
For men will kiss even by their own direction."

This said, impatience chokes her pleading tongue,
And swelling passion doth provoke a pause;

[1] *Unkind.* Milton applies the same epithet, in the same way, in his "Doctrine of Divorce:" "The desire and longing to put off an *unkindly* solitariness by uniting another body, but not without a fit soul, to his, in the cheerful society of wedlock."

[2] *Contemn* is here used in the sense of throw aside; as Malone explains it, "contemptuously refuse this favor."

Red cheeks and fiery eyes blaze forth her wrong;
Being judge in love, she cannot right her cause;
  And now she weeps, and now she fain would speak,
  And now her sobs do her intendments[1] break.

Sometimes she shakes her head, and then his hand,
Now gazeth she on him, now on the ground;
Sometimes her arms enfold him like a band,
She would, he will not in her arms be bound;
  And when from thence he struggles to be gone,
  She locks her lily fingers one in one.

"Fondling," she saith, "since I have hemmed thee here,
Within the circuit of this ivory pale,
I'll be a park, and thou shalt be my deer;
Feed where thou wilt, on mountain or in dale:
  Graze on my lips; and if those hills be dry,
  Stray lower, where the pleasant fountains lie.

"Within this limit is relief enough,
Sweet bottom-grass, and high delightful plain,
Round rising hillocks, brakes obscure and rough,
To shelter thee from tempest and from rain;
  Then be my deer, since I am such a park;
  No dog shall rouse thee, though a thousand bark."

At this Adonis smiles as in disdain,
That in each cheek appears a pretty dimple:
Love made those hollows, if himself were slain,
He might be buried in a tomb so simple;

1 *Intendments*, intentions. So in Othello, Act IV. Sc. II.: "I have said nothing but what I protest *intendment* of doing" The word continued to be used long after the time of Shakspeare.

Foreknowing well if there he came to lie,
Why there Love lived and there he could not die.

These lovely caves, these round-enchanting pits,
Opened their mouths to swallow Venus' liking:
Being mad before, how doth she now for wits?
Struck dead at first, what needs a second striking?
Poor queen of love, in thine own law forlorn,
To love a cheek that smiles at thee in scorn!

Now which way shall she turn? what shall she say?
Her words are done, her woes the more increasing,
The time is spent, her object will away,
And from her twining arms doth urge releasing:
"Pity" — she cries — "some favor — some remorse —"[1]
Away he springs, and hasteth to his horse.

But lo, from forth a copse that neighbors by,
A breeding jennet, lusty, young, and proud,
Adonis' trampling courser doth espy,
And forth she rushes, snorts, and neighs aloud:
The strong-necked steed, being tied unto a tree,
Breaketh his rein, and to her straight goes he.

Imperiously he leaps, he neighs, he bounds,
And now his woven girths he breaks asunder;
The bearing earth with his hard hoof he wounds,
Whose hollow womb resounds like heaven's thunder;
The iron bit he crushes 'tween his teeth,
Controlling what he was controlled with.

[1] *Remorse*, tenderness.

His ears up pricked; his braided hanging mane
Upon his compassed[1] crest now stand on end;[2]
His nostrils drink the air, and forth again,
As from a furnace, vapors doth he send:
  His eye, which scornfully glisters like fire,
  Shows his hot courage and his high desire.

Sometime he trots, as if he told the steps,
With gentle majesty, and modest pride;
Anon he rears upright, curvets, and leaps,
As who should say, Lo![3] thus my strength is tried;
  And this I do to captivate the eye
  Of the fair breeder that is standing by.

What recketh he his rider's angry stir,
His flattering "holla,"[4] or his "Stand, I say"?
What cares he now for curb, or pricking spur?
For rich caparisons, or trapping gay?
  He sees his love, and nothing else he sees,
  Nor nothing else with his proud sight agrees.

[1] *Compassed*, arched.

[2] *Mane* is here used as a plural noun. In a note on Othello, Act II. Sc. I., Knight justifies the adoption of a new reading —

"The wind-shaked serge, with high and monstrous *mane*" —

upon the belief that in this line we have a picture which was probably suggested in the noble passage of Job, "Hast thou given the horse strength? Hast thou clothed his neck with thunder?" The passage before us shows that the image was familiar to the mind of Shakspeare, of the majesty of the war-horse erecting his mane under the influence of passion.

[3] This is a faint echo of the wonderful passage in Job, "He saith among the trumpets, Ha, ha!"

[4] *Holla. Ho* is the ancient interjection, giving notice to stop. The word before us is certainly the same as the French *hola*, and is explained in Cotgrave's French Dictionary as meaning "enough, soft, soft, no more of that."

Look, when a painter would surpass the life,
In limning out a well-proportioned steed,
His art with nature's workmanship at strife,
As if the dead the living should exceed;
  So did this horse excel a common one,
  In shape, in courage, color, pace, and bone.

Round-hoofed, short-jointed, fetlocks shag and long,
Broad breast, full eye, small head, and nostril wide,
High crest, short ears, straight legs, and passing strong,
Thin mane, thick tail, broad buttock, tender hide:
  Look what a horse should have, he did not lack,
  Save a proud rider on so proud a back.

Sometime he scuds far off, and there he stares;
Anon he starts at stirring of a feather;
To bid the wind a base[1] he now prepares,
And whe'r he run, or fly, they knew not whether;
  For through his mane and tail the high wind sings,
  Fanning the hairs, who wave like feathered wings.

He looks upon his love and neighs unto her;
She answers him as if she knew his mind:
Being proud, as females are, to see him woo her,
She puts on outward strangeness, seems unkind;
  Spurns at his love, and scorns the heat he feels,
  Beating his kind embracements with her heels.

[1] In the game of *base*, or *prison base*, one runs and challenges another to pursue. "To bid the wind a base" is therefore to challenge the wind to speed. We have the same expression in the early play of the Two Gentlemen of Verona: —

"Indeed, *I bid the base* for Proteus."

Then, like a melancholy malecontent,
He vails[1] his tail, that, like a falling plume,
Cool shadow to his melting buttock lent;
He stamps, and bites the poor flies in his fume:
  His love, perceiving how he is enraged,
  Grew kinder, and his fury was assuaged.

His testy master goeth about to take him;
When lo, the unbacked breeder, full of fear,
Jealous of catching, swiftly doth forsake him,
With her the horse, and left Adonis there;
  As they were mad unto the wood they hie them
  Out-stripping crows that strive to over-fly them.

All swoln with chasing down Adonis sits,
Banning his boisterous and unruly beast;
And now the happy season once more fits,
That love-sick Love by pleading may be blest;
  For lovers say the heart hath treble wrong,
  When it is barred the aidance of the tongue.

An oven that is stopped, or river stayed,
Burneth more hotly, swelleth with more rage:
So of concealed sorrow may be said;
Free vent of words love's fire doth assuage;
  But when the heart's attorney[2] once is mute,
  The client breaks, as desperate in his suit.

He sees her coming, and begins to glow,
Even as a dying coal revives with wind,

1 *Vails*, lowers.
2 In Richard III. we have, —

> "Why should calamity be full of words?
> Windy attorneys to their client woes."

The tongue, in the passage before us, is the *attorney* to the heart.

And with his bonnet hides his angry brow;
Looks on the dull earth with disturbed mind;
  Taking no notice that she is so nigh,
  For all askance he holds her in his eye.

O, what a sight it was, wistly to view
How she came stealing to the wayward boy!
To note the fighting conflict of her hue!
How white and red each other did destroy!
  But now her cheek was pale, and by and by
  It flashed forth fire, as lightning from the sky.

Now was she just before him as he sat,
And like a lowly lover down she kneels;
With one fair hand she heaveth up his hat,
Her other tender hand his fair cheek feels:
  His tenderer cheek receives her soft hand's print,
  As apt as new-fallen snow takes any dint.

O, what a war of looks was then between them!
Her eyes, petitioners, to his eyes suing;
His eyes saw her eyes as they had not seen them;
Her eyes wooed still, his eyes disdained the wooing:
  And all this dumb play had his[1] acts made plain
  With tears, which, chorus-like, her eyes did rain.

Full gently now she takes him by the hand,
A lily prisoned in a gaol of snow,
Or ivory in an alabaster band;
So white a friend engirts so white a foe:
  This beauteous combat, wilful and unwilling,
  Showed like two silver doves that sit a billing.

[1] *His* for *its*.

Once more the engine of her thoughts began:
"O fairest mover on this mortal round,
Would thou wert as I am, and I a man,
My heart all whole as thine, thy heart my wound;[1]
For one sweet look thy help I would assure thee,
Though nothing but my body's bane would cure thee."

"Give me my hand," saith he; "why dost thou feel it?"
"Give me my heart," saith she, "and thou shalt have it;
O, give it me, lest thy hard heart do steel it,
And being steeled, soft sighs can never grave it:[2]
Then love's deep groans I never shall regard,
Because Adonis' heart hath made mine hard."

"For shame," he cries; "let go, and let me go;
My day's delight is past, my horse is gone,
And 'tis your fault I am bereft him so;
I pray you hence, and leave me here alone:
For all my mind, my thought, my busy care,
Is how to get my palfrey from the mare."

Thus she replies: "Thy palfrey, as he should,
Welcomes the warm approach of sweet desire.
Affection is a coal that must be cooled;
Else, suffered, it will set the heart on fire:
The sea hath bounds, but deep desire hath none,
Therefore no marvel though thy horse be gone.

[1] Malone explains this "thy heart wounded as mine is."
[2] *Grave*, engrave.

"How like a jade he stood, tied to the tree,
Servilely mastered with a leathern rein!
But when he saw his love, his youth's fair fee,
He held such petty bondage in disdain;
  Throwing the base thong from his bending crest,
  Enfranchising his mouth, his back, his breast.

"Who sees his true love in her naked bed,
Teaching the sheets a whiter hue than white,
But, when his glutton eye so full hath fed,
His other agents aim at like delight?
  Who is so faint that dare not be so bold
  To touch the fire, the weather being cold?

"Let me excuse thy courser, gentle boy;
And learn of him, I heartily beseech thee,
To take advantage on presented joy;
Though I were dumb, yet his proceedings teach thee.
  O, learn to love; the lesson is but plain,
  And, once made perfect, never lost again."

"I know not love," quoth he, "nor will not know it,
Unless it be a boar, and then I chase it:
'Tis much to borrow, and I will not owe it;
My love to love is love but to disgrace it;
  For I have heard it is a life in death,
  That laughs, and weeps, and all but with a breath.

"Who wears a garment shapeless and unfinished?
Who plucks the bud before one leaf put forth?
If springing things be any jot diminished,
They wither in their prime, prove nothing worth:
  The colt that's backed and burthened being young
  Loseth his pride, and never waxeth strong.

"You hurt my hand with wringing; let us part,
And leave this idle theme, this bootless chat:
Remove your siege from my unyielding heart;
To love's alarm it will not ope the gate.
Dismiss your vows, your feigned tears, your flattery;
For where a heart is hard, they make no battery."

"What! canst thou talk," quoth she, "hast thou a tongue?
O, would thou hadst not, or I had no hearing!
Thy mermaid's voice [1] hath done me double wrong;
I had my load before, now pressed with bearing:
Melodious discord, heavenly tune harsh sounding,
Ear's deep-sweet music, and heart's deep-sore wounding.

"Had I no eyes, but ears, my ears would love
That inward beauty and invisible;
Or, were I deaf, thy outward parts would move
Each part in me that were but sensible:
Though neither eyes nor ears, to hear nor see,
Yet should I be in love, by touching thee.

"Say, that the sense of feeling were bereft me,
And that I could not see, nor hear, nor touch,
And nothing but the very smell were left me,
Yet would my love to thee be still as much;

[1] *Mermaid's voice.* *Mermaid* and *siren* were formerly used as synonymous. So in The Comedy of Errors, Act III. Scene II.:

"O, train me not, sweet *mermaid*, with thy note,
To drown me in thy sister's flood of tears;
Sing, *siren*, for thyself, and I will dote."

For from the still'tory of thy face excelling
Comes breath perfumed, that breedeth love by smelling.

"But O, what banquet wert thou to the taste,
Being nurse and feeder of the other four!
Would they not wish the feast might ever last,
And bid Suspicion double-lock the door?
Lest Jealousy, that sour unwelcome guest,
Should, by his stealing in, disturb the feast."

Once more the ruby-colored portal opened,
Which to his speech did honey passage yield;
Like a red morn, that ever yet betokened
Wreck to the seaman, tempest to the field,
Sorrow to shepherds, woe unto the birds,
Gusts and foul flaws[1] to herdmen and to herds.

This ill presage advisedly she marketh:
Even as the wind is hushed before it raineth,
Or as the wolf doth grin before he barketh,
Or as the berry breaks before it staineth,
Or like the deadly bullet of a gun,
His meaning struck her ere his words begun.

And at his look she flatly falleth down,
For looks kill love, and love by looks reviveth:
A smile recures the wounding of a frown,
But blessed bankrupt, that by love so thriveth!
The silly boy, believing she is dead,
Claps her pale cheek, till clapping makes it red;

[1] *Flaws* is here used in the sense of violent blasts.

And all-amazed brake off his late intent,
For sharply he did think to reprehend her,
Which cunning love did wittily prevent:
Fair fall the wit that can so well defend her!
  For on the grass she lies as she were slain,
  Till his breath breatheth life in her again.

He wrings her nose, he strikes her on the cheeks,
He bends her fingers, holds her pulses hard;
He chafes her lips, a thousand ways he seeks
To mend the hurt that his unkindness marred;
  He kisses her; and she, by her good will,
  Will never rise so he will kiss her still.

The night of sorrow now is turned to day:
Her two blue windows [1] faintly she upheaveth,
Like the fair sun, when in his fresh array
He cheers the morn, and all the world relieveth:
  And as the bright sun glorifies the sky,
  So is her face illumined with her eye;

Whose beams upon his hairless face are fixed,
As if from thence they borrowed all their shine.
Were never four such lamps together mixed,
Had not his clouded with his brows' repine; [2]

[1] The windows are doubtless the eyelids, but the epithet blue is somewhat startling. We must remember that Shakspeare has described violets as

"Sweeter than the lids of Juno's eyes."

The propriety of this epithet is fully noticed by us in Cymbeline, Act II. Scene II.

[2] *Repine.* Used as a substantive. Chaucer employs *pine* in the same manner.

But hers, which through the crystal tears gave light,
Shone like the moon in water seen by night.[1]

"O, where am I?" quoth she, "in earth or heaven,
Or in the ocean drenched, or in the fire?
What hour is this? or morn or weary even?
Do I delight to die, or life desire?
But now I lived, and life was death's annoy;
But now I died, and death was lively joy.

"O, thou didst kill me; —kill me once again:
Thy eyes' shrewd tutor, that hard heart of thine,
Hath taught them scornful tricks, and such disdain
That they have murdered this poor heart of mine;
And these mine eyes, true leaders to their queen,
But for thy piteous lips no more had seen.

"Long may they kiss each other, for this cure!
O, never let their crimson liveries wear!
And as they last, their verdure still endure,
To drive infection[2] from the dangerous year!
That the star-gazers, having writ on death,
May say the plague is banished by thy breath.

"Pure lips, sweet seals in my soft lips imprinted,
What bargains may I make, still to be sealing?

[1] In Shakspeare's early plays we frequently meet the same image that is found in these early poems. Thus in Love's Labor's Lost: —

"Nor shines the silver moon one half so bright
Through the transparent bosom of the deep
As doth thy face through tears of mine give light;
Thou shin'st in every tear that I do weep."

[2] The custom of strewing houses with fragrant herbs was universal at a period when the constant recurrence of the plague habituated families to the use of what they considered preventives. It

To sell myself I can be well contented,
So thou wilt buy, and pay, and use good dealing;
  Which purchase if thou make, for fear of slips,
  Set thy seal-manual on my wax-red lips.

"A thousand kisses buys my heart from me;
And pay them at thy leisure, one by one.
What is ten hundred touches unto thee?
Are they not quickly told, and quickly gone?
  Say, for non-payment that the debt should double,[1]
  Is twenty hundred kisses such a trouble?"

"Fair queen," quoth he, "if any love you owe me,
Measure my strangeness[2] with my unripe years;
Before I know myself seek not to know me;
No fisher but the ungrown fry forbears:
  The mellow plum doth fall, the green sticks fast,
  Or, being early plucked, is sour to taste.

"Look, the world's comforter, with weary gait,
His day's hot task hath ended in the west:
The owl, night's herald, shrieks, — 'tis very late;
The sheep are gone to fold, birds to their nest;
  And coal-black clouds that shadow heaven's light
  Do summon us to part, and bid good night.

"Now let me say 'good night,' and so say you;
If you will say so, you shall have a kiss."

was this cause which rendered Bucklersbury at simpling time such a crowded mart.

[1] Here is one of the many traces of Shakspeare's legal studies — an allusion to the penalty for non-payment which formed the condition of a money-bond.

[2] *Strangeness*, coyness or bashfulness.

"Good night," quoth she; and, ere he says "adieu,"
The honey fee of parting tendered is;
  Her arms do lend his neck a sweet embrace;
  Incorporate then they seem; face grows to face.

Till, breathless, he disjoined, and backward drew
The heavenly moisture, that sweet coral mouth,
Whose precious taste her thirsty lips well knew,
Whereon they surfeit yet complain on drouth;
  He with her plenty pressed, she faint with dearth,
  (Their lips together glued,) fall to the earth.

Now quick Desire hath caught the yielding prey,
And glutton-like she feeds, yet never filleth:
Her lips are conquerors, his lips obey,
Paying what ransom the insulter willeth;
  Whose vulture thought doth pitch the price so high,
  That she will draw his lips' rich treasure dry.

And having felt the sweetness of the spoil,
With blindfold fury she begins to forage;
Her face doth reek and smoke, her blood doth boil,
And careless lust stirs up a desperate courage;
  Planting oblivion, beating reason back,
  Forgetting shame's pure blush, and honor's wrack.

Hot, faint, and weary, with her hard embracing,
Like a wild bird being tamed with too much handling,
Or as the fleet-foot roe that's tired with chasing,
Or like the froward infant stilled with dandling,
  He now obeys, and now no more resisteth,
  While she takes all she can, not all she listeth.

What wax so frozen but dissolves with tempering,
And yields at last to every light impression?[1]
Things out of hope are compassed oft with venturing,
Chiefly in love, whose leave[2] exceeds commission;
  Affection faints not like a pale-faced coward,
  But then woos best when most his choice is froward.

When he did frown, O, had she then gave over,
Such nectar from his lips she had not sucked.
Foul words and frowns must not repel a lover;
What though the rose have prickles, yet 'tis plucked:
  Were beauty under twenty locks kept fast
  Yet love breaks through, and picks them all at last.

For pity now she can no more detain him;
The poor fool[3] prays her that he may depart:
She is resolved no longer to restrain him;
Bids him farewell, and look well to her heart,
  The which, by Cupid's bow she doth protest,
  He carries thence incagéd in his breast.

"Sweet boy," she says, "this night I'll waste in sorrow,
For my sick heart commands mine eyes to watch.
Tell me, love's master, shall we meet to-morrow?
Say, shall we? shall we? wilt thou make the match?"

[1] The soft wax upon which the seal attached to a legal instrument was impressed, required to be tempered before the impression was made upon it. So Falstaff says of Justice Shallow, "I have him already tempering between my finger and my thumb, and shortly will I seal with him."

[2] *Leave*, license.

[3] No reader of Shakspeare can forget the pathos with which he has employed this expression in another place: "And my poor fool is hanged."

He tells her no; to-morrow he intends
To hunt the boar with certain of his friends.

"The boar!" quoth she; whereat a sudden pale,
Like lawn being spread upon the blushing rose,
Usurps her cheeks; she trembles at his tale,
And on his neck her yoking arms she throws:
She sinketh down, still hanging by his neck,
He on her belly falls, she on her back.

Now is she in the very lists of love,
Her champion mounted for the hot encounter:
All is imaginary she doth prove,
He will not manage her, although he mount her;
That worse than Tantalus' is her annoy,
To clip Elysium, and to lack her joy.

Even as poor birds, deceived with painted grapes,[1]
Do surfeit by the eye, and pine the maw,
Even so she languisheth in her mishaps,
As those poor birds that helpless[2] berries saw:
The warm effects which she in him finds missing,
She seeks to kindle with continual kissing.

But all in vain; good queen, it will not be:
She hath assayed as much as may be proved;
Her pleading hath deserved a greater fee;
She's Love, she loves, and yet she is not loved.
"Fie, fie," he says, "you crush me; let me go;
You have no reason to withhold me so."

[1] The allusion is to the picture of Zeuxis, mentioned by Pliny. We may observe that there was no English translation of Pliny so early as the date of this poem.

[2] *Helpless*, that afford no help.

"Thou hadst been gone," quoth she, "sweet boy, ere this,
But that thou told'st me thou wouldst hunt the boar.
O, be advised! thou know'st not what it is
With javelin's point a churlish swine to gore,
Whose tushes never-sheathed he whetteth still,
Like to a mortal[1] butcher, bent to kill.

"On his bow-back he hath a battle set
Of bristly pikes, that ever threat his foes;
His eyes like glowworms shine when he doth fret:
His snout digs sepulchres where'er he goes
Being moved, he strikes whate'er is in his way,
And whom he strikes, his cruel tushes slay.

"His brawny sides, with hairy bristles armed,
Are better proof than thy spear's point can enter;
His short thick neck cannot be easily harmed;
Being ireful, on the lion he will venture:
The thorny brambles and embracing bushes,
As fearful of him, part; through whom he rushes.

"Alas! he nought esteems that face of thine,
To which Love's eyes pay tributary gazes;
Nor thy soft hands, sweet lips, and crystal eyne,
Whose full perfection all the world amazes;
But having thee at vantage, (wondrous dread!)
Would root these beauties as he roots the mead.

"O, let him keep his loathsome cabin still!
Beauty hath nought to do with such foul fiends:

[1] *Mortal*, deadly.

Come not within his danger[1] by thy will;
They that thrive well take counsel of their friends.
  When thou didst name the boar, not to dissemble,
  I feared thy fortune, and my joints did tremble.

"Didst thou not mark my face? Was it not white?
Saw'st thou not signs of fear lurk in mine eye?
Grew I not faint? And fell I not downright?
Within my bosom, whereon thou dost lie,
  My boding heart pants, beats, and takes no rest,
  But like an earthquake, shakes thee on my breast.

"For where Love reigns, disturbing Jealousy
Doth call himself Affection's sentinel;
Gives false alarms, suggesteth mutiny,
And in a peaceful hour doth cry, 'Kill, kill;'
  Distempering gentle Love in his desire,
  As air and water do abate the fire.

"This sour informer, this bate-breeding[2] spy,
This canker that eats up love's tender spring,[3]
This carry-tale, dissentious jealousy,
That sometime true news, sometime false doth bring,
  Knocks at my heart, and whispers in mine ear,
  That if I love thee I thy death should fear:

"And, more than so, presenteth to mine eye
The picture of an angry-chafing boar,

[1] *Danger*, power of doing harm. So in the Merchant of Venice, Act IV. Sc. I.: —

"You stand within his danger."

See note on that passage.

[2] *Bate* signifies strife. Mrs. Quickly says that John Rugby is no breed-bate.

[3] *Spring*, bud, or young shoot.

Under whose sharp fangs on his back doth lie
An image like thyself, all stained with gore;
  Whose blood upon the fresh flowers being shed
  Doth make them droop with grief, and hang the head.

"What should I do, seeing thee so indeed,
That tremble at the imagination?
The thought of it doth make my faint heart bleed,
And fear doth teach it divination:
  I prophesy thy death, my living sorrow,
  If thou encounter with the boar to-morrow.

"But if thou needs wilt hunt, be ruled by me;
Uncouple at the timorous, flying hare,
Or at the fox, which lives by subtilty,
Or at the roe, which no encounter dare:
  Pursue these fearful creatures o'er the downs,
  And on thy well-breathed horse keep with thy hounds.

"And when thou hast on foot the purblind hare,
Mark the poor wretch, to overshoot[1] his troubles,
How he outruns the wind, and with what care
He cranks[2] and crosses with a thousand doubles:
  The many musits[3] through the which he goes
  Are like a labyrinth to amaze his foes.

1 *Overshoot.* The original editions read *overshut.* This reading is retained by Malone.

2 *Cranks*, winds. So in Henry IV. Part I.: —

"See how this river comes me cranking in."

3 *Musits.* The term is explained in Markham's "Gentlemen's Academy," 1595: "We term the place where she [the hare] sitteth her form; the place through which she goes to relief her musit."

"Sometime he runs among a flock of sheep,
To make the cunning hounds mistake their smell,
And sometime where earth-delving conies keep,[1]
To stop the loud pursuers in their yell;
And sometime sorteth[2] with a herd of deer;
Danger deviseth shifts; wit waits on fear:

"For there his smell with others being mingled,
The hot scent-snuffing hounds are driven to doubt,
Ceasing their clamorous cry till they have singled
With much ado the cold fault cleanly out;
Then do they spend their mouths: Echo replies,
As if another chase were in the skies.

"By this, poor Wat, far off upon a hill,
Stands on his hinder legs with listening ear,
To hearken if his foes pursue him still;
Anon their loud alarums he doth hear;
And now his grief may be comparéd well
To one sore sick that hears the passing-bell.

"Then shalt thou see the dew-bedabbled wretch
Turn, and return, indenting with the way;
Each envious brier his weary legs doth scratch,
Each shadow makes him stop, each murmur stay:
For misery is trodden on by many,
And being low, never relieved by any.

"Lie quietly, and hear a little more;
Nay, do not struggle, for thou shalt not rise;
To make thee hate the hunting of the boar,
Unlike myself thou hear'st me moralize,[3]

1 *Keep*, dwell. 2 *Sorteth*, consorteth.
3 *Moralize*, comment.

Applying this to that, and so to so;
For love can comment upon every woe.

"Where did I leave?"—"No matter where," quoth he;
"Leave me, and then the story aptly ends:
The night is spent."—"Why, what of that?" quoth she.
"I am," quoth he, "expected of my friends;
And now 'tis dark, and going I shall fall."
"In night," quoth she, "desire sees best of all.

"But if thou fall, O, then imagine this,
The earth in love with thee thy footing trips,
And all is but to rob thee of a kiss.
Rich preys make true men thieves; so do thy lips
Make modest Dian cloudy and forlorn,
Lest she should steal a kiss, and die forsworn.

"Now of this dark night I perceive the reason:
Cynthia for shame obscures her silver shine,
Till forging nature be condemn'd of treason,
For stealing mounds from heaven that were divine,
Wherein she framed thee in high heaven's despite,
To shame the sun by day, and her by night.

"And therefore hath she bribed the Destinies,
To cross the curious workmanship of nature,
To mingle beauty with infirmities,
And pure perfection with impure defeature;
Making it subject to the tyranny
Of mad mischances and much misery;

"As burning fevers, agues pale and faint,
Life-poisoning pestilence, and frenzies wood,[1]

[1] *Wood*, mad.

The marrow-eating sickness, whose attaint
Disorder breeds by heating of the blood:
  Surfeits, imposthumes, grief, and damned despair,
  Swear Nature's death for framing thee so fair.

"And not the least of all these maladies,
But in one minute's fight brings beauty under:
Both favor, savor, hue, and qualities,
Whereat the impartial gazer late did wonder,
  Are on the sudden wasted, thawed, and done,[1]
  As mountain-snow melts with the midday sun.

"Therefore despite of fruitless chastity,
Love-lacking vestals, and self-loving nuns,
That on the earth would breed a scarcity
And barren dearth of daughters and of sons,
  Be prodigal: the lamp that burns by night
  Dries up his oil to lend the world his light.

"What is thy body but a swallowing grave,
Seeming to bury that posterity
Which by the rights of time thou needs must have,
If thou destroy them not in dark obscurity?
  If so, the world will hold thee in disdain,
  Sith in thy pride so fair a hope is slain.

"So in thyself thyself art made away;
A mischief worse than civil home-bred strife,
Or theirs whose desperate hands themselves do slay,
Or butcher-sire, that reaves his son of life
  Foul cankering rust the hidden treasure frets,
  But gold that's put to use more gold begets.'

[1] *Done*, destroyed.

"Nay, then," quoth Adon, "you will fall again
Into your idle, over-handled theme;
The kiss I gave you is bestowed in vain,
And all in vain you strive against the stream;
For by this blacked-faced night, desire's foul nurse,
Your treatise makes me like you worse and worse.

"If love have lent you twenty thousand tongues,
And every tongue more moving than your own,
Bewitching like the wanton mermaid's songs,
Yet from mine ear the tempting tune is blown;
For know, my heart stands armèd in mine ear,
And will not let a false sound enter there;

"Lest the deceiving harmony should run
Into the quiet closure of my breast;
And then my little heart were quite undone,
In his bedchamber to be barred of rest.
No, lady, no; my heart longs not to groan,
But soundly sleeps, while now it sleeps alone.

"What have you urged that I cannot reprove?
The path is smooth that leadeth on to danger;
I hate not love, but your device in love,
That lends embracements unto every stranger.
You do it for increase; O strange excuse!
When reason is the bawd to lust's abuse.

"Call it not love, for love to heaven is fled,
Since sweating lust on earth usurped his name;
Under whose simple semblance he hath fed
Upon fresh beauty, blotting it with blame;
Which the hot tyrant stains, and soon bereaves,
As caterpillars do the tender leaves.

"Love comforteth like sunshine after rain,
But lust's effect is tempest after sun;
Love's gentle spring doth always fresh remain,
Lust's winter comes ere summer half be done.
  Love surfeits not; lust like a glutton dies:
  Love is all truth; lust full of forgéd lies.

"More I could tell, but more I dare not say;
The text is old, the orator too green.
Therefore in sadness, now I will away;
My face is full of shame, my heart of teen;[1]
  Mine ears that to your wanton talk attended
  Do burn themselves for having so offended."

With this he breaketh from the sweet embrace
Of those fair arms which bound him to her breast,
And homeward through the dark laund[2] runs apace;
Leaves Love upon her back deeply distressed.
  Look how a bright star shooteth from the sky,
  So glides he in the night from Venus' eye;

Which after him she darts, as one on shore
Gazing upon a late-embarkéd friend,
Till the wild waves will have him seen no more,
Whose ridges with the meeting clouds contend;
  So did the merciless and pitchy night
  Fold in the object that did feed her sight.

1 *Teen*, grief.

2 *Laund*, lawn. Camden describes a lawn as a plain among trees, and the epithet *dark* confirms this explanation. We have such a scene in Henry VI. Part III. Act III.: —

"Under this thick-grown brake we'll shroud ourselves,
For through this laund anon the deer will come."

Whereat amazed, as one that unaware
Hath dropped a precious jewel in the flood,
Or 'stonished as night-wanderers often are,
Their light blown out in some mistrustful wood;
  Even so confounded in the dark she lay,
  Having lost the fair discovery of her way.

And now she beats her heart, whereat it groans,
That all the neighbor-caves, as seeming troubled,
Make verbal repetition of her moans;
Passion on passion deeply is redoubled:
  "Ah me!" she cries, and twenty times, "woe, woe!"
  And twenty echoes twenty times cry so.

She, marking them, begins a wailing note,
And sings extemp'rally a woful ditty;
How love makes young men thrall, and old men dote;
How love is wise in folly, foolish-witty:
  Her heavy anthem still concludes in woe,
  And still the choir of echoes answer[1] so.

Her song was tedious, and outwore the night,
For lovers' hours are long, though seeming short:

[1] *Answer.* So the original. Mr. Dyce, who is a careful collator of copies, prints *answers.* No doubt, according to the rules of modern construction, answers is more correct, and Malone talks of Shakspeare having fallen into the error of "hasty writers, who are deceived by the noun immediately preceding the verb being in the plural number." We hold that to be a false refinement which destroys the landmarks of an age's phraseology. Ben Jonson, in his "English Grammar," lays down as a rule that "nouns signifying a multitude, though they be of the singular number, require a verb plural." The rule would appear still more reasonable when the plural is more apparently expressed in the noun of multitude, as in the form before us — "the choir of echoes."

If pleased themselves, others, they think, delight
In such like circumstance, with such like sport:
  Their copious stories, oftentimes begun,
  End without audience, and are never done.

For who hath she to spend the night withal,
But idle sounds resembling parasites,
Like shrill-tongued tapsters answering every call,
Soothing the humor of fantastic wits?
  She says, "'tis so:" they answer all, "'tis so;"
  And would say after her if she said "no."

Lo! here the gentle lark, weary of rest,
From his moist cabinet mounts up on high,
And wakes the morning, from whose silver breast
The sun ariseth in his majesty;
  Who doth the world so gloriously behold,
  The cedar-tops and hills seem burnished gold.

Venus salutes him with this fair good-morrow:
"O thou clear god, and patron of all light,
From whom each lamp and shining star doth borrow
The beauteous influence that makes him bright,
  There lives a son, that sucked an earthly mother,
  May lend thee light, as thou dost lend to other."

This said, she hasteth to a myrtle grove,
Musing the morning is so much o'erworn,
And yet she hears no tidings of her love:
She harkens for his hounds, and for his horn:
  Anon she hears them chant it lustily,
  And all in haste she coasteth[1] to the cry.

[1] *Coasteth*, advanceth.

And as she runs, the bushes in the way
Some catch her by the neck, some kiss her face,
Some twine about her thigh to make her stay;
She wildly breaketh from their strict embrace,
 Like a milch doe, whose swelling dugs do ache,
 Hasting to feed her fawn, hid in some brake.

By this she hears the hounds are at a bay,
Whereat she starts, like one that spies an adder
Wreathed up in fatal folds, just in his way,
The fear whereof doth make him shake and shudder;
 Even so the timorous yelping of the hounds
 Appals her senses, and her spright confounds.

For now she knows it is no gentle chase,
But the blunt boar, rough bear, or lion proud,
Because the cry remaineth in one place,
Where fearfully the dogs exclaim aloud:
 Finding their enemy to be so curst,
 They all strain court'sy who shall cope him first.

This dismal cry rings sadly in her ear,
Through which it enters to surprise her neart,
Who, overcome by doubt and bloodless fear,
With cold-pale[1] weakness numbs each feeling part:
 Like soldiers, when their captain once doth yield,
 They basely fly, and dare not stay the field.

Thus stands she in a trembling ecstasy;
Till, cheering up her senses sore-dismayed,

[1] *Cold-pale.* The hyphen denoting the compound adjective is marked in the original edition of 1593.

[2] *Sore-dismayed.* This is the reading of the edition of 1596. The original has *all* dismayed.

She tells them 'tis a causeless fantasy,
And childish error that they are afraid;
Bids them leave quaking, bids them fear no more; —
And with that word she spied the hunted boar;

Whose frothy mouth, bepainted all with red,
Like milk and blood being mingled both together,
A second fear through all her sinews spread,
Which madly hurries her she knows not whither:
This way she runs, and now she will no further,
But back retires, to rate the boar for murther.

A thousand spleens bear her a thousand ways;
She treads the path that she untreads again;
Her more than haste is mated[1] with delays,
Like the proceedings of a drunken brain,
Full of respect,[2] yet nought at all respecting,
In hand with all things, nought at all effecting.

Here kennelled in a brake she finds a hound,
And asks the weary caitiff for his master;
And there another licking of his wound,
'Gainst venomed sores the only sovereign plaster;
And here she meets another sadly scowling,
To whom she speaks, and he replies with howling.

When he hath ceased his ill-resounding noise,
Another flap-mouthed mourner, black and grim,
Against the welkin volleys out his voice;
Another and another answer him,
Clapping their proud tails to the ground below,
Shaking their scratched ears, bleeding as they go.

[1] *Mated*, confounded.

[2] *Respect*, circumspection.

Look, how the world's poor people are amazed,
At apparitions, signs, and prodigies,
Whereon with fearful eyes they long have gazed,
Infusing them with dreadful prophecies:
  So she at these sad signs draws up her breath,
  And, sighing it again, exclaims on Death.

"Hard-favored tyrant, ugly, meagre, lean,
Hateful divorce of love," (thus chides she Death,)
"Grim-grinning ghost, earth's worm, what, dost thou mean
To stifle beauty, and to steal his breath,
  Who when he lived, his breath and beauty set
  Gloss on the rose, smell to the violet?

"If he be dead, — O, no, it cannot be,
Seeing his beauty, thou shouldst strike at it —
O, yes, it may; thou hast no eyes to see,
But hatefully at random dost thou hit.
  Thy mark is feeble age; but thy false dart
  Mistakes that aim, and cleaves an infant's heart.

"Hadst thou but bid beware, then he had spoke,
And hearing him thy power had lost his [1] power.
The Destinies will curse thee for this stroke;
They bid thee crop a weed, thou pluck'st a flower:
  Love's golden arrow at him should have fled,
  And not Death's ebon dart, to strike him dead.[2]

[1] *His* for *its*.

[2] Boswell has quoted a passage from Massinger's "Virgin Martyr," alluding, as Shakspeare here does, to the beautiful fable of Cupid and death exchanging arrows: —

> "Strange affecticn!
> Cupid once more hath changed his shafts with Death,
> And kills, instead of giving life."

"Dost thou drink tears, that thou provok'st such
weeping?
What may a heavy groan advantage thee?
Why hast thou cast into eternal sleeping
Those eyes that taught all other eyes to see?
Now Nature cares not for thy mortal vigor,
Since her best work is ruined with thy rigor."

Here overcome, as one full of despair,
She vailed[1] her eyelids, who, like sluices, stopped
The crystal tide that from her two cheeks fair
In the sweet channel of her bosom dropped;
But through the floodgates breaks the silver rain,
And with his strong course opens them again.

O, how her eyes and tears did lend and borrow!
Her eyes seen in the tears, tears in her eye;
Both crystals, where they viewed each other's sorrow,
Sorrow, that friendly sighs sought still to dry;
But like a stormy day, now wind, now rain,
Sighs dry her cheeks, tears make them wet again.

Variable passions throng her constant woe,
As striving who should best become her grief;
All entertained, each passion labors so
That every present sorrow seemeth chief,
But none is best; then join they all together,
Like many clouds consulting for foul weather.

By this, far off she hears some huntsmen hollo:[2]
A nurse's song ne'er pleased her babe so well:

[1] *Vailed*, lowered.

[2] *Hollo*, or hollow, is not quite the same word as *holla*, which we have already noticed, although the usual spelling of this word in the passage before us is *holla*.

The dire imagination she did follow
This sound of hope doth labor to expel;
  For now reviving joy bids her rejoice,
  And flatters her it is Adonis' voice.

Whereat her tears began to turn their tide,
Being prisoned in her eye, like pearls in glass;
Yet sometimes falls an orient drop beside,
Which her cheek melts, as scorning it should pass,
  To wash the foul face of the sluttish ground,
  Who is but drunken when she seemeth drowned.

O, hard-believing love, how strange it seems
Not to believe, and yet too credulous!
Thy weal and woe are both of them extremes,
Despair and hope make thee ridiculous:
  The one doth flatter thee in thoughts unlikely,
  In likely thoughts the other kills thee quickly.

Now she unweaves the web that she hath wrought;
Adonis lives, and Death is not to blame;
It was not she that called him all-to[1] naught;
Now she adds honors to his hateful name;
  She clepes him king of graves, and grave for kings,
  Imperious supreme of all mortal things.

"No, no," quoth she, "sweet Death, I did but jest;
Yet pardon me, I felt a kind of fear,
Whenas I met the boar, that bloody beast,
Which knows no pity, but is still severe;
  Then, gentle shadow, (truth I must confess,)
  I railed on thee, fearing my love's decease.

[1] *All-to.* Mr. Dyce explains this as entirely, altogether.

"'Tis not my fault: the boar provoked my tongue;
Be wreaked on him, invisible commander;
'Tis he, foul creature, that hath done thee wrong;
I did but act, he's author of thy slander;
Grief hath two tongues, and never woman yet
Could rule them both, without ten women's wit."

Thus, hoping that Adonis is alive,
Her rash suspect she doth extenuate;
And that his beauty may the better thrive,
With Death she humbly doth insinuate;
Tells him of trophies, statues, tombs; and stories
His victories, his triumphs, and his glories.

"O Jove," quoth she, "how much a fool was I,
To be of such a weak and silly mind,
To wail his death who lives, and must not die,
Till mutual overthrow of mortal kind!
For he being dead, with him is beauty slain,
And, beauty dead, black chaos comes again.[1]

"Fie, fie, fond love, thou art so full of fear
As one with treasure laden, hemmed with thieves;
Trifles, unwitnesséd with eye or ear,
Thy coward heart with false bethinking grieves."
Even at this word she hears a merry horn,
Whereat she leaps that was but late forlorn.

As falcon to the lure away she flies;
The grass stoops not, she treads on it so light;

[1] Shakspeare, in his greater works, was not ashamed to recur to the treasury of his early thoughts: —

"Excellent wretch! Perdition catch my soul,
But I do love thee! and when I love thee not
Chaos is come again."

And in her haste unfortunately spies
The foul boar's conquest on her fair delight;
  Which seen, her eyes, as murdered with the view,
  Like stars ashamed of day, themselves withdrew.

Or, as the snail, whose tender horns being hit,
Shrinks backward in his shelly cave with pain,
And there, all smothered up, in shade doth sit,
Long after fearing to creep forth again;
  So, at his bloody view, her eyes are fled
  Into the deep, dark cabins of her head;

Where they resign their office and their light
To the disposing of her troubled brain;
Who bids them still consort with ugly night,
And never wound the heart with looks again;
  Who, like a king perplexéd in his throne,
  By their suggestion gives a deadly groan,

Whereat each tributary subject quakes:
As when the wind, imprisoned in the ground,
Struggling for passage, earth's foundation shakes,
Which with cold terror doth men's minds confound,
  The mutiny each part doth so surprise,
  That from their dark beds once more leap her eyes;

And, being opened, threw unwilling light
Upon the wide wound that the boar had trenched
In his soft flank; whose wonted lily white
With purple tears, that his wound wept, was drenched:
  No flower was nigh, no grass, herb, leaf, or weed,
  But stole his blood, and seemed with him to bleed

This solemn sympathy poor Venus noteth;
Over one shoulder doth she hang her head;
Dumbly she passions, franticly she doteth;
She thinks he could not die, he is not dead.
  Her voice is stopped, her joints forget to bow;
  Her eyes are mad that they have wept till now.

Upon his hurt she looks so steadfastly
That her sight dazzling makes the wound seem three;
And then she reprehends her mangling eye
That makes more gashes where no breach should be:
  His face seems twain, each several limb is doubled;
  For oft the eye mistakes, the brain being troubled.

"My tongue cannot express my grief for one,
And yet," quoth she, "behold two Adons dead!
My sighs are blown away, my salt tears gone,
Mine eyes are turned to fire, my heart to lead:
  Heavy heart's lead melt at mine eyes' red fire!
  So shall I die by drops of hot desire.

"Alas, poor world, what treasure hast thou lost!
What face remains alive that's worth the viewing?
Whose tongue is music now? what canst thou boast
Of things long since, or any thing ensuing?
  The flowers are sweet, their colors fresh and trim;
  But true-sweet beauty lived and died with him.

"Bonnet nor veil henceforth no creature wear!
Nor sun nor wind will ever strive to kiss you:
Having no fair[1] to lose, you need not fear;
The sun doth scorn you, and the wind doth hiss
  you:

[1] *Fair*, beauty.

But when Adonis lived, sun and sharp air
Lurked like two thieves to rob him of his fair;

"And therefore would he put his bonnet on,
Under whose brim the gaudy sun would peep;
The wind would blow it off, and, being gone,
Play with his locks; then would Adonis weep:
And straight, in pity of his tender years,
They both would strive who first should dry his tears.

"To see his face the lion walked along
Behind some hedge, because he would not fear him:
To recreate himself, when he hath sung,
The tiger would be tame and gently hear him:
If he had spoke the wolf would leave his prey,
And never fright the silly lamb that day.

"When he beheld his shadow in the brook
The fishes spread on it their golden gills;
When he was by the birds such pleasure took,
That some would sing, some other in their bills
Would bring him mulberries, and ripe-red cherries;
He fed them with his sight, they him with berries.

"But this foul, grim, and urchin-snouted[1] boar,
Whose downward eye still looketh for a grave,
Ne'er saw the beauteous livery that he wore:
Witness the entertainment that he gave;
If he did see his face, why then I know
He thought to kiss him, and hath killed him so.

[1] *Urchin-snouted*, with the snout of the urchin, or hedgehog.

"'Tis true, 'tis true; thus was Adonis slain;
He ran upon the boar with his sharp spear,
Who did not whet his teeth at him again,
But by a kiss thought to persuade him there;
And nuzzling in his flank the loving swine
Sheathed, unaware, the tusk in his soft groin.

"Had I been toothed like him I must confess
With kissing him I should have killed him first;
But he is dead, and never did he bless
My youth with his; the more am I accurst."
With this she falleth in the place she stood,
And stains her face with his congealéd blood.

She looks upon his lips, and they are pale;
She takes him by the hand, and that is cold;
She whispers in his ears a heavy tale,
As if they heard the woful words she told:
She lifts the coffer-lids that close his eyes,
Where, lo! two lamps, burnt out, in darkness lies:

Two glasses where herself herself beheld
A thousand times, and now no more reflect;
Their virtue lost, wherein they late excelled,
And every beauty robbed of his effect:
"Wonder of time," quoth she, "this is my spite,
That you being dead the day should yet be light.

"Since thou art dead, lo! here I prophesy,
Sorrow on love hereafter shall attend;
It shall be waited on with jealousy,
Find sweet beginning but unsavory end;
Ne'er settled equally, but high or low;
That all love's pleasure shall not match his woe.

"It shall be fickle, false, and full of fraud;
Bud and be blasted in a breathing while;
The bottom poison, and the top o'erstrawed[1]
With sweets that shall the truest sight beguile:
  The strongest body shall it make most weak,
  Strike the wise dumb, and teach the fool to speak.

"It shall be sparing, and too full of riot,
Teaching decrepit age to tread the measures;[2]
The staring ruffian shall it keep in quiet,
Pluck down the rich, enrich the poor with treasures:
  It shall be raging mad, and silly mild,
  Make the young old, the old become a child.

"It shall suspect, where is no cause of fear;
It shall not fear where it should most mistrust;
It shall be merciful, and too severe,
And most deceiving when it seems most just;
  Perverse it shall be where it shows most toward,
  Put fear to valor, courage to the coward.

"It shall be cause of war and dire events,
And set dissension 'twixt the son and sire;
Subject and servile to all discontents,
As dry combustious matter is to fire;
  Sith in his prime death doth my love destroy,
  They that love best their love shall not enjoy."

By this, the boy that by her side lay killed
Was melted like a vapor from her sight,

[1] *O'erstrawed*, o'erstrewed.
[2] *Measures*, grave dances suited to age.

And in his blood that on the ground lay spilled,
A purple flower sprung up, checkered with white,
  Resembling well his pale cheeks, and the blood
  Which in round drops upon their whiteness stood.

She bows her head, the new sprung flower to smell,
Comparing it to her Adonis' breath;
And says, within her bosom it shall dwell,
Since he himself is reft from her by death:
  She crops the stalk, and in the breach appears
  Green dropping sap, which she compares to tears.

"Poor flower," quoth she, "this was thy father's guise,
(Sweet issue of a more sweet smelling sire,)
For every little grief to wet his eyes:
To grow unto himself was his desire,
  And so 'tis thine; but know, it is as good
  To wither in my breast as in his blood.

"Here was thy father's bed, here in my breast;
Thou art the next of blood, and 'tis thy right:
Lo! in this hollow cradle take thy rest,
My throbbing heart shall rock thee, day and night:
  There shall not be one minnte in an hour
  Wherein I will not kiss my sweet love's flower."

Thus weary of the world, away she hies,
And yokes her silver doves; by whose swift aid
Their mistress mounted, through the empty skies
In her light chariot quickly is conveyed,
  Holding their course to Paphos, where their queen
  Means to immure herself, and not be seen.

THE RAPE OF LUCRECE.

TO THE

RIGHT HONORABLE HENRY WRIOTHESLY,

EARL OF SOUTHAMPTON, AND BARON OF TITCHFIELD.

The love I dedicate to your Lordship is without end; whereof this pamphlet, without beginning, is but a superfluous moiety.[1] The warrant I have of your honorable disposition, not the worth of my untutored lines, makes it assured of acceptance. What I have done is yours, what I have to do is yours; being part in all I have, devoted yours. Were my worth greater, my duty would show greater: meantime, as it is, it is bound to your Lordship, to whom I wish long life, still lengthened with all happiness.

Your Lordship's in all duty,

William Shakspeare.

[1] *Moiety.* In Henry IV. Part I., and in Lear, Shakspeare uses *moiety* as it is here used, meaning a portion, not a half.

THE ARGUMENT.

Lucius Tarquinius, (for his excessive pride surnamed Superbus,) after he had caused his own father-in-law, Servius Tullius, to be cruelly murdered, and, contrary to the Roman laws and customs, not requiring or staying for the people's suffrages, had possessed himself of the kingdom, went, accompanied with his sons and other noblemen of Rome, to besiege Ardea; during which siege, the principal men of the army meeting one evening at the tent of Sextus Tarquinius, the king's son, in their discourses after supper, every one commended the virtues of his own wife; among whom, Collatinus extolled the incomparable chastity of his wife Lucretia. In that pleasant humor they all posted to Rome; and intending, by their secret and sudden arrival, to make trial of that which every one had before avouched, only Collatinus finds his wife (though it were late in the night) spinning with her maids: the other ladies were all found dancing and revelling, or in several disports. Whereupon the noblemen yielded Collatinus the victory, and his wife the fame. At that time Sextus Tarquinius, being inflamed with Lucrece's beauty, yet smothering his passions for the present, departed with the rest back to the camp; from whence he shortly after privily withdrew himself, and was (according to his estate) royally entertained and lodged by Lucrece at Collatium. The same night he treacherously stealeth into her chamber, violently ravished her, and early in the morning speedeth away. Lucrece, in this lamentable plight, hastily despatcheth messengers, one to Rome for her father, another to the camp for Collatine. They came, the one accompanied with Junius Brutus, the other by Publius Valerius; and finding Lucrece attired in mourning habit, demanded the cause of her sorrow. She, first taking an oath of them for her revenge, revealed the actor, and whole manner of his dealing, and withal suddenly stabbed herself. Which done, with one consent they all vowed to root out the whole hated family of the Tarquins; and, bearing the dead body to Rome, Brutus acquainted the people with the doer and manner of the vile deed, with a bitter invective against the tyranny of the king; wherewith the people were so moved, that with one consent and a general acclamation the Tarquins were all exiled, and the state government changed from kings to consuls.

THE RAPE OF LUCRECE.

From the besieged Ardea all in post,
Borne by the trustless wings of false desire,
Lust-breathéd Tarquin leaves the Roman host,
And to Collatium bears the lightless fire
Which, in pale embers hid, lurks to aspire,
  And girdle with embracing flames the waist
  Of Collatine's fair love, Lucrece the chaste.

Haply that name of chaste unhapp'ly set
This bateless edge on his keen appetite;
When Collatine unwisely did not let[1]
To praise the clear unmatched red and white
Which triumphed in that sky of his delight,
  Where mortal stars, as bright as heaven's beauties,
  With pure aspécts did him peculiar duties.

For he the night before, in Tarquin's tent,
Unlocked the treasure of his happy state;
What priceless wealth the heavens had him lent

[1] *Let*, forbear.

In the possession of his beauteous mate;
Reckoning his fortune at such high-proud rate,
That kings might be espouséd to more fame,
But king nor peer to such a peerless dame.

O, happiness enjoyed but of a few!
And, if possessed, as soon decayed and done[1]
As is the morning's silver-melting dew
Against the golden splendor of the sun!
An expired date, cancelled ere well begun:
Honor and beauty, in the owner's arms,
Are weakly fortressed from a world of harms.

Beauty itself doth of itself persuade
The eyes of men without an orator;
What needeth then apologies be made
To set forth that which is so singular?
Or why is Collatine the publisher
Of that rich jewel he should keep unknown
From thievish ears, because it is his own?

Perchance his boast of Lucrece' sovereignty
Suggested[2] this proud issue of a king;
For by our ears our hearts oft tainted be:
Perchance that envy of so rich a thing,
Braving compare, disdainfully did sting
His high-pitched thoughts, that meaner men should vaunt
That golden hap which their superiors want.

1 *Done.* The word is here used as in a previous passage of the Venus and Adonis: —

"Wasted, thawed, and *done*,
As mountain snow melts with the midday sun."

2 *Suggested*, tempted.

But some untimely thought did instigate
His all-too-timeless speed, if none of those:
His honor, his affairs, his friends, his state,
Neglected all, with swift intent he goes,
To quench the coal which in his liver glows.
O rash, false heat, wrapped in repented cold,
Thy hasty spring still blasts,[1] and ne'er grows old!

When at Collatium this false lord arrived,
Well was he welcomed by the Roman dame,
Within whose face beauty and virtue strived
Which of them both should underprop her fame:
When virtue bragged, beauty would blush for shame;
When beauty boasted blushes, in despite
Virtue would stain that or[2] with silver white.

But beauty, in that white intituled,[3]
From Venus' doves doth challenge that fair field:
Then virtue claims from beauty beauty's red,

1 *Blasts* is here used as a verb neuter. It is so used in the poem ascribed to Raleigh, entitled "The Farewell:" —

"Tell age, it daily wasteth;
Tell honor, how it alters;
Tell beauty that it *blasteth*."

2 *Or*. The line usually stands thus: —

"Virtue would stain that *o'er* with silver white."

The original has *ore*. Malone has suggested, but he does not act upon the suggestion, that "the word intended was perhaps *or*, *i. e.* gold, to which the poet compares the deep color of a blush." We have no doubt whatever of the matter. The lines in the subsequent stanza complete the heraldic allusion: —

"Then virtue claims from beauty beauty's *red*,
Which virtue gave the *golden* age, to *gild*
Their *silver* cheeks, and called it then their shield."

3 *Intituled*, having a title to, or in.

Which virtue gave the golden age to gild
Their silver cheeks, and called it then their shield;
  Teaching them thus to use it in the fight,—
  When shame assailed, the red should fence the
      white.

This heraldry in Lucrece's face was seen,
Argued by beauty's red, and virtue's white:
Of either's color was the other queen,
Proving from world's minority their right:
Yet their ambition makes them still to fight;
  The sovereignty of either being so great,
  That oft they interchange each other's seat.

This silent war of lilies and of roses
Which Tarquin viewed in her fair face's field,
In their pure ranks his traitor eye encloses;
Where, lest between them both it should be killed,
The coward captive vanquishéd doth yield
  To those two armies that would let him go,
  Rather than triumph in so false a foe.

Now thinks he that her husband's shallow tongue
(The niggard prodigal that praised her so)
In that high task hath done her beauty wrong,
Which far exceeds his barren skill to show:
Therefore that praise which Collatine doth owe,[1]
  Enchanted Tarquin answers with surmise,
  In silent wonder of still gazing eyes.

This earthly saint, adored by this devil,
Little suspecteth the false worshipper;

[1] The object of praise which Collatine doth possess.

For unstained thoughts do seldom dream on evil;
Birds never limed no secret bushes fear:
So guiltless she securely gives good cheer
And reverend welcome to her princely guest,
Whose inward ill no outward harm expressed:

For that he colored with his high estate,
Hiding base sin in plaits of majesty;
That nothing in him seemed inordinate,
Save sometime too much wonder of his eye,
Which, having all, all could not satisfy;
But poorly rich, so wanteth in his store
That cloyed with much he pineth still for more.

But she, that never coped with stranger eyes,
Could pick no meaning from their parling[1] looks,
Nor read the subtle-shining secrecies
Writ in the glassy margents of such books;[2]
She touched no unknown baits, nor feared no hooks;
Nor could she moralize[3] his wanton sight,
More than his eyes were opened to the light.

He stories to her ears her husband's fame,
Won in the fields of fruitful Italy;
And decks with praises Collatine's high name,
Made glorious by his manly chivalry,
With bruisèd arms and wreaths of victory;
Her joy with heaved-up hand she doth express,
And, wordless, so greets Heaven for his success.

1 *Parling*, speaking.
2 See Romeo and Juliet. Illustrations of Act I.
3 *Moralize*, interpret.

Far from the purpose of his coming thither,
He makes excuses for his being there.
No cloudy show of stormy blustering weather
Doth yet in his fair welkin once appear;
Till sable Night, mother of Dread and Fear,
 Upon the world dim darkness doth display,
 And in her vaulty prison stows the day.

For then is Tarquin brought unto his bed,
Intending[1] weariness with heavy spright;
For, after supper, long he questionéd[2]
With modest Lucrece, and wore out the night:
Now leaden slumber with life's strength doth fight;
 And every one to rest himself betakes,
 Save thieves, and cares, and troubled minds, that wakes.

As one of which doth Tarquin lie revolving
The sundry dangers of his will's obtaining;
Yet ever to obtain his will resolving,
Though weak-built hopes persuade him to abstaining;
Despair to gain doth traffic oft for gaining;
 And when great treasure is the meed proposed,
 Though death be adjunct, there's no death supposed.

Those that much covet are with gain so fond,
That what they have not, that which they possess
They scatter and unloose it from their bond,[3]

[1] *Intending*, pretending.
[2] *Questioned*, conversed.
[3] This is the reading of the original edition of 1594. That of 1616 reads,

> "are with gain so fond,
> That *oft* they have not that which they possess;
> They scatter and unloose it."

Malone adopts the reading of the original, and he thus explains it:

And so, by hoping more, they have but less;
Or, gaining more, the profit of excess
  Is but to surfeit, and such griefs sustain,
  That they prove bankrupt in this poor-rich gain.

The aim of all is but to nurse the life
With honor, wealth, and ease, in waning age,
And in this aim there is such thwarting strife,
That one for all, or all for one, we gage;
As life for honor in fell battles' rage;
  Honor for wealth; and oft that wealth doth cost
  The death of all, and all together lost.

So that in venturing ill we leave to be
The things we are, for that which we expect;
And this ambitious foul infirmity,
In having much, torments us with defect
Of that we have: so then we do neglect
  The thing we have, and, all for want of wit,
  Make something nothing, by augmenting it.

Such hazard now must doting Tarquin make,
Pawning his honor to obtain his lust;
And for himself himself he must forsake:
Then where is truth if there be no self-trust?
When shall he think to find a stranger just,

"Poetically speaking, they may be said to scatter *what they have not*, *i. e.* what they cannot be *truly* said to have; what they do not *enjoy*, though *possessed* of it." This is clearly a misinterpretation. The reasoning of the two following stanzas is directed against the folly of venturing a certainty for an expectation, by which we "make something nothing." The meaning, then, though obscurely expressed, is, that the covetous are so fond of gaining what they have not, that they scatter and unloose from their bond (safe hold) that which they possess.

When he himself himself confounds,[1] betrays
To slanderous tongues, and wretched, hateful days?

Now stole upon the time the dead of night,
When heavy sleep had closed up mortal eyes;
No comfortable star did lend his light,
No noise but owls' and wolves' death-boding cries;
Now serves the season that they may surprise
The silly lambs; pure thoughts are dead and still,
While lust and murder wake to stain and kill.

And now this lustful lord leaped from his bed,
Throwing his mantle rudely o'er his arm;
Is madly tossed between desire and dread;
Th' one sweetly flatters, th' other feareth harm;
But honest Fear, bewitched with lust's foul charm,
Doth too oft betake him to retire,
Beaten away by brain-sick, rude Desire.

His falchion on a flint he softly smiteth,
That from the cold stone sparks of fire do fly,
Whereat a waxen torch forthwith he lighteth,
Which must be lode-star to his lustful eye;
And to the flame thus speaks advisedly:
"As from this cold flint I enforced this fire,
So Lucrece must I force to my desire."

Here pale with fear he doth premeditate
The dangers of his loathsome enterprise,
And in his inward mind he doth debate

[1] *Confounds.* Malone interprets this as *destroys;* but the meaning is sufficiently clear if we accept *confounds* in its usual sense.

What following sorrow may on this arise;
Then looking scornfully, he doth despise
His naked armor of still-slaughtered lust,
And justly thus controls his thoughts unjust:

"Fair torch, burn out thy light, and lend it not
To darken her whose light excelleth thine!
And die unhallowed thoughts, before you blot
With your uncleanness that which is divine!
Offer pure incense to so pure a shrine:
Let fair humanity abhor the deed
That spots and stains love's modest snow-white weed.[1]

"O, shame to knighthood and to shining arms!
O, foul dishonor to my household's grave!
O, impious act, including all foul harms!
A martial man to be soft fancy's slave;[2]
True valor still a true respect should have;
Then my digression[3] is so vile, so base,
That it will live engraven in my face.

"Yea, though I die, the scandal will survive,
And be an eyesore in my golden coat;
Some loathsome dash the herald will contrive,[4]

[1] *Weed*, garment. The word is more commonly used in the plural, as in Milton's "Paradise Regained:" —

"But now an aged man in rural *weeds*."

But in the same scene of Coriolanus (Act II. Sc. III.) we have both *weed* and *weeds*.

[2] *Fancy's slave*, love's slave.

[3] *Digression* is here used in the sense of *transgression*.

[4] Here is one of the frequent examples with which the works of Shakspeare and his contemporaries abound, of applying the usages of chivalry to the more remote antiquity of Greece and

To cipher me how fondly I did dote;
That my posterity, shamed with the note,
  Shall curse my bones, and hold it for no sin
  To wish that I their father had not been.

"What win I if I gain the thing I seek?
A dream, a breath, a froth of fleeting joy:
Who buys a minute's mirth to wail a week?
Or sells eternity to get a toy?
For one sweet grape who will the vine destroy?
  Or what fond beggar, but to touch the crown,
  Would with the sceptre straight be strucken down?

"If Collatinus dream of my intent,
Will he not wake, and in a desperate rage
Post hither, this vile purpose to prevent?
This siege that hath engirt his marriage,
This blur to youth, this sorrow to the sage,
  This dying virtue, this surviving shame,
  Whose crime will bear an ever-during blame?

"O, what excuse can my invention make,
When thou shalt charge me with so black a deed?
Will not my tongue be mute, my frail joints shake?
Mine eyes forego their light, my false heart bleed?
The guilt being great the fear doth still exceed;

Rome. The poem of Lucrece contains many such allusions. In particular, towards the close we have this line: —

"*Knights* by their oaths should right poor ladies' harms."

This was indeed an anticipation of chivalry; but the poet could in no way so forcibly express the spirit which animated the avengers of Lucrece, and which the injured lady here invokes, as by employing the language of chivalry. The use of the word *ladies* in this line is as much an anachronism as that of *knights;* but what other words will express the meaning intended?

And extreme fear can neither fight nor fly,
But, coward-like, with trembling terror die.

"Had Collatinus killed my son or sire,
Or lain in ambush to betray my life,
Or were he not my dear friend, this desire
Might have excuse to work upon his wife;
As in revenge or quittal of such strife:
But as he is my kinsman, my dear friend,
The shame and fault finds no excuse nor end.

"Shameful it is; — ay, if the fact be known:
Hateful it is; — there is no hate in loving:
I'll beg her love; — but she is not her own;[1]
The worst is but denial, and reproving:
My will is strong, past reason's weak removing.
Who fears a sentence or an old man's saw
Shall by a painted cloth[2] be kept in awe."

Thus, graceless, holds he disputation
'Tween frozen conscience and hot-burning will,
And with good thoughts makes dispensation,
Urging the worser sense for vantage still;
Which in a moment doth confound and kill
All pure effects, and doth so far proceed,
That what is vile shows like a virtuous deed.

Quoth he, "She took me kindly by the hand,
And gazed for tidings in my eager eyes,

1 Malone says the words such as *shameful it is* are "supposed to be spoken by some airy monitor." Surely the poet only meant to express that contest of thoughts which goes forward in a mind distracted between reason and passion; and which the dramatic poet can only represent by soliloquy, as it is here represented.

2 See As You Like It, Illustrations of Act III.

Fearing some hard news from the warlike band
Where her belovéd Collatinus lies.
O, how her fear did make her color rise!
  First red as roses that on lawn we lay,
  Then white as lawn the roses took away.[1]

"And how her hand, in my hand being locked,
Forced it to tremble with her loyal fear;
Which struck her sad, and then it faster rocked,
Until her husband's welfare she did hear;
Whereat she smiléd with so sweet a cheer,
  That had Narcissus seen her as she stood,
  Self-love had never drowned him in the flood.

"Why hunt I then for color or excuses?
All orators are dumb when beauty pleadeth;
Poor wretches have remorse in poor abuses;
Love thrives not in the heart that shadows dread-
eth:
Affection is my captain, and he leadeth;
  And when his gaudy banner is displayed,
  The coward fights, and will not be dismayed.

"Then, childish fear, avaunt! debating, die!
Respect[2] and reason wait on wrinkled age!
My heart shall never countermand mine eye:
Sad[3] pause and deep regard beseem the sage;
My part is youth, and beats these from the stage:
  Desire my pilot is, beauty my prize;
  Then who fears sinking where such treasure lies?"

[1] *Took away*, being taken away.
[2] *Respect*, prudence, — in the sense of the original Latin, looking again.
[3] *Sad*, grave.

As corn o'ergrown by weeds, so heedful fear
Is almost choked by unresisted lust.
Away he steals with open, listening ear,
Full of foul hope, and full of fond mistrust;
Both which, as servitors to the unjust,
So cross him with their opposite persuasion,
That now he vows a league, and now invasion.

Within his thought her heavenly image sits,
And in the selfsame seat sits Collatine:
That eye which looks on her confounds his wits;
That eye which him beholds, as more divine,
Unto a view so false will not incline;
But with a pure appeal seeks to the heart,
Which once corrupted takes the worser part;

And therein heartens up his servile powers,
Who, flattered by their leader's jocund show,
Stuff up his lust, as minutes fill up hours;
And as their captain, so their pride doth grow,
Paying more slavish tribute than they owe.
By reprobate desire thus madly led,
The Roman lord marcheth to Lucrece' bed.

The locks between her chamber and his will,
Each one by him enforced, retires his ward;
But as they open they all rate his ill,
Which drives the creeping thief to some regard;
The threshold grates the door to have him heard;
Night-wandering weasels shriek to see him there;
They fright him, yet he still pursues his fear.

As each unwilling portal yields him way,
Through little vents and crannies of the place

The wind wars with his torch, to make him stay,
And blows the smoke of it into his face,
Extinguishing his conduct[1] in this case;
But his hot heart, which fond desire doth scorch,
Puffs forth another wind that fires the torch:

And being lighted, by the light he spies
Lucretia's glove, wherein her needle sticks;
He takes it from the rushes where it lies,
And griping it, the neeld[2] his finger pricks:
As who should say, this glove to wanton tricks
Is not inured; return again in haste;
Thou seest our mistress' ornaments are chaste.

But all these poor forbiddings could not stay him;
He in the worst sense construes their denial;
The doors, the wind, the glove that did delay him,
He takes for accidental things of trial;
Or as those bars which stop the hourly dial,
Who with a lingering stay his course doth let,[3]
Till every minute pays the hour his debt.

"So, so," quoth he, "these lets attend the time,
Like little frosts that sometime threat the spring,
To add a more rejoicing to the prime,
And give the sneapéd[4] birds more cause to sing.
Pain pays the income of each precious thing;

1 *Conduct*, conductor.
2 *Neeld*, needle.
3 *Let*, obstruct.
4 *Sneaped*, checked. So in Love's Labor's Lost, Act I. Sc. I.: —

"Birón is like an envious *sneaping* frost,
That bites the first-born infants of the spring."

Huge rocks, high winds, strong pirates, shelves, and
sands,
The merchant fears, ere rich at home he lands."

Now is he come unto the chamber door
That shuts him from the heaven of his thought,
Which with a yielding latch, and with no more,
Hath barred him from the blessèd thing he sought.
So from himself impiety hath wrought,
That for his prey to pray he doth begin,
As if the heavens should countenance his sin.

But in the midst of his unfruitful prayer,
Having solicited the eternal power
That his foul thoughts might compass his fair fair,
And they would stand auspicious to the hour,
Even there he starts: — quoth he, "I must deflower;
The powers to whom I pray abhor this fact,
How can they then assist me in the act?

"Then Love and Fortune be my gods, my guide!
My will is backed with resolution;
Thoughts are but dreams till their effects be tried,
The blackest sin is cleared with absolution;
Against love's fire fear's frost hath dissolution.
The eye of heaven is out, and misty night
Covers the shame that follows sweet delight."

This said, his guilty hand plucked up the latch,
And with his knee the door he opens wide;
The dove sleeps fast that this night-owl will catch;
Thus treason works ere traitors be espied.
Who sees the lurking serpent steps aside;
But she, sound sleeping, fearing no such thing,
Lies at the mercy of his mortal sting.

Into the chamber wickedly he stalks,[1]
And gazeth on her yet unstainéd bed.
The curtains being close, about he walks,
Rolling his greedy eyeballs in his head:
By their high treason is his heart misled;
  Which gives the watchword to his hand full soon,
  To draw the cloud that hides the silver moon.

Look, as the fair and fiery-pointed sun,
Rushing from forth a cloud, bereaves our sight;
Even so, the curtain drawn, his eyes begun
To wink, being blinded with a greater light:
Whether it is that she reflects so bright,
  That dazzleth them, or else some shame supposed;
  But blind they are, and keep themselves enclosed.

O, had they in that darksome prison died,
Then had they seen the period of their ill!
Then Collatine again by Lucrece' side
In his clear bed might have reposéd still:
But they must ope, this blessed league to kill;

[1] *Stalks.* Malone says, "That the poet meant by the word *stalk* to convey the notion, not of a boisterous, but quiet movement, appears from a subsequent passage:—

> 'For in the dreadful dark of deep midnight
> With shining falchion in my chamber came
> A *creeping* creature.'"

Malone appears from a subsequent part of his note to confound *stalk* with *stride.* He says, "A person apprehensive of being discovered naturally takes *long steps*, the sooner to arrive at his point." But long steps are noisy steps; and therefore "Tarquin's ravishing *strides*" cannot be the true reading of the famous passage in Macbeth. But *stalk*, on the contrary, literally means, *to go warily or softly.* It is the Anglo-Saxon *stælcan*—*pedetentim ire.* The fowler who creeps upon the birds *stalks*, and his *stalking*-horse derives its name from the character of the fowler's movement.

And holy-thoughted Lucrece to their sight
Must sell her joy, her life, her world's delight.

Her lily hand her rosy cheek lies under,
Cozening the pillow of a lawful kiss;
Who therefore angry, seems to part in sunder,
Swelling on either side to want his bliss;
Between whose hills her head entombéd is:
Where, like a virtuous monument, she lies,
To be admired of lewd unhallowed eyes.

Without the bed her other fair hand was,
On the green coverlet; whose perfect white
Showed like an April daisy on the grass,
With pearly sweat, resembling dew of night.
Her eyes, like marigolds, had sheathed their light,
And canopied in darkness sweetly lay,
Till they might open to adorn the day.

Her hair, like golden threads, played with her breath;
O modest wantons! wanton modesty!
Showing life's triumph in the map of death,
And death's dim look in life's mortality:
Each in her sleep themselves so beautify
As if between them twain there were no strife,
But that life lived in death, and death in life.

Her breasts, like ivory globes circled with blue,
A pair of maiden worlds unconqueréd,
Save of their lord no bearing yoke they knew,
And him by oath they truly honoréd.
These worlds in Tarquin new ambition bred:
Who, like a foul usurper, went about
From this fair throne to heave the owner out.

What could he see but mightily he noted?
What did he note but strongly he desired?
What he beheld on that he firmly doted,
And in his will his wilful eye he tired.[1]
With more than admiration he admired
  Her azure veins, her alabaster skin,
  Her coral lips, her snow-white dimpled chin.

As the grim lion fawneth o'er his prey,
Sharp hunger by the conquest satisfied,
So o'er this sleeping soul doth Tarquin stay,
His rage of lust by gazing qualified;
Slacked, not suppressed; for standing by her side,
  His eye, which late this mutiny restrains,
  Unto a greater uproar tempts his veins:

And they, like straggling slaves for pillage fighting,
Obdurate vassals, fell exploits effecting,
In bloody death and ravishment delighting,
Nor children's tears, nor mother's groans respecting,
Swell in their pride, the onset still expecting:
  Anon his beating heart, alarum striking,
  Gives the hot charge, and bids them do their
      liking.

His drumming heart cheers up his burning eye,
His eye commends the leading to his hand;
His hand, as proud of such a dignity,
Smoking with pride, marched on to make his stand
On her bare breast, the heart of all her land;
  Whose ranks of blue veins, as his hand did scale,
  Left their round turrets destitute and pale.

[1] *Tired*, satiated, glutted — as a falcon *tires* on his prey.

They, mustering to the quiet cabinet
Where their dear governess and lady lies,
Do tell her she is dreadfully beset,
And fright her with confusion of their cries:
She, much amazed, breaks ope her locked-up eyes,
  Who, peeping forth this tumult to behold,
  Are by his flaming torch dimmed and controlled.

Imagine her as one in dead of night
From forth dull sleep by dreadful fancy waking,
That thinks she hath beheld some ghastly sprite,
Whose grim aspéct sets every joint a shaking;
What terror 'tis! but she, in worser taking,
  From sleep disturbed, heedfully doth view
  The sight which makes supposéd terror true.

Wrapped and confounded in a thousand fears,
Like to a new-killed bird she trembling lies;
She dares not look; yet, winking, there appears
Quick-shifting antics, ugly in her eyes:
Such shadows are the weak brain's forgeries:
  Who, angry that the eyes fly from their lights,
  In darkness daunts them with more dreadful sights

His hand, that yet remains upon her breast,
(Rude ram, to batter such an ivory wall!)
May feel her heart, poor citizen, distressed,
Wounding itself to death, rise up and fall,
Beating her bulk,[1] that his hand shakes withal.

[1] *Bulk*, the body, the whole mass. Johnson, however, defines the word as the breast, or largest part of a man; deriving it from the Dutch *bulcke*. A passage in Hamlet employs the word in the same way as in the text before us:—

"He raised a sigh so piteous and profound
As it did seem to shatter all his *bulk*."

This moves in him more rage, and lesser pity,
To make the breach, and enter this sweet city.

First, like a trumpet, doth his tongue begin
To sound a parley to his heartless foe,
Who o'er the white sheet peers her whiter chin,
The reason of this rash alarm to know,
Which he by dumb demeanor seeks to show;
But she with vehement prayers urgeth still
Under what color he commits this ill.

Thus he replies: "The color in thy face
(That even for anger makes the lily pale,
And the red rose blush at her own disgrace)
Shall plead for me, and tell my loving tale:
Under that color am I come to scale
Thy never-conquered fort; the fault is thine,
For those thine eyes betray thee unto mine.

"Thus I forestall thee, if thou mean to chide:
Thy beauty hath ensnared thee to this night,
Where thou with patience must my will abide,
My will that marks thee for my earth's delight,
Which I to conquer sought with all my might;
But as reproof and reason beat it dead,
By thy bright beauty was it newly bred.

"I see what crosses my attempt will bring;
I know what thorns the growing rose defends:
I think the honey guarded with a sting:
All this, beforehand, counsel comprehends:
But will is deaf, and hears no heedful friends;

Turbervile, who preceded Shakspeare about twenty years, has this line: —

"My liver leapt within my *bulk*."

Only he hath an eye to gaze on beauty,
And dotes on what he looks, 'gainst law or duty.

"I have debated, even in my soul,
What wrong, what shame, what sorrow I shall breed:
But nothing can Affection's course control,
Or stop the headlong fury of his speed.
I know repentant tears ensue the deed,
Reproach, disdain, and deadly enmity;
Yet strive I to embrace mine infamy."

This said, he shakes aloft his Roman blade,
Which, like a falcon towering in the skies,
Coucheth[1] the fowl below with his wing's shade,
Whose crooked beak threats, if he mount he dies:
So under his insulting falchion lies
Harmless Lucretia, marking what he tells
With trembling fear, as fowl hear falcon's bells.[2]

"Lucrece," quoth he, "this night I must enjoy thee
If thou deny, then force must work my way,
For in thy bed I purpose to destroy thee;
That done, some worthless slave of thine I'll slay,
To kill thine honor with thy life's decay;
And in thy dead arms do I mean to place him,
Swearing I slew him, seeing thee embrace him.

"So thy surviving husband shall remain
The scornful mark of every open eye;
Thy kinsmen hang their heads at this disdain,

1 *Coucheth*, causes to couch.
2 We have the same image in Henry VI. Part III.:—

"Not he that loves him best
Dares stir a wing if Warwick *shake his bells*"

Thy issue blurred with nameless bastardy.
And thou, the author of their obloquy,
  Shalt have thy trespass cited up in rhymes,
  And sung by children in succeeding times.

"But if thou yield, I rest thy secret friend:
The fault unknown is as a thought unacted;
A little harm, done to a great good end,
For lawful policy remains enacted.
The poisonous simple sometimes is compacted
  In a pure compound; being so applied,
  His venom in effect is purified.

"Then for thy husband and thy children's sake,
Tender[1] my suit: bequeath not to their lot
The shame that from them no device can take,
The blemish that will never be forgot;
Worse than a slavish wipe, or birth-hour's blot:[2]
  For marks descried in men's nativity
  Are nature's faults, not their own infamy."

Here with a cockatrice' dead-killing eye
He rouseth up himself, and makes a pause;
While she, the picture of pure piety,
Like a white hind under the grype's[3] sharp claws,
Pleads in a wilderness, where are no laws,

[1] *Tender*, heed, regard.

[2] *Birth-hour's blot*, corporal blemish. So in A Midsummer Night's Dream: —

> "And the *blots* of nature's hand
> Shall not in their issue stand;
> Never mole, hare-lip, nor scar,
> Nor mark prodigious."

[3] Steevens says the *grype* is properly the griffin. But in the passage before us, as in the early English writers, the word is applied to birds of prey, — the eagle especially.

To the rough beast that knows no gentle right,
Nor aught obeys but his foul appetite.

But[1] when a black-faced cloud the world doth threat,
In his dim mist the aspiring mountains hiding,
From earth's dark womb some gentle gust doth get,
Which blows these pitchy vapors from their biding,
Hindering their present fall by this dividing;
So his unhallowed haste her words delays,
And moody Pluto winks while Orpheus plays.

Yet, foul night-waking cat, he doth but dally,
While in his hold-fast foot the weak mouse panteth;
Her sad behavior feeds his vulture folly,
A swallowing gulf that even in plenty wanteth:
His ear her prayers admits, but his heart granteth
No penetrable entrance to her plaining:
Tears harden lust, though marble wear with rain-
ing.

Her pity-pleading eyes are sadly fixed
In the remorseless wrinkles of his face;
Her modest eloquence with sighs is mixed,
Which to her oratory adds more grace.
She puts the period often from his place,[2]
And 'midst the sentence so her accent breaks,
That twice she doth begin ere once she speaks.

[1] Malone, who has certainly made very few deviations from the original text of this poem, here changes *but* to *look*, "there being no opposition whatsoever between this and the preceding passage." An opposition is, however, intended. Lucretia pleads to the "rough beast" that "knows no right;" *but*, as the gentle gust divides the black cloud,

"So his unhallowed haste her words delays."

[2] Shakspeare, whose knowledge of the outward effects of the passions was universal, makes the terror of poor Lucrece display

She conjures him by high almighty Jove,
By knighthood, gentry, and sweet friendship's oath,
By her untimely tears, her husband's love,
By holy human law, and common troth,
By heaven and earth, and all the power of both,
  That to his borrowed bed he make retire,
  And stoop to honor, not to foul desire.

Quoth she, "Reward not hospitality
With such black payment as thou hast pretended;[1]
Mud not the fountain that gave drink to thee;
Mar not the thing that cannot be amended;
End thy ill aim, before thy shoot[2] be ended:
  He is no woodman that doth bend his bow
  To strike a poor unseasonable doe.

"My husband is thy friend, for his sake spare me;
Thyself art mighty, for thine own sake leave me;
Myself a weakling, do not then ensnare me;
Thou look'st not like deceit; do not deceive me:
My sighs, like whirlwinds, labor hence to heave thee.
  If ever man were moved with woman's moans,
  Be movéd with my tears, my sighs, my groans:

itself in the same manner as that of "great clerks" greeting their prince with "premeditated welcomes." They also

> "Make periods in the midst of sentences,
> Throttle their practised accent in their fears,
> And, in conclusion, dumbly have broke off."
> (Midsummer Night's Dream, Act v. Sc. I.)

1 *Pretended*, proposed.

2 *Shoot.* Malone says that the author intended this word to be taken in a double sense, *suit* and *shoot* being in his time pronounced alike. We doubt this. *Suit* is not the word that the indignation of Lucrece would have used; nor is the double sense carried forward at all.

"All which together, like a troubled ocean,
Beat at thy rocky and wreck-threatening heart;
To soften it with their continual motion;
For stones dissolved to water do convert.
O, if no harder than a stone thou art,
   Melt at my tears, and be compassionate!
   Soft pity enters at an iron gate.

"In Tarquin's likeness I did entertain thee;
Hast thou put on his shape to do him shame?
To all the host of heaven I complain me,
Thou wrong'st his honor, wound'st his princely name.
Thou art not what thou seem'st; and if the same
   Thou seem'st not what thou art, a god, a king;
   For kings, like gods, should govern every thing.

"How will thy shame be seeded in thine age,
When thus thy vices bud before thy spring?
If in thy hope thou dar'st do such outrage,
What dar'st thou not when once thou art a king!
O, be remembered, no outrageous thing
   From vassal actors can be wiped away;
   Then kings' misdeeds cannot be hid in clay.

"This deed will make thee only loved for fear,
But happy monarchs still are feared for love:
With foul offenders thou perforce must bear,
When they in thee the like offences prove:
If but for fear of this thy will remove;
   For princes are the glass, the school, the book,
   Where subjects' eyes do learn, do read, do look.

"And wilt thou be the school where Lust shall learn?
Must he in thee read lectures of such shame?
Wilt thou be glass, wherein it shall discern

Authority for sin, warrant for blame,
To privilege dishonor in thy name?
  Thou back'st reproach against long-livéd laud,
  And mak'st fair reputation but a bawd.

"Hast thou command? by him that gave it thee,
From a pure heart command thy rebel will:
Draw not thy sword to guard iniquity,
For it was lent thee all that brood to kill.
Thy princely office how canst thou fulfil,
  When, patterned by thy fault, foul Sin may say,
  He learned to sin, and thou didst teach the way?

"Think but how vile a spectacle it were
To view thy present trespass in another.
Men's faults do seldom to themselves appear;
Their own transgressions partially they smother:
This guilt would seem death-worthy in thy brother.
  O, how are they wrapped in with infamies,
  That from their own misdeeds askance their eyes!

"To thee, to thee, my heaved-up hands appeal,
Not to seducing lust, thy rash relier;
I sue for exiled majesty's repeal;[1]
Let him return, and flattering thoughts retire:
His true respect will 'prison false desire,
  And wipe the dim mist from thy doting eyne,
  That thou shalt see thy state, and pity mine."

"Have done," quoth he; "my uncontrolléd tide
Turns not, but swells the higher by this let.
Small lights are soon blown out, huge fires abide,

[1] *Repeal*, recall; from the French *rappeler*.

And with the wind in greater fury fret:
The petty streams that pay a daily debt
  To their salt sovereign, with their fresh falls' haste,
  Add to his flow, but alter not his taste."

"Thou art," quoth she, "a sea, a sovereign king;
And lo, there falls into thy boundless flood
Black lust, dishonor, shame, misgoverning,
Who seek to stain the ocean of thy blood.
If all these petty ills shall change thy good,
  Thy sea within a puddle's womb is hearsed,
  And not the puddle in thy sea dispersed.

"So shall these slaves be king, and thou their slave;
Thou nobly base, they basely dignified;
Thou their fair life, and they thy fouler grave;
Thou loathéd in their shame, they in thy pride:
The lesser thing should not the greater hide;
  The cedar stoops not to the base shrub's foot,
  But low shrubs wither at the cedar's root.

"So let thy thoughts, low vassals to thy state—"
"No more," quoth he; "by Heaven, I will not hear thee:
Yield to my love; if not, enforcéd hate,
Instead of love's coy touch, shall rudely tear thee;
That done, despitefully I mean to bear thee
  Unto the base bed of some rascal groom,
  To be thy partner in this shameful doom."

This said, he sets his foot upon the light,
For light and lust are deadly enemies:
Shame folded up in blind concealing night,
When most unseen, then most doth tyrannize.
The wolf hath seized his prey, the poor lamb cries

Till with her own white fleece her voice controlled
Entombs her outcry in her lips' sweet fold:

For with the nightly linen that she wears
He pens her piteous clamors in her head;
Cooling his hot face in the chastest tears
That ever modest eyes with sorrow shed.
O that prone[1] lust should stain so pure a bed!
The spots whereof could weeping purify,
Her tears should drop on them perpetually.

But she hath lost a dearer thing than life,
And he hath won what he would lose again.
This forcéd league doth force a further strife,
This momentary joy breeds months of pain,
This hot desire converts to cold disdain;
Pure Chastity is rifled of her store,
And Lust, the thief, far poorer than before.

Look, as the full-fed hound or gorgéd hawk,
Unapt for tender smell or speedy flight,
Make slow pursuit, or altogether balk
The prey wherein by nature they delight,
So surfeit-taking Tarquin fares this night:
His taste delicious, in digestion souring,
Devours his will that lived by foul devouring.

O, deeper sin than bottomless conceit
Can comprehend in still imagination!
Drunken desire must vomit his receipt,

[1] *Prone*, having inclination or propensity, and so self-willed, headstrong.

Ere he can see his own abomination.
While lust is in his pride no exclamation
 Can curb his heat, or rein his rash desire,
 Till, like a jade, self-will himself doth tire.

And then with lank and lean discolored cheek,
With heavy eye, knit brow, and strengthless pace,
Feeble desire, all recreant, poor, and meek,
Like to a bankrupt beggar wails his case:
The flesh being proud, desire doth fight with grace,
 For there it revels; and when that decays,
 The guilty rebel for remission prays.

So fares it with this faultful lord of Rome,
Who this accomplishment so hotly chased;
For now against himself he sounds this doom,
That through the length of times he stands disgraced:
Besides, his soul's fair temple is defaced;
 To whose weak ruins muster troops of cares,
 To ask the spotted princess how she fares.

She says, her subjects with foul insurrection
Have battered down her consecrated wall,
And by their mortal fault brought in subjection
Her immortality, and make her thrall
To living death, and pain perpetual:
 Which in her prescience she controllèd still,
 But her foresight could not forestall their will.

Even in this thought through the dark night he steal-
 eth,
A captive victor that hath lost in gain;
Bearing away the wound that nothing healeth,
The scar that will, despite of cure, remain,
Leaving his spoil perplexed in greater pain.

She bears the load of lust he left behind,
And he the burthen of a guilty mind.

He like a thievish dog creeps sadly thence;
She like a wearied lamb lies panting there;
He scowls, and hates himself for his offence;
She, desperate, with her nails her flesh doth tear;
He faintly flies, sweating with guilty fear;
She stays exclaiming on the direful night;
He runs, and chides his vanished, loathed delight.

He thence departs a heavy convertite;
She there remains a hopeless castaway:
He in his speed looks for the morning light;
She prays she never may behold the day;
"For day," quoth she, "night's scapes doth open lay;
And my true eyes have never practised how
To cloak offences with a cunning brow.

"They think not but that every eye can see
The same disgrace which they themselves behold;
And therefore would they still in darkness be,
To have their unseen sin remain untold;
For they their guilt with weeping will unfold,
And grave, like water, that doth eat in steel,
Upon my cheeks what helpless shame I feel.

Here she exclaims against repose and rest,
And bids her eyes hereafter still be blind.
She wakes her heart by beating on her breast,
And bids it leap from thence, where it may find
Some purer chest, to close so pure a mind.
Frantic with grief thus breathes she forth her spite
Against the unseen secrecy of night:

"O comfort-killing night, image of hell!
Dim register and notary of shame!
Black stage for tragedies and murders fell!
Vast sin-concealing chaos! nurse of blame!
Blind muffled bawd! dark harbor for defame!
  Grim cave of death, whispering conspirator,
  With close-tongued treason and the ravisher!

"O hateful, vaporous, and foggy night,
Since thou art guilty of my cureless crime,
Muster thy mists to meet the eastern light,
Make war against proportioned course of time!
Or if thou wilt permit the sun to climb
  His wonted height, yet, ere he go to bed,
  Knit poisonous clouds about his golden head.

"With rotten damps ravish the morning air;
Let their exhaled unwholesome breaths make sick
The life of purity, the supreme fair,
Ere he arrive his weary noontide prick;[1]
And let thy misty vapors march so thick,
  That in their smoky ranks his smothered light
  May set at noon, and make perpetual night.

"Were Tarquin night, (as he is but night's child,)
The silver-shining queen he would distain;
Her twinkling handmaids too, by him defiled,
Through night's black bosom should not peep again;
So should I have copartners in my pain:
  And fellowship in woe doth woe assuage,
  As palmers' chat makes short their pilgrimage.

1 *Noontide prick*, the point of noon.

"Where[1] now I have no one to blush with me,
To cross their arms, and hang their heads with mine,
To mask their brows, and hide their infamy;
But I alone alone must sit and pine,
Seasoning the earth with showers of silver brine,
  Mingling my talk with tears, my grief with groans,
  Poor wasting monuments of lasting moans.

"O night, thou furnace of foul-reeking smoke,
Let not the jealous day behold that face
Which underneath thy black all-hiding cloak
Immodestly lies martyred with disgrace!
Keep still possession of thy gloomy place,
  That all the faults which in thy reign are made
  May likewise be sepúlchred[2] in thy shade!

"Make me not object to the telltale day!
The light will show, charáctered[3] in my brow,
The story of sweet chastity's decay,
The impious breach of holy wedlock vow:
Yea, the illiterate, that know not how
  To 'cipher what is writ in learnéd books,
  Will quote[4] my loathsome trespass in my looks.

1 *Where*, whereas.

2 *Sepúlchred.* Milton uses the word with the same accent, in his lines on Shakspeare: —

"And so sepúlchred in such pomp dost lie,
That kings for such a tomb would wish to die."

3 *Charáctered.* Here again is an accentuation different from the present, but which is common to all Shakspeare's contemporaries. Malone has observed that this is still the pronunciation of the Irish people; and he adds, with great truth, that much of the pronunciation of Queen Elizabeth's age is yet retained in Ireland.

4 *Quote*, observe.

"The nurse, to still her child, will tell my story,
And fright her crying babe with Tarquin's name;
The orator, to deck his oratory,
Will couple my reproach to Tarquin's shame:
Feast-finding minstrels, tuning my defame,
    Will tie the hearers to attend each line,
    How Tarquin wrongéd me, I Collatine.

"Let my good name, that senseless reputation,
For Collatine's dear love be kept unspotted:
If that be made a theme for disputation,
The branches of another root are rotted,
And undeserved reproach to him allotted,
    That is as clear from this attaint of mine,
    As I, ere this, was pure to Collatine.

"O unseen shame! invisible disgrace!
O unfelt sore! crest-wounding, private scar!
Reproach is stamped in Collatinus' face,
And Tarquin's eye may read the mot[1] afar,
How he in peace is wounded, not in war.
    Alas, how many bear such shameful blows,
    Which not themselves but he that gives them knows!

"If, Collatine, thine honor lay in me,
From me by strong assault it is bereft.
My honey lost, and I, a drone-like bee,
Have no perfection of my summer left,
But robbed and ransacked by injurious theft:
    In thy weak hive a wandering wasp hath crept,
    And sucked the honey which thy chaste bee kept.

[1] *Mot*, motto.

"Yet am I guilty of thy honor's wrack,[1] —
Yet for thy honor did I entertain him;[2]
Coming from thee, I could not put him back,
For it had been dishonor to disdain him:
Besides of weariness he did complain him,
And talked of virtue: — O, unlooked-for evil,
When virtue is profaned in such a devil!

"Why should the worm intrude the maiden bud?
Or hateful cuckoos hatch in sparrows' nests?
Or toads infect fair founts with venom mud?
Or tyrant folly lurk in gentle breasts?[3]
Or kings be breakers of their own behests?
But no perfection is so absolute,
That some impurity doth not pollute.

"The aged man that coffers up his gold
Is plagued with cramps, and gouts, and painful fits,
And scarce hath eyes his treasure to behold,

1 *Wrack.* Mr. Hunter, in his "Disquisition on the Tempest," pointed out the necessity of restoring to Shakspeare's text the old word *wrack*, instead of the modern *wreck*. He asks, "What could editors, who proceed upon principles which lead to such a substistution, do with this couplet of the Lucrece: —

'O, this dread night, wouldst thou one hour come back,
I could prevent this storm, and shun thy *wrack!*'"

In this particular instance they have preserved the original word; but in that before us, where *wrack* is equally required to rhyme with *back*, they have substituted *wreck*. Even Mr. Dyce herein copies Malone without alteration. This is probably mere carelessness; but it shows the danger of tampering with an original reading.

2 This is again an instance of the dramatic crowding of thought upon thought, and making one thought answer and repel the other, which render Shakspeare's soliloquies such matchless revelations of the heart. Malone, not perceiving this dramatic power, changes *guilty* to *guiltless;* because the idea of the first line does not correspond with that of the second.

3 *Folly* is here used in the sense of wickedness; and *gentle* in that of well-born.

But like still-pining Tantalus he sits.
And useless barns the harvest of his wits;
  Having no other pleasure of his gain
  But torment that it cannot cure his pain.

" So then he hath it, when he cannot use it,
And leaves it to be mastered by his young,
Who in their pride do presently abuse it:
Their father was too weak, and they too strong,
To hold their curséd-blesséd fortune long.
  The sweets we wish for turn to loathéd sours,
  Even in the moment that we call them ours.

" Unruly blasts wait on the tender spring;
Unwholesome weeds take root with precious flowers;
The adder hisses where the sweet birds sing;
What virtue breeds iniquity devours:
We have no good that we can say is ours.
  But ill-annexéd Opportunity
  Or kills his life, or else his quality.

" O Opportunity! thy guilt is great:
'Tis thou that execut'st the traitor's treason;
Thou sett'st the wolf where he the lamb may get;
Whoever plots the sin, thou 'point'st the season;
'Tis thou that spurn'st at right, at law, at reason;
  And in thy shady cell, where none may spy him,
  Sits Sin, to seize the souls that wander by him.

" Thou mak'st the vestal violate her oath;
Thou blow'st the fire when temperance is thawed;
Thou smother'st honesty, thou murther'st troth;
Thou foul abetter! thou notorious bawd!
Thou plantest scandal, and displacest laud:

Thou ravisher, thou traitor, thou false thief,
Thy honey turns to gall, thy joy to grief!

"Thy secret pleasure turns to open shame,
Thy private feasting to a public fast;
Thy smoothing[1] titles to a ragged[2] name;
Thy sugared tongue to bitter wormwood taste:
Thy violent vanities can never last.
How comes it then, vile Opportunity,
Being so bad, such numbers seek for thee?

"When wilt thou be the humble suppliant's friend,
And bring him where his suit may be obtained?
When wilt thou sort[3] an hour great strifes to end?
Or free that soul which wretchedness hath chained?
Give physic to the sick, ease to the pained?
The poor, lame, blind, halt, creep, cry out for thee;
But they ne'er meet with Opportunity.

"The patient dies while the physician sleeps;
The orphan pines while the oppressor feeds;
Justice is feasting while the widow weeps;
Advice is sporting while infection breeds;[4]
Thou grant'st no time for charitable deeds:

1 *Smoothing*, flattering.

2 *Ragged* is here used in the sense of contemptible. It means something broken, torn, and therefore worthless. See Note on Henry IV. Part II. Act I. Sc. I.

3 *Sort*, assign, appropriate. So in Richard III.: —

"But I will *sort* a pitchy day for thee."

4 The constant allusions of the Elizabethan poets to that familiar terror, the plague, show how completely the evil, whether present or absent, was associated with the habitual thoughts of the people. *Advice* is here used in the sense of government, municipal or civil; and the line too correctly describes the carelessness of those in high places, who abated not their feasting and their revelry while pestilence was doing its terrible work around them.

Wrath, envy, treason, rape, and murder's rages,
Thy heinous hours wait on them as their pages.

"When truth and virtue have to do with thee,
A thousand crosses keep them from thy aid;
They buy thy help: but Sin ne'er gives a fee,
He gratis comes; and thou art well appayed [1]
As well to hear as grant what he hath said.
My Collatine would else have come to me
When Tarquin did, but he was stayed by thee.

"Guilty thou art of murder and of theft;
Guilty of perjury and subornation;
Guilty of treason, forgery, and shift;
Guilty of incest, that abomination;
An accessory by thine inclination
To all sins past, and all that are to come,
From the creation to the general doom.

"Misshapen Time, copesmate of ugly night,
Swift subtle post, carrier of grisly care,
Eater of youth, false slave to false delight,
Base watch of woes, sin's packhorse, virtue's snare;
Thou nursest all, and murtherest all that are.
O, hear me then, injurious, shifting Time!
Be guilty of my death, since of my crime.

"Why hath thy servant, Opportunity,
Betrayed the hours thou gav'st me to repose?
Cancelled my fortunes, and enchainéd me
To endless date of never-ending woes?
Time's office is to fine [2] the hate of foes;

[1] *Appayed*, satisfied, pleased. *Well appayed*, *ill appayed*, are constantly used by Chaucer and other ancient writers.
[2] *To fine*, to bring to an end.

To eat up errors by opinion bred,
Not spend the dowry of a lawful bed.

"Time's glory is to calm contending kings,
To unmask falsehood, and bring truth to light,
To stamp the seal of time in aged things,
To wake the morn and sentinel the night,
To wrong the wronger till he render right;
To ruinate proud buildings with thy hours,
And smear with dust their glittering golden towers;

"To fill with worm-holes stately monuments,
To feed oblivion with decay of things,
To blot old books, and alter their contents,
To pluck the quills from ancient ravens' wings,
To dry the old oak's sap, and cherish springs;[1]
To spoil antiquities of hammered steel,
And turn the giddy round of Fortune's wheel;

"To show the beldame daughters of her daughter,
To make the child a man, the man a child,
To slay the tiger that doth live by slaughter,
To tame the unicorn and lion wild,
To mock the subtle, in themselves beguiled;
To cheer the ploughman with increaseful crops,
And waste huge stones with little water-drops.

"Why work'st thou mischief in thy pilgrimage,
Unless thou couldst return to make amends?
One poor retiring[2] minute in an age

[1] *Springs*, shoots, saplings. Time, which dries up the old oak's sap, cherishes the young plants.

[2] *Retiring* is here used in the sense of coming back again.

Would purchase thee a thousand thousand friends,
Lending him wit that to bad debtors lends:
O, this dread night, wouldst thou one hour come back,
I could prevent this storm, and shun thy wrack!

"Thou ceaseless lackey to eternity,
With some mischance cross Tarquin in his flight:
Devise extremes beyond extremity,
To make him curse this curséd crimeful night:
Let ghastly shadows his lewd eyes affright;
And the dire thought of his committed evil
Shape every bush a hideous, shapeless devil.

"Disturb his hours of rest with restless trances,
Afflict him in his bed with bedrid groans;
Let there bechance him pitiful mischances,
To make him moan, but pity not his moans:
Stone him with hardened hearts, harder than stones;
And let mild women to him lose their mildness,
Wilder to him than tigers in their wildness.

"Let him have time to tear his curléd hair,[1]
Let him have time against himself to rave,
Let him have time of Time's help to despair,
Let him have time to live a loathéd slave,
Let him have time a beggar's orts to crave;
And time to see one that by alms doth live
Disdain to him disdainéd scraps to give.

[1] *Curled hair* is the characteristic of Tarquin, as it was of all men of high rank in Shakspeare's time. Perhaps it implied a notion of luxuriousness. In this way we have "the *curled* Anthony;" and in Othello,

'The wealthy *curled* darlings of our nation."

"Let him have time to see his friends his foes,
And merry fools to mock at him resort;
Let him have time to mark how slow time goes
In time of sorrow, and how swift and short
His time of folly and his time of sport:
And ever let his unrecalling[1] crime
Have time to wail the abusing of his time.

"O Time, thou tutor both to good and bad,
Teach me to curse him that thou taught'st this ill!
At his own shadow let the thief run mad!
Himself himself seek every hour to kill!
Such wretched hands such wretched blood should spill;
For who so base would such an office have
As slanderous death's-man to so base a slave?

"The baser is he, coming from a king,
To shame his hope with deeds degenerate.
The mightier man, the mightier is the thing
That makes him honored, or begets him hate;
For greatest scandal waits on greatest state.
The moon being clouded presently is missed,
But little stars may hide them when they list.

"The crow may bathe his coal-black wings in mire,
And unperceived fly with the filth away;
But if the like the snow-white swan desire,
The stain upon his silver down will stay.
Poor grooms are sightless night, kings glorious day.
Gnats are unnoted wheresoe'er they fly,
But eagles gazed upon with every eye.

[1] *Unrecalling*, not to be recalled. The elder writers use the participle with much more license than we do.

"Out, idle words, servants to shallow fools!
Unprofitable sounds, weak arbitrators!
Busy yourselves in skill-contending schools,
Debate where leisure serves with dull debaters;
To trembling clients be you mediators:
For me, I force[1] not argument a straw,
Since that my case is past the help of law.

"In vain I rail at Opportunity,
At Time, at Tarquin, and uncheerful night;
In vain I cavil with my infamy,
In vain I spurn at my confirmed despite:
This helpless smoke of words doth me no right.
The remedy indeed to do me good,
Is to let forth my foul, defiléd blood.

"Poor hand, why quiver'st thou at this decree?
Honor thyself to rid me of this shame;
For if I die my honor lives in thee,
But if I live thou liv'st in my defame:
Since thou couldst not defend thy loyal dame,
And wast afeard to scratch her wicked foe,
Kill both thyself and her for yielding so."

This said, from her betumbled couch she starteth,
To find some desperate instrument of death:
But this no-slaughter-house no tool imparteth
To make more vent for passage of her breath,
Which thronging through her lips so vanisheth
As smoke from Ætna, that in air consumes,
Or that which from dischargéd cannon fumes.

1. *Force* is here used in the sense of value or regard.

"In vain," quoth she, "I live, and seek in vain
Some happy mean to end a hapless life.
I feared by Tarquin's falchion to be slain,
Yet for the selfsame purpose seek a knife:
But when I feared I was a loyal wife;
  So am I now: — O no, that cannot be;
  Of that true type hath Tarquin rifled me.

"O! that is gone for which I sought to live,
And therefore now I need not fear to die.
To clear this spot by death, at least I give
A badge of fame to slander's livery;[1]
A dying life to living infamy;
  Poor helpless help, the treasure stolen away,
  To burn the guiltless casket where it lay!

"Well, well, dear Collatine, thou shalt not know
The stainéd taste of violated troth;
I will not wrong thy true affection so
To flatter thee with an infringéd oath;
This bastard graff shall never come to growth;
  He shall not boast who did thy stock pollute
  That thou art doting father of his fruit.

"Nor shall he smile at thee in secret thought,
Nor laugh with his companions at thy state;
But thou shalt know thy interest was not bought
Basely with gold, but stolen from forth thy gate.
For me, I am the mistress of my fate,
  And with my trespass never will dispense,
  Till life to death acquit my forced offence.

[1] An allusion to the badges which servants or retainers of families of rank wore on their liveries.

"I will not poison thee with my attaint,
Nor fold my fault in cleanly-coined excuses;
My sable ground of sin I will not paint,
To hide the truth of this false night's abuses:
My tongue shall utter all; mine eyes like sluices,
As from a mountain-spring that feeds a dale,
Shall gush pure streams to purge my impure tale."

By this, lamenting Philomel had ended
The well-tuned warble of her nightly sorrow,
And solemn night with slow-sad gait descended
To ugly hell; when, lo, the blushing morrow
Lends light to all fair eyes that light will borrow:
But cloudy Lucrece shames herself to see,
And therefore still in night would cloistered be.

Revealing day through every cranny spies,
And seems to point her out where she sits weeping;
To whom she sobbing speaks: "O eye of eyes,
Why pry'st thou through my window? leave thy peeping;
Mock with thy tickling beams eyes that are sleeping:
Brand not my forehead with thy piercing light,
For day hath nought to do what's done by night."

Thus cavils she with every thing she sees:
True grief is fond [1] and testy as a child,
Who wayward once, his mood with nought agrees.
Old woes, not infant sorrows, bear them mild;
Continuance tames the one; the other wild,
Like an unpractised swimmer plunging still
With too much labor drowns for want of skill.

[1] *Fond*, foolish.

So she, deep-drenchéd in a sea of care,
Holds disputation with each thing she views,
And to herself all sorrow doth compare;
No object but her passion's strength renews;
And as one shifts, another straight ensues:
  Sometime her grief is dumb, and hath no words;
  Sometime 'tis mad, and too much talk affords.

The little birds that tune their morning's joy
Make her moans mad with their sweet melody.
For mirth doth search the bottom of annoy;
Sad souls are slain in merry company;
Grief best is pleased with grief's society:
  True sorrow then is feelingly sufficed
  When with like semblance it is sympathized.

'Tis double death to drown in ken of shore;
He ten times pines, that pines beholding food;
To see the salve doth make the wound ache more;
Great grief grieves most at that would do it good;
Deep woes roll forward like a gentle flood,
  Who, being stopped, the bounding banks o'erflows:
  Grief dallied with nor law nor limit knows.

"You mocking birds," quoth she, "your tunes entomb
Within your hollow-swelling feathered breasts,
And in my hearing be you mute and dumb!
(My restless discord loves no stops nor rests;
A woful hostess brooks not merry guests:)
  Relish your nimble notes to pleasing ears;
  Distress likes dumps[1] when time is kept with tears.

[1] *Dumps*, melancholy airs.

"Come, Philomel, that sing'st of ravishment,
Make thy sad grove in my dishevelled hair.
As the dank earth weeps at thy languishment,
So I at each sad strain will strain a tear,
And with deep groans the diapason bear:
  For burthen-wise I'll hum on Tarquin still,
  While thou on Tereus descant'st better skill.[1]

"And whiles against a thorn thou bear'st thy part,
To keep thy sharp woes waking, wretched I,
To imitate thee well, against my heart
Will fix a sharp knife, to affright mine eye;
Who, if it wink, shall thereon fall and die.
  These means, as frets upon an instrument,
  Shall tune our heartstrings to true languishment.

"And for, poor bird, thou sing'st not in the day,
As shaming any eye should thee behold,
Some dark deep desert, seated from the way,
That knows nor parching heat nor freezing cold,
We will find out; and there we will unfold
  To creatures stern sad tunes, to change their kinds:
  Since men prove beasts, let beasts bear gentle minds."

As the poor frighted deer, that stands at gaze,
Wildly determining which way to fly,
Or one encompassed with a winding maze,
That cannot tread the way out readily;
So with herself is she in mutiny,
  To live or die which of the twain were better,
  When life is shamed, and Death reproach's debtor.

[1] *Better skill.* We must probably here understand *with* better skill.

"To kill myself," quoth she, "alack! what were it,
But with my body my poor soul's pollution?
They that lose half with greater patience bear it
Than they whose whole is swallowed in confusion.
That mother tries a merciless conclusion
Who, having two sweet babes, when death takes one,
Will slay the other, and be nurse to none.

"My body or my soul, which was the dearer?
When the one pure, the other made divine.
Whose love of either to myself was nearer?
When both were kept for heaven and Collatine.
Ah me! the bark peeled from the lofty pine,
His leaves will wither and his sap decay;
So must my soul, her bark being peeled away.

"Her house is sacked, her quiet interrupted,
Her mansion battered by the enemy;
Her sacred temple spotted, spoiled, corrupted,
Grossly engirt with daring infamy;
Then let it not be called impiety
If in this blemished fort I make some hole
Through which I may convey this troubled soul.

"Yet die I will not till my Collatine
Have heard the cause of my untimely death;
That he may vow in that sad hour of mine,
Revenge on him that made me stop my breath.
My stainéd blood to Tarquin I'll bequeath,
Which by him tainted shall for him be spent,
And as his due writ in my testament.

"My honor I'll bequeath unto the knife
That wounds my body so dishonoréd

'Tis honor to deprive dishonored life;
The one will live, the other being dead;
So of shame's ashes shall my fame be bred;
For in my death I murther shameful scorn;
My shame so dead, mine honor is new-born.

"Dear lord of that dear jewel I have lost,
What legacy shall I bequeath to thee?
My resolution, Love, shall be thy boast,
By whose example thou revenged mayst be.
How Tarquin must be used, read it in me:
Myself, thy friend, will kill myself, thy foe,
And, for my sake, serve thou false Tarquin so

"This brief abridgment of my will I make:
My soul and body to the skies and ground;
My resolution, husband, do thou take;
Mine honor be the knife's that makes my wound;
My shame be his that did my fame confound;
And all my fame that lives disburséd be
To those that live and think no shame of me.

"Thou, Collatine, shalt oversee this will;[1]
How was I overseen that thou shalt see it!
My blood shall wash the slander of mine ill;
My life's foul deed my life's fair end shall free it.
Faint not faint heart, but stoutly say, 'So be it.'
Yield to my hand; my hand shall conquer thee;
Thou dead, both die, and both shall victors be."

[1] The executor of a will was sometimes called the *overseer;* but our ancestors often appointed overseers as well as executors. Shakspeare's own will contains such an appointment.

This plot of death when sadly she had laid,
And wiped the brinish pearl from her bright eyes,
With untuned tongue she hoarsely called her maid,
Whose swift obedience to her mistress hies;
For fleet-winged duty with thought's feathers flies.
  Poor Lucrece' cheeks unto her maid seem so
  As winter meads when sun doth melt their snow.

Her mistress she doth give demure good-morrow,
With soft-slow tongue, true mark of modesty,
And sorts a sad look to her lady's sorrow,
(For why? her face wore sorrow's livery,)
But durst not ask of her audaciously
  Why her two suns were cloud-eclipséd so,
  Nor why her fair cheeks over-washed with woe.

But as the earth doth weep, the sun being set,[1]
Each flower moistened like a melting eye;
Even so the maid with swelling drops 'gan wet
Her circled eyne, enforced by sympathy
Of those fair suns, set in her mistress' sky,
  Who in a salt-waved ocean quench their light,
  Which makes the maid weep like the dewy night.

[1] In the folio edition of Romeo and Juliet, as well as in the quarto of 1597, we find the line —

"When the sun sets, the *earth* doth drizzle dew."

Here the image completely agrees with that in the text before us. But in the undated quarto, which the modern editors follow, we have "the *air* doth drizzle dew." Science was long puzzled to decide whether the earth or the air produced dew; but it was reserved for the accurate experiments of modern times to show that the earth and the air must unite to produce this effect under particular circumstances of temperature and radiation. The correction of the undated edition of Romeo and Juliet was certainly unnecessary.

A pretty while these pretty creatures stand,
Like ivory conduits coral cisterns filling:
One justly weeps; the other takes in hand
No cause, but company, of her drops spilling:
Their gentle sex to weep are often willing;
Grieving themselves to guess at others' smarts,
And then they drown their eyes, or break their hearts.

For men have marble, women waxen minds,
And therefore are they formed as marble will;[1]
The weak oppressed, the impression of strange kinds
Is formed in them by force, by fraud, or skill:
Then call them not the authors of their ill,
No more than wax shall be accounted evil,
Wherein is stamped the semblance of a devil.

Their smoothness, like a goodly champaign plain,
Lays open all the little worms that creep;
In men, as in a rough-grown grove, remain
Cave-keeping evils that obscurely sleep:
Through crystal walls each little mote will peep:
Though men can cover crimes with bold, stern looks,
Poor women's faces are their own faults' books.

No man inveigh against the withered flower,
But chide rough winter that the flower hath killed!
Not that devoured, but that which doth devour,
Is worthy blame. O, let it not be hild[2]
Poor women's faults that they are so fulfilled[3]

[1] *Marble* here stands for men whose minds have just been compared to marble.

[2] *Hild*, held. Such a change for the sake of rhyme is frequent in Spenser.

[3] *Fulfilled*, completely filled.

With men's abuses! those proud lords, to blame,
Make weak-made women tenants to their shame.

The precedent whereof in Lucrece view,
Assailed by night with circumstances strong
Of present death, and shame that might ensue
By that her death, to do her husband wrong:
Such danger to resistance did belong,
That dying fear through all her body spread;
And who cannot abuse a body dead?

By this, mild patience bid fair Lucrece speak
To the poor counterfeit[1] of her complaining:
"My girl," quoth she, "on what occasion break
Those tears from thee, that down thy cheeks are raining?
If thou dost weep for grief of my sustaining,
Know, gentle wench, it small avails my mood:
If tears could help, mine own would do me good.

"But tell me, girl, when went" (and there she stayed
Till after a deep groan) "Tarquin from hence?"
"Madam, ere I was up," replied the maid,
"The more to blame my sluggard negligence:
Yet with the fault I thus far can dispense;
Myself was stirring ere the break of day,
And, ere I rose, was Tarquin gone away.

"But, lady, if your maid may be so bold,
She would request to know your heaviness."
"O peace!" quoth Lucrece; "if it should be told,

[1] *Counterfeit*, a likeness or copy.

The repetition cannot make it less;
For more it is than I can well express:
  And that deep torture may be called a hell,
  When more is felt than one hath power to tell.

"Go, get me hither paper, ink, and pen —
Yet save that labor, for I have them here.
What should I say?— One of my husband's men
Bid thou be ready, by and by, to bear
A letter to my lord, my love, my dear;
  Bid him with speed prepare to carry it:
  The cause craves haste, and it will soon be writ."

Her maid is gone, and she prepares to write,
First hovering o'er the paper with her quill:
Conceit and grief an eager combat fight;
What wit sets down is blotted straight with will;
This is too curious-good, this blunt and ill:
  Much like a press of people at a door,
  Throng her inventions, which shall be before.

At last she thus begins: "Thou worthy lord
Of that unworthy wife that greeteth thee,
Health to thy person! next vouchsafe t' afford
(If ever, love, thy Lucrece thou wilt see)
Some present speed to come and visit me:
  So I commend me from our house in grief;[1]
  My woes are tedious, though my words are brief."

[1] The simplicity of this letter is exquisitely beautiful; and its pathos is deeper from the circumstance that it is scarcely raised above the tone of ordinary correspondence.

"So I commend me from our house in grief"

is such a formula as we constantly find in ancient correspondence. In the "Paston Letters" we have such conclusions as this: "Written at ——, when I was not well at ease."

Here folds she up the tenor of her woe,
Her certain sorrow writ uncertainly.
By this short schedule Collatine may know
Her grief, but not her grief's true quality;
She dares not thereof make discovery,
  Lest he should hold it her own gross abuse,
  Ere she with blood had stained her stained excuse.

Besides, the life and feeling of her passion
She hoards, to spend when he is by to hear her;
When sighs, and groans, and tears may grace the fashion
Of her disgrace, the better so to clear her
From that suspicion which the world might bear her.
  To shun this blot, she would not blot the letter
  With words, till action might become them better.

To see sad sights moves more than hear them told;
For then the eye interprets to the ear
The heavy motion that it doth behold,[1]
When every part a part of woe doth bear.
'Tis but a part of sorrow that we hear:
  Deep sounds[2] make lesser noise than shallow fords,
  And sorrow ebbs, being blown with wind of words.

Her letter now is sealed, and on it writ,
"At Ardea to my lord with more than haste:"
The post attends, and she delivers it,
Charging the sour-faced groom to hie as fast
As lagging fowls before the northern blast.

1 *Motion*, dumb show.

2 *Sounds.* Malone proposes to read *floods.* This Steevens resists, and says that *sound* is such a part of the sea as may be sounded. To this Malone replies that a sound cannot be deep, and therefore sounds is not here intended. A sound is a bay or frith;

Speed more than speed but dull and slow she deems:
Extremity still urgeth such extremes.

The homely villein court'sies to her low;
And blushing on her, with a steadfast eye
Receives the scroll, without or yea or no,
And forth with bashful innocence doth hie.
But they whose guilt within their bosoms lie
Imagine every eye beholds their blame;
For Lucrece thought he blushed to see her shame;

When, silly groom! God wot, it was defect
Of spirit, life, and bold audacity.
Such harmless creatures have a true respect
To talk in deeds, while others saucily
Promise more speed, but do it leisurely:
Even so, this pattern of the worn-out age
Pawned honest looks, but laid no words to gage.

His kindled duty kindled her mistrust,
That two red fires in both their faces blazed:
She thought he blushed, as knowing Tarquin's lust,
And, blushing with him, wistly on him gazed;
Her earnest eye did make him more amazed:
The more she saw the blood his cheeks replenish,
The more she thought he spied in her some blemish.

But long she thinks till he return again,
And yet the duteous vassal scarce is gone.
The weary time she cannot entertain,

and Dampier, who is better authority than the commentators on nautical matters, mentions a *sound* as "large and deep." The stillness of a sound, in consequence of being land-locked, testifies to the correctness of the poet's image.

For now 'tis stale to sigh, to weep, and groan:
So woe hath wearied woe, moan tired moan,
That she her plaints a little while doth stay,
Pausing for means to mourn some newer way.

At last she calls to mind where hangs a piece
Of skilful painting, made for Priam's Troy;
Before the which is drawn [1] the power of Greece,
For Helen's rape the city to destroy,
Threatening cloud-kissing Ilion with annoy;
Which the conceited [2] painter drew so proud,
As heaven (it seemed) to kiss the turrets bowed.

A thousand lamentable objects there,
In scorn of Nature, Art gave lifeless life:
Many a dry drop seemed a weeping tear,
Shed for the slaughtered husband by the wife:
The red blood reeked to show the painter's strife;
And dying eyes gleamed forth their ashy lights,
Like dying coals burnt out in tedious nights.

There might you see the laboring pioneer
Begrimed with sweat, and smearéd all with dust;
And from the towers of Troy there would appear
The very eyes of men through loopholes thrust,
Gazing upon the Greeks with little lust:
Such sweet observance in this work was had,
That one might see those far-off eyes look sad.

In great commanders grace and majesty
You might behold, triúmphing in their faces;
In youth, quick bearing and dexterity;

[1] *Drawn*, drawn out into the field.
[2] *Conceited*, ingenious, imaginative

And here and there the painter interlaces
Pale cowards, marching on with trembling paces;
  Which heartless peasants did so well resemble,
  That one would swear he saw them quake and
      tremble.

In Ajax and Ulysses, O, what art
Of physiognomy might one behold!
The face of either 'ciphered either's heart;
Their face their manners most expressly told:
In Ajax' eyes blunt rage and rigor rolled;
  But the mild glance that sly Ulysses lent
  Showed deep regard and smiling government.

There pleading might you see grave Nestor stand,
As 'twere encouraging the Greeks to fight;
Making such sober action with his hand
That it beguiled attention, charmed the sight:
In speech, it seemed, his beard all silver white
  Wagged up and down, and from his lips did fly
  Thin winding breath, which purled up[1] to the
      sky.

About him were a press of gaping faces,
Which seemed to swallow up his sound advice;
All jointly listening, but with several graces,
As if some mermaid did their ears entice;
Some high, some low, the painter was so nice:

[1] *Purled.* The meaning of *purl*, as applied to a sound, is familiar to all. Bacon, in speaking of the sound of a pipe, mentions "a sweet degree of sibilation or purling." Thus, in the passage before us, the thin winding breath of Nestor, the soft flowing words, *purled* up to the sky. But the commentators believe that purled here expresses motion, and not sound; and Steevens proposes to substitute *curled.*

The scalps of many, almost hid behind,
To jump up higher seemed to mock the mind.

Here one man's hand leaned on another's head,
His nose being shadowed by his neighbor's ear;
Here one being thronged bears back, all boll'n[1] and red;
Another smothered seems to pelt[2] and swear;
And in their rage such signs of rage they bear,
As, but for loss of Nestor's golden words,
It seemed they would debate with angry swords.

For much imaginary work was there;
Conceit deceitful, so compact, so kind,[3]
That for Achilles' image stood his spear,
Griped in an arméd hand; himself, behind,
Was left unseen, save to the eye of mind:
A hand, a foot, a face, a leg, a head,
Stood for the whole to be imaginéd.

And from the walls of strong besiegéd Troy
When their brave hope, bold Hector, marched to field,
Stood many Trojan mothers, sharing joy
To see their youthful sons bright weapons wield;
And to their hope they such odd action yield,
That through their light joy seeméd to appear
(Like bright things stained) a kind of heavy fear.

And, from the strond of Dardan where they fought,
To Simois' reedy banks, the red blood ran,
Whose waves to imitate the battle sought

1 *Boll'n*, swollen.
2 *Pelt*, to be clamorous, to discharge hasty words as pellets.
3 *Kind*, natural.

With swelling ridges; and their ranks began
To break upon the gallèd shore, and than[1]
  Retire again, till meeting greater ranks
  They join, and shoot their foam at Simois' banks.

To this well-painted piece is Lucrece come
To find a face where all distress is stel'd.[2]
Many she sees where cares have carvèd some,
But none where all distress and dolor dwelled,
Till she despairing Hecuba beheld,
  Staring on Priam's wounds with her old eyes,
  Which bleeding under Pyrrhus' proud foot lies.

In her the painter had anatomized
Time's ruin, beauty's wrack, and grim care's reign;
Her cheeks with chaps and wrinkles were disguised;

1 *Than*, used for *then*. This is another example (we had one before in *hild*) of changing a termination for the sake of rhyme. In Fairfax's "Tasso" there is a parallel instance:—

> "Time was, (for each one hath his doting time,
>   These silver locks were golden tresses *than*,)
> That country life I hated as a crime,
>   And from the forest's sweet contentment ran."

2 *Stel'd*. A passage in the twenty-fourth Sonnet may explain the lines in the text:—

> "Mine eye hath played the painter, and hath *stel'd*
> Thy beauty's form in table of my heart."

The word *stel'd*, in both instances, has a distinct association with something painted: but *to stell* is interpreted as to fix, from *stell*, a fixed place of abode. It appears to us that the word is connected in Shakspeare's mind with the word *stile*, the pencil by which forms are traced and copied. The application does not appear forced, when we subsequently find the poet using the expression of "*pencilled* pensiveness." We constantly use the term *stile* as applied to painting; but we all know that *stile*, as describing the manner of delineating forms, is derived from the instrument by which characters were anciently *written*. *Stel'd* is probably then *stil'd*, the word being slightly changed to suit the rhyme.

Of what she was no semblance did remain:
Her blue blood, changed to black in every vein,
  Wanting the spring that those shrunk pipes had fed,
  Showed life imprisoned in a body dead.

On this sad shadow Lucrece spends her eyes,
And shapes her sorrow to the beldame's woes,
Who nothing wants to answer her but cries,
And bitter words to ban her cruel foes:
The painter was no God to lend her those;
  And therefore Lucrece swears he did her wrong,
  To give her so much grief and not a tongue.

"Poor instrument," quoth she, "without a sound,
I'll tune thy woes with my lamenting tongue;
And drop sweet balm in Priam's painted wound,
And rail on Pyrrhus that hath done him wrong,
And with my tears quench Troy that burns so long;
  And with my knife scratch out the angry eyes
  Of all the Greeks that are thine enemies.

"Show me the strumpet that began this stir,
That with my nails her beauty I may tear.
Thy heat of lust, fond Paris, did incur
This load of wrath that burning Troy doth bear;
Thy eye kindléd the fire that burneth here:
  And here in Troy, for trespass of thine eye,
  The sire, the son, the dame, and daughter die.

"Why should the private pleasure of some one
Become the public plague of many mo?[1]
Let sin, alone committed, light alone

[1] *Mo*, more.

Upon his head that hath transgresséd so.
Let guiltless souls be freed from guilty woe:
  For one's offence, why should so many fall,
  To plague a private sin in general?

"Lo, here weeps Hecuba, here Priam dies,
Here manly Hector faints, here Troilus swounds:[1]
Here friend by friend in bloody channel lies,
And friend to friend gives unadviséd[2] wounds,
And one man's lust these many lives confounds:[3]
  Had doting Priam checked his son's desire,
  Troy had been bright with fame, and not with fire."

Here feelingly she weeps Troy's painted woes:
For sorrow, like a heavy-hanging bell,
Once set on ringing, with his own weight goes;
Then little strength rings out the doleful knell:
So Lucrece set a-work sad tales doth tell
  To pencilled pensiveness and colored sorrow;
  She lends them words, and she their looks doth borrow.

She throws her eyes about the painting, round,
And whom she finds forlorn she doth lament:
At last she sees a wretched image bound,
That piteous looks to Phrygian shepherds lent;
His face, though full of cares, yet showed content:
  Onward to Troy with the blunt swains he goes,
  So mild that Patience seemed to scorn his woes.

1 *Swounds*, swoons. It is probable that the word was so usually pronounced. In Drayton *swound* rhymes to wound.

2 *Unadvised*, unknowing.

3 *Confounds* is here used in the sense of destroys.

In him the painter labored with his skill
To hide deceit, and give the harmless show
An humble gait, calm looks, eyes wailing still,
A brow unbent, that seemed to welcome woe;
Cheeks neither red nor pale, but mingled so
 That blushing red no guilty instance gave,
 Nor ashy pale the fear that false hearts have.

But, like a constant and confirméd devil,
He entertained a show so seeming just,
And therein so ensconced his secret evil,
That jealousy itself could not mistrust
False-creeping craft and perjury should thrust
 Into so bright a day such black-faced storms,
 Or blot with hell-born sin such saint-like forms.

The well-skilled workman this mild image drew
For perjured Sinon, whose enchanting story
The credulous old Priam after slew;
Whose words, like wildfire, burnt the shining glory
Of rich-built Ilion, that the skies were sorry,
 And little stars shot from their fixéd places,
 When their glass fell wherein they viewed their faces.[1]

This picture she advisedly[2] perused,
And chid the painter for his wondrous skill;
Saying, some shape in Sinon's was abused,

[1] Malone objects to this image of Priam's palace being the mirror in which the fixed stars beheld themselves. Boswell has answered Malone by quoting Lydgate's description of the same wonderful edifice: —

"That verely when so the sonne shone
Upon the golde meynt amonge the stone,
They gave a lyght withouten any were,
As doth Apollo in his mid-day sphere."

[2] *Advisedly*, attentively.

So fair a form lodged not a mind so ill;
And still on him she gazed, and gazing still,
  Such signs of truth in his plain face she spied,
  That she concludes the picture was belied.

"It cannot be," quoth she, "that so much guile"
(She would have said) "can lurk in such a look;"
But Tarquin's shape came in her mind the while,
And from her tongue "can lurk" from "cannot" took;
"It cannot be" she in that sense forsook,
  And turned it thus: "It cannot be, I find,
  But such a face should bear a wicked mind:

"For even as subtle Sinon here is painted,
So sober-sad, so weary, and so mild,
(As if with grief or travail he had fainted,)
To me came Tarquin armèd; so beguiled[1]
With outward honesty, but yet defiled
  With inward vice: as Priam him did cherish,
  So did I Tarquin; so my Troy did perish.

"Look, look, how listening Priam wets his eyes,
To see those borrowed tears that Sinon sheds.
Priam, why art thou old, and yet not wise?
For every tear he falls[2] a Trojan bleeds;
His eye drops fire, no water thence proceeds:
  Those round clear pearls of his that move thy pity
  Are balls of quenchless fire to burn thy city.

[1] *So beguiled.* The original has *to beguiled.* Beguiled is masked with fraud. In The Merchant of Venice we have,—

"Thus ornament is but the *guiled* shore
To a most dangerous sea."

[2] *Falls*, lets fall.

"Such devils steal effects from lightless hell;
For Sinon in his fire doth quake with cold,
And in that cold hot-burning fire doth dwell;
These contraries such unity do hold
Only to flatter fools, and make them bold:
So Priam's trust false Sinon's tears doth flatter,
That he finds means to burn his Troy with water."

Here, all enraged, such passion her assails,
That patience is quite beaten from her breast.
She tears the senseless Sinon with her nails,
Comparing him to that unhappy guest
Whose deed hath made herself herself detest:
At last she smilingly with this gives o'er;
"Fool! fool!" quoth she, "his wounds will not be sore."

Thus ebbs and flows the current of her sorrow,
And time doth weary time with her complaining.
She looks for night, and then she longs for morrow,
And both she thinks too long with her remaining:
Short time seems long in sorrow's sharp sustaining.
Though woe be heavy, yet it seldom sleeps;
And they that watch see time how slow it creeps.

Which all this time hath overslipped her thought,
That she with painted images hath spent:
Being from the feeling of her own grief brought
By deep surmise of others' detriment;
Losing her woes in shows of discontent.
It easeth some, though none it ever cured,
To think their dolor others have endured.

But now the mindful messenger, come back,
Brings home his lord and other company;
Who finds his Lucrece clad in mourning black;
And round about her tear-distained eye
Blue circles streamed, like rainbows in the sky.
These water-galls [1] in her dim element
Foretell new storms to those already spent.

Which when her sad-beholding husband saw,
Amazedly in her sad face he stares:
Her eyes, though sod in tears, looked red and raw,
Her lively color killed with deadly cares.
He hath no power to ask her how she fares,
But stood, like old acquaintance in a trance,
Met far from home, wondering each other's chance.

At last he takes her by the bloodless hand,
And thus begins: "What uncouth ill event
Hath thee befallen, that thou dost trembling stand?
Sweet love, what spite hath thy fair color spent?
Why art thou thus attired in discontent?
Unmask, dear dear, this moody heaviness,
And tell thy grief, that we may give redress."

Three times with sighs she gives her sorrow fire
Ere once she can discharge one word of woe:
At length addressed [2] to answer his desire,
She modestly prepares to let them know
Her honor is ta'en prisoner by the foe;
While Collatine and his consorted lords
With sad attention long to hear her words.

[1] *Water-galls.* Steevens says the word is current among the shepherds on Salisbury Plain.
[2] *Addressed*, prepared.

And now this pale swan in her watery nest
Begins the sad dirge of her certain ending:
"Few words," quoth she, "shall fit the trespass best,
Where no excuse can give the fault amending:
In me more woes than words are now depending;
And my laments would be drawn out too long,
To tell them all with one poor tiréd tongue.

"Then be this all the task it hath to say: —
Dear husband, in the interest of thy bed
A stranger came, and on that pillow lay
Where thou wast wont to rest thy weary head;
And what wrong else may be imaginéd
By foul enforcement might be done to me,
From that, alas, thy Lucrece is not free.

"For in the dreadful dead of dark midnight,
With shining falchion in my chamber came
A creeping creature, with a flaming light,
And softly cried, Awake, thou Roman dame,
And entertain my love; else lasting shame
On thee and thine this night I will inflict,
If thou my love's desire do contradict.

"For some hard-favored groom of thine, quoth he,
Unless thou yoke thy liking to my will,
I'll murder straight, and then I'll slaughter thee,
And swear I found you where you did fulfil
The loathsome act of lust, and so did kill
The lechers in their deed: this act will be
My fame, and thy perpetual infamy.

"With this I did begin to start and cry,
And then against my heart he set his sword,
Swearing, unless I took all patiently

I should not live to speak another word:
So should my shame still rest upon record,
  And never be forgot in mighty Rome
  The adulterate death of Lucrece and her groom.

"Mine enemy was strong, my poor self weak,
And far the weaker with so strong a fear:
My bloody judge forbade my tongue to speak;
No rightful plea might plead for justice there:
His scarlet lust came evidence to swear
  That my poor beauty had purloined his eyes,
  And when the judge is robbed, the prisoner dies.

"O, teach me how to make mine own excuse!
Or, at the least, this refuge let me find;
Though my gross blood be stained with this abuse,
Immaculate and spotless is my mind;
That was not forced; that never was inclined
  To accessory yieldings, but still pure
  Doth in her poisoned closet yet endure."

Lo here, the hopeless merchant of this loss,
With head declined, and voice dammed up with woe,
With sad-set eyes, and wretched arms across,
From lips new-waxen pale begins to blow
The grief away that stops his answer so:
  But wretched as he is, he strives in vain;
  What he breathes out his breath drinks up again.

As through an arch the violent roaring tide
Outruns the eye that doth behold his haste;
Yet in the eddy boundeth in his pride
Back to the strait that forced him on so fast;
In rage sent out, recalled in rage, being past:

Even so he sighs, his sorrows make a saw,
To push grief on, and back the same grief draw.

Which speechless woe of his poor she attendeth,
And his untimely frenzy thus awaketh:
"Dear lord, thy sorrow to my sorrow lendeth
Another power; no flood by raining slaketh.
My woe too sensible, thy passion maketh
More feeling-painful: let it then suffice
To drown one woe, one pair of weeping eyes.

"And for my sake, when I might charm thee so,
For she that was thy Lucrece, — now attend me;
Be suddenly revengéd on my foe,
Thine, mine, his own; suppose thou dost defend me
From what is past: the help that thou shalt lend me
Comes all too late, yet let the traitor die;
For sparing justice feeds iniquity.

"But ere I name him, you, fair lords," quoth she,
(Speaking to those that came with Collatine,)
"Shall plight your honorable faiths to me,
With swift pursuit to venge this wrong of mine;
For 'tis a meritorious fair design
To chase injustice with revengeful arms:
Knights, by their oaths, should right poor ladies' harms."

At this request, with noble disposition
Each present lord began to promise aid,
As bound in knighthood to her imposition,
Longing to hear the hateful foe bewrayed.
But she, that yet her sad task hath not said,
The protestation stops. "O speak," quoth she,
"How may this forcéd stain be wiped from me?

"What is the quality of mine offence,
Being constrained with dreadful circumstance?
May my pure mind with the foul act dispense,
My low-declinéd honor to advance?
May any terms acquit me from this chance?
  The poisoned fountain clears itself again;
  And why not I from this compelléd stain?"

With this, they all at once began to say,
Her body's stain her mind untainted clears;
While with a joyless smile she turns away
The face, that map which deep impression bears
Of hard misfortune, carved in it with tears.
  "No, no," quoth she; "no dame, hereafter living,
  By my excuse shall claim excuse's giving."

Here with a sigh, as if her heart would break,
She throws forth Tarquin's name: "He, he," she says,
But more than "he" her poor tongue could not speak;
Till after many accents and delays,
Untimely breathings, sick and short assays,
  She utters this: "He, he, fair lords, 'tis he,
  That guides this hand to give this wound to me."

Even here she sheathéd in her harmless breast
A harmful knife, that thence her soul unsheathed:
That blow did bail it from the deep unrest
Of that polluted prison where it breathed:
Her contrite sighs unto the clouds bequeathed
  Her wingéd sprite, and through her wounds doth fly
  Life's lasting date from cancelled destiny.

Stone-still, astonished with this deadly deed,
Stood Collatine and all his lordly crew;
Till Lucrece' father, that beholds her bleed,
Himself on her self-slaughtered body threw;
And from the purple fountain Brutus drew
  The murderous knife, and as it left the place,
  Her blood, in poor revenge, held it in chase;

And bubbling from her breast, it doth divide
In two slow rivers, that the crimson blood
Circles her body in on every side,
Who like a late-sacked island vastly[1] stood
Bare and unpeopled, in this fearful flood.
  Some of her blood still pure and red remained,
  And some looked black, and that false Tarquin stained.

About the mourning and congealéd face
Of that black blood a watery rigol[2] goes,
Which seems to weep upon the tainted place:
And ever since, as pitying Lucrece' woes,
Corrupted blood some watery token shows;
  And blood untainted still doth red abide,
  Blushing at that which is so putrefied.

"Daughter, dear daughter," old Lucretius cries,
"That life was mine which thou hast here deprived.
If in the child the father's image lies,
Where shall I live now Lucrece is unlived?
Thou wast not to this end from me derived.
  If children predecease progenitors,
  We are their offspring, and they none of ours.

1 *Vastly*, like a waste.

2 *Rigol*, circle.

"Poor broken glass, I often did behold
In thy sweet semblance my old age new born;
But now that fair, fresh mirror, dim and old,
Shows me a bareboned death by time outworn;
O, from thy cheek my image thou hast torn!
And shivered all the beauty of my glass,
That I no more can see what once I was.

"O Time, cease thou thy course, and last no longer,
If they surcease to be that should survive.
Shall rotten death make conquest of the stronger,
And leave the faltering, feeble souls alive?
The old bees die, the young possess their hive:
Then live, sweet Lucrece, live again, and see
Thy father die, and not thy father thee."

By this starts Collatine as from a dream,
And bids Lucretius give his sorrow place;
And then in key-cold[1] Lucrece' bleeding stream
He falls and bathes the pale fear in his face,
And counterfeits to die with her a space;
Till manly shame bids him possess his breath,
And live, to be revengéd on her death.

The deep vexation of his inward soul
Hath served a dumb arrest upon his tongue;
Who, mad that sorrow should his use control,
Or keep him from heart-easing words so long,
Begins to talk; but through his lips do throng

[1] *Key-cold.* So in Richard III. Act I. Sc. II.:—

"Poor *key-cold* figure of a holy king."

See note on that passage; which, however, we do not strictly adhere to, conceiving, upon some discussion of the matter with a friend, that *key-cold* simply means cold as a key.

Weak words, so thick come, in his poor heart's aid,
That no man could distinguish what he said.

Yet sometime Tarquin was pronouncéd plain,
But through his teeth, as if the name he tore.
This windy-tempest, till it blow up rain,
Held back his sorrow's tide, to make it more.
At last it rains, and busy winds give o'er:
Then son and father weep with equal strife,
Who should weep most for daughter or for wife.

The one doth call her his, the other his,
Yet neither may possess the claim they lay.
The father says, "She 's mine." "O, mine she is,"
Replies her husband: "do not take away
My sorrow's interest; let no mourner say
He weeps for her, for she was only mine,
And only must be wailed by Collatine."

"O," quoth Lucretius, "I did give that life
Which she too early and too late[1] hath spilled."
"Woe, woe," quoth Collatine, "she was my wife,
I owed her, and 'tis mine that she hath killed."
"My daughter" and "my wife" with clamours filled
The dispersed air, who, holding Lucrece' life,
Answered their cries, "my daughter" and "my wife."

Brutus, who plucked the knife from Lucrece' side,
Seeing such emulation in their woe,
Began to clothe his wit in state and pride,

[1] *Too late*, too recently.

Burying in Lucrece' wound his folly's show.
He with the Romans was esteeméd so
As silly jeering idiots are with kings,
For sportive words, and uttering foolish things.

But now he throws that shallow habit by,
Wherein deep policy did him disguise;
And armed his long-hid wits advisedly,
To check the tears in Collatinus' eyes,
"Thou wrongéd lord of Rome," quoth he, "arise;
Let my unsounded self, supposed a fool,
Now set thy long-experienced wit to school.

"Why, Collatine, is woe the cure for woe?
Do wounds help wounds, or grief help grievous deeds?
Is it revenge to give thyself a blow,
For his foul act by whom thy fair wife bleeds?
Such childish humor from weak minds proceeds:
Thy wretched wife mistook the matter so,
To slay herself, that should have slain her foe.

"Courageous Roman, do not steep thy heart
In such relenting dew of lamentations,
But kneel with me, and help to bear thy part,
To rouse our Roman gods with invocations,
That they will suffer these abominations,
(Since Rome herself in them doth stand disgraced,)
By our strong arms from forth her fair streets chased.

"Now, by the Capitol that we adore,
And by this chaste blood so unjustly stained,
By Heaven's fair sun that breeds the fat earth's store,

By all our country rights in Rome maintained,
And by chaste Lucrece' soul that late complained [1]
  Her wrongs to us, and by this bloody knife,
  We will revenge the death of this true wife."

This said, he struck his hand upon his breast,
And kissed the fatal knife to end his vow;
And to his protestation urged the rest,
Who, wondering at him, did his words allow: [2]
Then jointly to the ground their knees they bow;
  And that deep vow which Brutus made before,
  He doth again repeat, and that they swore.

When they had sworn to this advisèd doom,
They did conclude to bear dead Lucrece thence;
To show her bleeding body thorough Rome,
And so to publish Tarquin's foul offence:
Which being done with speedy diligence,
  The Romans plausibly [3] did give consent
  To Tarquin's everlasting banishment.

[1] *Complained* was formerly used without a subjoined preposition.
[2] *Allow*, approve.
[3] *Plausibly*, with expressions of applause; with acclamation. *Plausively*, applausively.

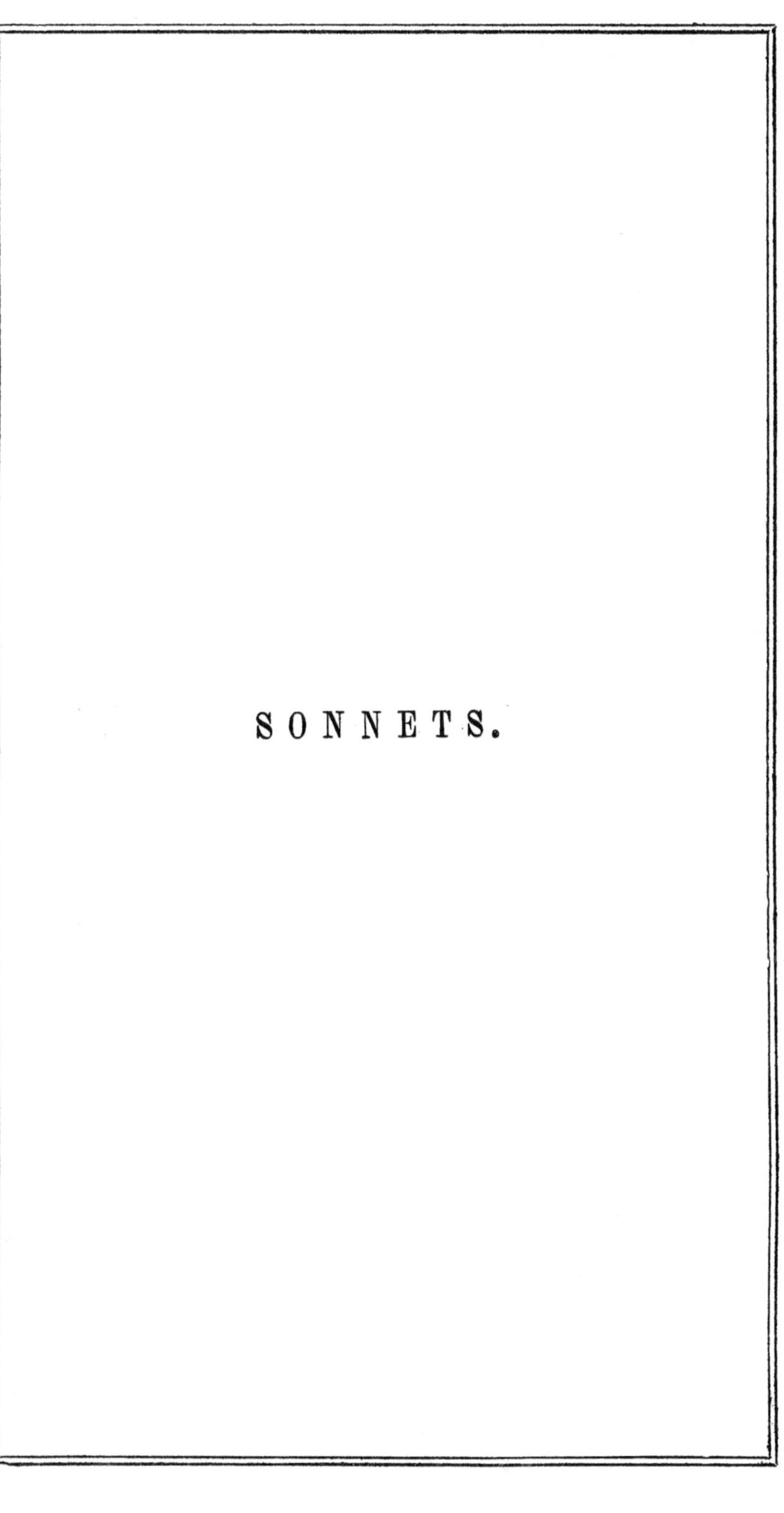

SONNETS.

TO

THE ONLY BEGETTER OF THESE ENSUING SONNETS,

MR. W. H.,

ALL HAPPINESS,

AND

THAT ETERNITY PROMISED BY OUR EVER-LIVING POET,

WISHETH

THE WELL-WISHING ADVENTURER

IN SETTING FORTH.

T. T.

SONNETS.

I.

FROM fairest creatures we desire increase,
That thereby beauty's rose might never die,
But as the riper should by time decease,
His tender heir might bear his memory:
But thou, contracted to thine own bright eyes,
Feed'st thy light's flame with self-substantial fuel,
Making a famine where abundance lies,
Thyself thy foe, to thy sweet self too cruel.
Thou that art now the world's fresh ornament,
And only herald to the gaudy spring,
Within thine own bud buriest thy content,
And, tender churl, mak'st waste in niggarding.
  Pity the world, or else this glutton be,
  To eat the world's due, by the grave and thee.

II.

When forty winters shall besiege thy brow,
And dig deep trenches in thy beauty's field,

Thy youth's proud livery, so gazed on now,
Will be a tattered weed[1] of small worth held:
Then being asked where all thy beauty lies,
Where all the treasure of thy lusty days;
To say, within thine own deep sunken eyes,
Were an all-eating shame and thriftless praise.
How much more praise deserved thy beauty's use,
If thou couldst answer, "This fair child of mine
Shall sum my count, and make my old excuse —"
Proving his beauty by succession thine!
  This were to be new-made when thou art old,
  And see thy blood warm when thou feel'st it cold.

III.

Look in thy glass, and tell the face thou viewest,
Now is the time that face should form another;
Whose fresh repair if now thou not renewest,
Thou dost beguile the world, unbless some mother.
For where is she so fair whose uneared[2] womb
Disdains the tillage of thy husbandry?
Or who is he so fond[3] will be the tomb
Of his self-love to stop posterity?
Thou art thy mother's glass, and she in thee
Calls back the lovely April of her prime:
So thou through windows of thine age shalt see,
Despite of wrinkles, this thy golden time.
  But if thou live, remembered not to be,
  Die single, and thine image dies with thee.

[1] *Weed*, garment. [2] *Uneared*, unploughed. [3] *Fond*, foolish.

IV.

Unthrifty loveliness, why dost thou spend
Upon thyself thy beauty's legacy?
Nature's bequest gives nothing, but doth lend,
And being frank, she lends to those are free.
Then, beauteous niggard, why dost thou abuse
The bounteous largess given thee to give?
Profitless usurer, why dost thou use
So great a sum of sums, yet canst not live?
For having traffic with thyself alone,
Thou of thyself thy sweet self dost deceive.
Then how, when nature calls thee to be gone,
What acceptable audit canst thou leave?
  The unused beauty must be tombed with thee,
  Which, used, lives thy executor to be.

V.

Those hours that with gentle work did frame
The lovely gaze where every eye doth dwell,
Will play the tyrants to the very same,
And that unfair[1] which fairly doth excel;
For never-resting time leads summer on
To hideous winter, and confounds him there;
Sap checked with frost, and lusty leaves quite gone,
Beauty o'ersnowed, and bareness every where:
Then, were not summer's distillation left,
A liquid prisoner pent in walls of glass,
Beauty's effect with beauty were bereft,
Nor it, nor no remembrance what it was.

[1] *Unfair*, a verb — deprive of fairness, of beauty.

But flowers distilled, though they with winter meet,
Leese[2] but their show; their substance still lives sweet.

VI.

Then let not winter's ragged hand deface
In thee thy summer, ere thou be distilled:
Make sweet some phial; treasure thou some place
With beauty's treasure, ere it be self-killed.
That use is not forbidden usury,
Which happies[2] those that pay the willing loan;
That's for thyself to breed another thee,
Or ten times happier, be it ten for one;
Ten times thyself were happier than thou art,
If ten of thine ten times refigured thee:
Then what could death do if thou shouldst depart,
Leaving thee living in posterity?
Be not self-willed, for thou art much too fair
To be Death's conquest, and make worms thine heir.

VII.

Lo, in the orient when the gracious light
Lifts up his burning head, each under eye
Doth homage to his new-appearing sight,
Serving with looks his sacred majesty;
And having climbed the steep-up heavenly hill,
Resembling strong youth in his middle age,
Yet mortal looks adore his beauty still,
Attending on his golden pilgrimage:

1 *Leese*, lose.
2 *Happies*, makes happy.

But when from high-most pitch, with weary car,
Like feeble age, he reeleth from the day,
The eyes, 'fore duteous, now converted are
From his low tract, and look another way:
  So thou, thyself outgoing in thy noon,
  Unlooked on diest, unless thou get a son.

VIII.

Music to hear, why hear'st thou music sadly?[1]
Sweets with sweets war not, joy delights in joy.
Why lov'st thou that which thou receiv'st not gladly?
Or else receiv'st with pleasure thine annoy?
If the true concord of well-tuned sounds,
By unions married, do offend thine ear,
They do but sweetly chide thee, who confounds
In singleness the parts that thou shouldst bear.
Mark how one string, sweet husband to another
Strikes each in each by mutual ordering;[2]
Resembling sire and child, and happy mother,
Who, all in one, one pleasing note do sing:
  Whose speechless song, being many, seeming one,
  Sings this to thee, "Thou single wilt prove none."

IX.

Is it for fear to wet a widow's eye
That thou consum'st thyself in single life?

[1] Malone thus explains this passage: — "O thou, whom to hear is music, why hear'st thou," &c.

[2] If two strings are tuned in perfect unison, and one only is struck, a very sensible vibration takes place in the other. This is called sympathetic vibration.

Ah! if thou issueless shalt hap to die,
The world will wail thee, like a makeless[1] wife:
The world will be thy widow, and still weep
That thou no form of thee hast left behind,
When every private widow well may keep,
By children's eyes, her husband's shape in mind.
Look, what an unthrift in the world doth spend
Shifts but his place, for still the world enjoys it;
But beauty's waste hath in the world an end,
And kept unused, the user so destroys it.
  No love toward others in that bosom sits,
  That on himself such murderous shame commits.

X.

For shame! deny that thou bear'st love to any,
Who for thyself art so unprovident.
Grant if thou wilt thou art beloved of many,
But that thou none lov'st is most evident;
For thou art so possessed with murderous hate,
That 'gainst thyself thou stick'st not to conspire,
Seeking that beauteous roof to ruinate,
Which to repair should be thy chief desire.
O, change thy thought, that I may change my mind!
Shall hate be fairer lodged than gentle love?
Be, as thy presence is, gracious and kind,
Or to thyself, at least, kind-hearted prove;
  Make thee another self, for love of me,
  That beauty still may live in thine or thee.

[1] *Makeless*, mateless. Make and mate are synonymous in our elder writers.

XI.

As fast as thou shalt wane, so fast thou grow'st
In one of thine, from that which thou departest;
And that fresh blood which youngly thou bestow'st,
Thou may'st call thine, when thou from youth convertest.
Herein lives wisdom, beauty, and increase;
Without this, folly, age, and cold decay:
If all were minded so the times should cease,
And threescore years would make the world away.
Let those whom Nature hath not made for store,
Harsh, featureless, and rude, barrenly perish:
Look whom she best endowed, she gave thee more;
Which bounteous gift thou shouldst in bounty cherish;
She carved thee for her seal, and meant thereby
Thou shouldst print more, nor let that copy die.

XII.

When I do count the clock that tells the time,
And see the brave day sunk in hideous night;
When I behold the violet past prime,
And sable curls, all [1] silvered o'er with white;
When lofty trees I see barren of leaves,
Which erst from heat did canopy the herd,
And summer's green all girded up in sheaves,
Borne on the bier with white and bristly beard;
Then of thy beauty do I question make,
That thou among the wastes of time must go,
Since sweets and beauties do themselves forsake,
And die as fast as they see others grow;

[1] *All.* The original has *or*.

And nothing 'gainst Time's scythe can make defence
Save breed, to brave him when he takes thee hence.

XIII.

O that you were yourself! but, love, you are
No longer yours than you yourself here live:
Against this coming end you should prepare,
And your sweet semblance to some other give.
So should that beauty which you hold in lease
Find no determination: then you were
Yourself again, after yourself's decease,
When your sweet issue your sweet form should bear.
Who lets so fair a house fall to decay,
Which husbandry in honor might uphold
Against the stormy gusts of winter's day,
And barren rage of death's eternal cold?
O! none but unthrifts:—Dear my love, you know
You had a father; let your son say so.

XIV.

Not from the stars do I my judgment pluck;
And yet methinks I have astronomy,
But not to tell of good or evil luck,
Of plagues, of dearths, or season's quality:
Nor can I fortune to brief minutes tell,
Pointing to each his thunder, rain, and wind,
Or say with princes if it shall go well,
By oft predict that I in heaven find:
But from thine eyes my knowledge I derive,
And (constant stars) in them I read such art,
As truth and beauty shall together thrive,
If from thyself to store thou wouldst convert:

Or else of thee this I prognosticate,
Thy end is truth's and beauty's doom and date.

XV.

When I consider every thing that grows
Holds in perfection but a little moment,
That this huge state presenteth nought but shows
Whereon the stars in secret influence comment:
When I perceive that men as plants increase,
Cheerèd and checked even by the selfsame sky;
Vaunt in their youthful sap, at height decrease,
And wear their brave state out of memory;
Then the conceit of this inconstant stay
Sets you most rich in youth before my sight,
Where wasteful time debateth with decay,
To change your day of youth to sullied night:
And all in war with Time, for love of you,
As he takes from you, I engraft you new.

XVI.

But wherefore do not you a mightier way
Make war upon this bloody tyrant Time?
And fortify yourself in your decay
With means more blessèd than my barren rhyme?
Now stand you on the top of happy hours;
And many maiden gardens, yet unset,
With virtuous wish would bear your [1] living flowers,
Much liker than your painted counterfeit: [2]
So should the lines of life that life repair,
Which this, Time's pencil, or my pupil pen,

[1] *Your*. The ordinary reading is *you*, Malone conceiving that *your* in the original is an error of the press.

[2] *Counterfeit*, portrait.

Neither in inward worth, nor outward fair,[1]
Can make you live yourself in eyes of men.
  To give away yourself keeps yourself still;
  And you must live drawn by your own sweet skill.

XVII.

Who will believe my verse in time to come,
If it were filled with your most high deserts?
Though yet, Heaven knows, it is but as a tomb
Which hides your life, and shows not half your parts.
If I could write the beauty of your eyes,
And in fresh numbers number all your graces,
The age to come would say, this poet lies,
Such heavenly touches ne'er touched earthly faces.
So should my papers, yellowed with their age,
Be scorned, like old men of less truth than tongue;
And your true rights be termed a poet's rage,
And stretchéd metre of an antique song:
  But were some child of yours alive that time,
  You should live twice; — in it, and in my rhyme.

XVIII.

Shall I compare thee to a summer's day?
Thou art more lovely and more temperate:
Rough winds do shake the darling buds of May,
And summer's lease hath all too short a date:
Sometime too hot the eye of heaven[2] shines,
And often is his gold complexion dimmed;

[1] *Fair*, beauty. The word is used in the same sense in the 18th Sonnet.

[2] So in Richard II.: —

"When the searching *eye of heaven* is hid
Behind the globe, and lights the lower world."

And every fair from fair sometime declines,
By chance, or nature's changing course, untrimmed;[1]
But thy eternal summer shall not fade,
Nor lose possession of that fair thou owest;
Nor shall Death brag thou wander'st in his shade,
When in eternal lines to time thou growest;
So long as men can breathe, or eyes can see,
So long lives this, and this gives life to thee.

XIX.

Devouring Time, blunt thou the lion's paws,
And make the earth devour her own sweet brood;
Pluck the keen teeth from the fierce tiger's jaws,
And burn the long-lived phœnix in her blood;
Make glad and sorry seasons, as thou fleet'st,
And do whate'er thou wilt, swift-footed Time,
To the wide world, and all her fading sweets;
But I forbid thee one most heinous crime;
O, carve not with thy hours my love's fair brow,
Nor draw no lines there with thine antique pen;
Him in thy course untainted do allow,
For beauty's pattern to succeeding men.
Yet do thy worst, old Time: despite thy wrong,
My love shall in my verse ever live young.

XX.

A woman's face, with nature's own hand painted,
Hast thou, the master-mistress of my passion;
A woman's gentle heart, but not acquainted
With shifting change, as is false women's fashion;

[1] *Untrimmed*, undecorated.

An eye more bright than theirs, less false in rolling,
Gilding the object whereupon it gazeth;
A man in hue, all hues in his controlling,
Which steals men's eyes, and women's souls amazeth.
And for a woman wert thou first created;
Till Nature, as she wrought thee, fell a-doting,
And by addition me of thee defeated,
By adding one thing to my purpose nothing.
But since she pricked thee out for women's pleasure,
Mine be thy love, and thy love's use their treasure.

XXI.

So is it not with me as with that muse,
Stirred by a painted beauty to his verse;
Who heaven itself for ornament doth use,
And every fair with his fair doth rehearse;
Making a couplement[1] of proud compare,
With sun and moon, with earth and sea's rich gems,
With April's first-born flowers, and all things rare
That heaven's air in his huge rondure[2] hems.
O, let me, true in love, but truly write,
And then believe me, my love is as fair
As any mother's child, though not so bright
As those gold candles fixed in heaven's air:
Let them say more that like of hearsay well;
I will not praise, that purpose not to sell.

[1] *Couplement*, union. So in Spenser: —

"Allied with bands of mutual *couplement*."

[2] *Rondure*, circumference.

XXII.

My glass shall not persuade me I am old,
So long as youth and thou are of one date;
But when in thee time's furrows I behold,
Then look I death my days should expiate.
For all that beauty that doth cover thee
Is but the seemly raiment of my heart,
Which in thy breast doth live, as thine in me;
How can I then be elder than thou art?
O, therefore, love, be of thyself so wary,
As I not for myself but for thee will;
Bearing thy heart, which I will keep so chary
As tender nurse her babe from faring ill.
  Presume not on thy heart when mine is slain;
  Thou gav'st me thine, not to give back again.

XXIII.

As an unperfect actor on the stage,
Who with his fear is put besides his part,
Or some fierce thing replete with too much rage,
Whose strength's abundance weakens his own heart
So I, for fear of trust, forget to say
The perfect ceremony of love's rite,
And in mine own love's strength seem to decay,
O'ercharged with burthen of mine own love's might.
O, let my books be then the eloquence
And dumb presagers of my speaking breast;
Who plead for love, and look for recompense,
More than that tongue that more hath more expressed.
  O, learn to read what silent love hath writ:
  To hear with eyes belongs to love's fine wit.

XXIV.

Mine eye hath played the painter, and hath stelled
Thy beauty's form in table[1] of my heart;
My body is the frame wherein 'tis held,
And perspective it is best painter's art.
For through the painter must you see his skill,
To find where your true image pictured lies,
Which in my bosom's shop is hanging still,
That hath his windows glazèd with thine eyes.
Now see what good turns eyes for eyes have done;
Mine eyes have drawn thy shape, and thine for me
Are windows to my breast, where-through the sun
Delights to peep, to gaze therein on thee;
  Yet eyes this cunning want to grace their art,
  They draw but what they see, know not the heart.

XXV.

Let those who are in favor with their stars,
Of public honor and proud titles boast,
Whilst I, whom fortune of such triumph bars,
Unlooked for joy in that I honor most.
Great princes' favorites their fair leaves spread
But as the marigold at the sun's eye;
And in themselves their pride lies buriéd,
For at a frown they in their glory die.

[1] *Table.* So in All's Well that Ends Well:—

"'Twas pretty, though a plague,
To see him every hour; to sit and draw
His arched brows, his hawking eye, his curls,
In our heart's *table.*"

Table, though sometimes used in the sense of a picture, more commonly means the tabular surface upon which a picture is painted.

The painful warrior famousèd for fight,[1]
After a thousand victories once foiled,
Is from the book of honor razèd quite,
And all the rest forgot for which he toiled:
 Then happy I, that love and am beloved
 Where I may not remove, nor be removed.

XXVI.

Lord of my love, to whom in vassalage
Thy merit hath my duty strongly knit,
To thee I send this written embassage,
To witness duty, not to show my wit.
Duty so great, which wit so poor as mine
May make seem bare, in wanting words to show it;
But that I hope some good conceit of thine
In thy soul's thought, all naked, will bestow it:
Till whatsoever star that guides by moving,
Points on me graciously with fair aspèct,
And puts apparel on my tattered loving,
To show me worthy of thy sweet respect:
 Then may I dare to boast how I do love thee;
 Till then, not show my head where thou mayst
  prove me.

XXVII.

Weary with toil, I haste me to my bed,
The dear repose for limbs with travel tired;

[1] *Fight*. The original has *worth*. Theobald, who saw that the alternate rhyme is invariably preserved in the other Sonnets, proposed to make one of two changes; to read *fight* instead of *worth*, or *forth* instead of *quite*. We are not perfectly satisfied with either change; but as the first has been adopted in all modern editions, we will not attempt to disturb the received reading, and we have no doubt that some error is involved in the original.

But then begins a journey in my head,
To work my mind, when body's work 's expired:
For then my thoughts (from far where I abide)
Intend a zealous pilgrimage to thee,
And keep my drooping eyelids open wide,
Looking on darkness which the blind do see:
Save that my soul's imaginary sight
Presents thy shadow to my sightless view,
Which, like a jewel hung in ghastly night,
Makes black night beauteous, and her old face new.
Lo, thus, by day my limbs, by night my mind,
For thee, and for myself, no quiet find.

XXVIII.

How can I then return in happy plight,
That am debarred the benefit of rest?
When day's oppression is not eased by night,
But day by night and night by day oppressed?
And each, though enemies to either's reign,
Do in consent shake hands to torture me,
The one by toil, the other to complain
How far I toil, still farther off from thee.
I tell the day, to please him, thou art bright,
And dost him grace when clouds do blot the heaven:
So flatter I the swart-complexioned night;
When sparkling stars twire[1] not, thou gild'st the even.

[1] *Twire.* Malone proposed to read *twirl*, and Steevens conjectured that *twire* means *quire.* Gifford, in a note upon Ben Jonson's "Sad Shepherd," explains that in the passage before us the meaning is "when the stars do not gleam or appear at intervals." He adds, "*Twire* should not have been suffered to grow obsolete, for we have no word now in use that can take its place, or be considered as precisely synonymous with it in sense: leer and twinkle are merely shades of it." Gifford quotes several pas-

But day doth daily draw my sorrows longer,
And night doth nightly make grief's length seem
stronger.

XXIX.

When in disgrace with fortune and men's eyes,
I all alone beweep my outcast state,
And trouble deaf Heaven with my bootless cries,
And look upon myself, and curse my fate,
Wishing me like to one more rich in hope,
Featured like him, like him with friends possessed,
Desiring this man's art, and that man's scope,
With what I most enjoy contented least;
Yet in these thoughts myself almost despising,
Haply I think on thee, — and then my state
(Like to the lark at break of day arising
From sullen earth) sings hymns at heaven's gate;[1]
For thy sweet love remembered such wealth brings,
That then I scorn to change my state with kings.

XXX.

When to the sessions of sweet silent thought
I summon up remembrance of things past,
I sigh the lack of many a thing I sought,
And with old woes new wail my dear times' waste:

sages from Jonson and Beaumont and Fletcher in confirmation of his opinion. But there are four lines in Drayton's "Polyolbion" which contain a parallel use of the word: —

"Suppose 'twixt noon and night the sun is half-way wrought,
(The shadows to be large, by his descending brought,)
Who with a fervent eye looks through the *twiring* glades,
And his disperséd rays commixeth with the shades."

[1] See Cymbeline, Illustrations of Act II.

Then can I drown an eye, unused to flow,
For precious friends hid in death's dateless [1] night,
And weep afresh love's long-since cancelled woe,
And moan the expense of many a vanished sight.[2]
Then can I grieve at grievances foregone,
And heavily from woe to woe tell o'er
The sad account of fore-bemoanéd moan,
Which I new pay as if not paid before.
But if the while I think on thee, dear friend,
All losses are restored, and sorrows end.

XXXI.

Thy bosom is endearéd with all hearts
Which I by lacking have supposéd dead;
And there reigns love and all love's loving parts,
And all those friends which I thought buriéd.
How many a holy and obsequious [3] tear
Hath dear religious love stolen from mine eye,
As interest of the dead, which now appear
But things removed, that hidden in thee lie!
Thou art the grave where buried love doth live,
Hung with the trophies of my lovers gone,
Who all their parts of me to thee did give;
That due of many now is thine alone:
Their images I loved I view in thee,
And thou (all they) hast all the all of me.

[1] *Dateless*, endless; having no certain time of expiration.

[2] If we understand *expense* to be used as analogous to *passing away*, there is no difficulty in this line. What we expend is gone from us; and so the poet moans the *expense* of many a vanished sight. Malone thinks that *sight* is used for *sigh;* but this is certainly a very strained conjecture.

[3] *Obsequious*, funereal.

XXXII.

If thou survive my well-contented day,
When that churl Death my bones with dust shall cover,
And shalt by fortune once more re-survey
These poor rude lines of thy deceased lover,
Compare them with the bettering of the time;
And though they be outstripped by every pen,
Reserve[1] them for my love, not for their rhyme,
Exceeded by the height of happier men.
O, then vouchsafe me but this loving thought!
"Had my friend's muse grown with this growing age,
A dearer birth than this his love had brought,
To march in ranks of better equipage:
  But since he died, and poets better prove,
  Theirs for their style I'll read, his for his love."

XXXIII.

Full many a glorious morning have I seen
Flatter the mountain-tops with sovereign eye,
Kissing with golden face the meadows green,
Gilding pale streams with heavenly alchymy;
Anon permit the basest clouds to ride
With ugly rack[2] on his celestial face,
And from the forlorn world his visage hide,
Stealing unseen to west with this disgrace:

[1] *Reserve*, the same as *preserve*. In Pericles we have, —

"*Reserve* that excellent complexion."

[2] *Rack*. Tooke, in his full discussion of the meaning of this word, ("Diversions of Purley," Part II. Chap. IV.,) holds that *rack* means "merely that which is *reeked;*" and that in all the instances of its use by Shakspeare the word signifies *vapor*. He illustrates the passage before us by quoting the lines in the First Part of Henry IV., where the Prince in some degree justifies his course of profligacy: —

Even so my sun one early morn did shine
With all triumphant splendor on my brow;
But out! alack! he was but one hour mine,
The region cloud hath masked him from me now.
  Yet him for this my love no whit disdaineth;
  Suns of the world may stain, when heaven's sun staineth.[1]

XXXIV.

Why didst thou promise such a beauteous day,
And make me travel forth without my cloak,
To let base clouds o'ertake me in my way,
Hiding their bravery in their rotten smoke?
'Tis not enough that through the cloud thou break,
To dry the rain on my storm-beaten face,
For no man well of such a salve can speak,
That heals the wound, and cures not the disgrace:
Nor can thy shame give physic to my grief;
Though thou repent, yet I have still the loss:
The offender's sorrow lends but weak relief
To him that bears the strong offence's cross.[2]
  Ah! but those tears are pearl which thy love sheds,
  And they are rich, and ransom all ill deeds.

"Yet herein will I imitate the sun,
Who doth permit the *base contagious clouds*
To smother up his beauty from the world,
That when he please again to be himself,
Being wanted, he may be more wondered at,
By breaking through the *foul and ugly mists*
Of vapors that did seem to strangle him."

[1] *Stain* and *staineth* are here used with the signification of a verb neuter. Suns of the world may be stained as heaven's sun is stained.

[2] *Cross.* The original has *loss* — evidently a mistake. Malone substituted *cross*.

XXXV.

No more be grieved at that which thou hast done:
Roses have thorns, and silver fountains mud;
Clouds and eclipses stain both moon and sun,
And loathsome canker lives in sweetest bud.
All men make faults, and even I in this,
Authórizing thy trespass with compare,
Myself corrupting, salving thy amiss,[1]
Excusing thy sins more than thy sins are:
For to thy sensual fault I bring in sense,
(Thy adverse party is thy advocate,)
And 'gainst myself a lawful plea commence:
Such civil war is in my love and hate,
That I an accessory needs must be
To that sweet thief which sourly robs from me.

XXXVI.

Let me confess that we two must be twain,
Although our undivided loves are one:
So shall those blots that do with me remain,
Without thy help, by me be borne alone.
In our two loves there is but one respect,
Though in our lives a separable[2] spite,
Which though it alter not love's sole effect,
Yet doth it steal sweet hours from love's delight.
I may not evermore acknowledge thee,
Lest my bewailéd guilt should do thee shame;
Nor thou with public kindness honor me,
Unless thou take that honor from thy name:

[1] *Amiss*, fault.

[2] *Separable*, separating.

But do not so; I love thee in such sort,
As, thou being mine, mine is thy good report.

XXXVII.

As a decrepit father takes delight
To see his active child do deeds of youth,
So I, made lame by fortune's dearest[1] spite,
Take all my comfort of thy worth and truth;
For whether beauty, birth, or wealth, or wit,
Or any of these all, or all, or more,
Entitled in thy parts do crownéd sit,
I make my love engrafted to this store:
So then I am not lame, poor, nor despised,
Whilst that this shadow doth such substance give,
That I in thy abundance am sufficed,
And by a part of all thy glory live.
Look what is best, that best I wish in thee;
This wish I have; then ten times happy me!

XXXVIII.

How can my muse want subject to invent,
While thou dost breathe, that pour'st into my verse
Thine own sweet argument, too excellent
For every vulgar paper to rehearse?
O, give thyself the thanks, if aught in me
Worthy perusal stand against thy sight;
For who 's so dumb that cannot write to thee,
When thou thyself dost give invention light?
Be thou the tenth muse, ten times more in worth
Than those old nine which rhymers invocate;

[1] *Dearest.* So in Hamlet:—
"Would I had met my *dearest* foe in Heaven!"

And he that calls on thee, let him bring forth
Eternal numbers to outlive long date
If my slight muse do please these curious days,
The pain be mine, but thine shall be the praise.

XXXIX.

O, how thy worth with manners may I sing,
When thou art all the better part of me?
What can mine own praise to mine own self bring?
And what is 't but mine own, when I praise thee?
Even for this let us divided live,
And our dear love lose name of single one,
That by this separation I may give
That due to thee, which thou deserv'st alone.
O absence, what a torment wouldst thou prove,
Were it not thy sour leisure gave sweet leave
To entertain the time with thoughts of love,
(Which time and thoughts so sweetly doth deceive,)
And that thou teachest how to make one twain,
By praising him here, who doth hence remain!

XL.

Take all my loves, my love, yea, take them all;
What hast thou then more than thou hadst before?
No love, my love, that thou mayst true love call;
All mine was thine, before thou hadst this more.
Then if for my love thou my love receivest,
I cannot blame thee for [1] my love thou usest
But yet be blamed, if thou thyself deceivest
By wilful taste of what thyself refusest.

[1] *For* here signifies *because.*

I do forgive thy robbery, gentle thief,
Although thou steal thee all my poverty;
And yet, love knows, it is a greater grief
To bear love's wrong, than hate's known injury.
  Lascivious grace, in whom all ill well shows,
  Kill me with spites; yet we must not be foes.

XLI.

Those pretty wrongs that liberty commits
When I am sometime absent from thy heart,
Thy beauty and thy years full well befits,
For still temptation follows where thou art.
Gentle thou art, and therefore to be won,
Beauteous thou art, therefore to be assailed;
And when a woman woos, what woman's son
Will sourly leave her till she have prevailed?
Ah me! but yet thou mightst my seat forbear,
And chide thy beauty and thy straying youth,
Who lead thee in their riot even there
Where thou art forced to break a twofold truth;
  Hers, by thy beauty tempting her to thee,
  Thine, by thy beauty being false to me.

XLII.

That thou hast her, it is not all my grief,
And yet it may be said I loved her dearly;
That she hath thee, is of my wailing chief,
A loss in love that touches me more nearly.
Loving offenders, thus I will excuse ye:—
Thou dost love her, because thou knew'st I love her;
And for my sake even so doth she abuse me,
Suffering my friend for my sake to approve her.

If I lose thee, my loss is my love's gain,
And, losing her, my friend hath found that loss;
Both find each other, and I lose both twain,
And both for my sake lay on me this cross:
But here's the joy; my friend and I are one;
Sweet flattery! then she loves but me alone.

XLIII.

When most I wink, then do mine eyes best see,
For all the day they view things unrespected;[1]
But when I sleep, in dreams they look on thee,
And, darkly bright, are bright in dark directed;
Then thou whose shadow shadows doth make bright,
How would thy shadow's form form happy show
To the clear day with thy much clearer light,
When to unseeing eyes thy shade shines so!
How would (I say) mine eyes be blessèd made
By looking on thee in the living day,
When in dead night thy fair imperfect shade
Through heavy sleep on sightless eyes doth stay?
All days are nights to see, till I see thee,
And nights bright days, when dreams ao show thee me.[2]

XLIV.

If the dull substance of my flesh were thought,
Injurious distance should not stop my way;
For then, despite of space, I would be brougnt
From limits far remote, where thou dost stay.
No matter then, although my foot did stand
Upon the farthest earth removed from thee,

[1] *Unrespected*, unregarded.

[2] *Thee me*, thee *to* me

For nimble thought can jump both sea and land,
As soon as think the place where he would be.
But ah! thought kills me that I am not thought,
To leap large lengths of miles when thou art gone,
But that, so much of earth and water wrought,[1]
I must attend time's leisure with my moan:
  Receiving nought by elements so slow
  But heavy tears, badges of either's woe:

XLV.

The other two, slight air and purging fire,
Are both with thee, wherever I abide;
The first my thought, the other my desire,
These present-absent with swift motion slide.
For when these quicker elements are gone
In tender embassy of love to thee,
My life, being made of four, with two alone
Sinks down to death, oppressed with melancholy;
Until life's composition be recurred
By those swift messengers returned from thee,
Who even but now come back again assured
Of thy fair health, recounting it to me:
  This told, I joy; but then no longer glad,
  I send them back again, and straight grow sad.

[1] A passage in Henry V. explains this:—"He is pure air and fire; and the dull elements of earth and water never appear in him." The thought is continued in the first line of the 45th Sonnet, in which Sonnet we also find "my life being made of four." This was the theory of life in Shakspeare's time; and Sir Toby, in Twelfth Night, speaks learnedly when he says "Does not our life consist of the four elements?" Shakspeare, however, somewhat laughs at the theory when he makes Sir Andrew reply, "Faith, so they say; but I think it rather consists of eating and drinking."

XLVI.

Mine eye and heart are at a mortal war,
How to divide the conquest of thy sight;
Mine eye my heart thy[1] picture's sight would bar,
My heart mine eye the freedom of that right.
My heart doth plead that thou in him dost lie,
(A closet never pierced with crystal eyes,)
But the defendant doth that plea deny,
And says in him thy fair appearance lies.
To 'cide[2] this title is impannelléd
A quest[3] of thoughts, all tenants to the heart;
And by their verdict is determinéd
The clear eye's moiety,[4] and the dear heart's part;
As thus; mine eye's due is thine outward part,
And my heart's right thine inward love of heart.

XLVII.

Betwixt mine eye and heart a league is took,
And each doth good turns now unto the other:
When that mine eye is famished for a look,
Or heart in love with sighs himself doth smother,
With my love's picture then my eye doth feast,
And to the painted banquet bids my heart;

1 *Thy.* The original has *their;* and it is remarkable that the same typographical error occurs four times in this one Sonnet — a pretty convincing proof that no competent or authorized person superintended the publication. Errors of this sort are very frequent in the original; but we have not thought it necessary to notice them when there can be no doubt of the meaning.

2 *'Cide.* Malone explains that this is a contraction of *decide.* The original reads *side.*

3 *Quest*, inquest or jury.

4 *Moïety*, portion.

Another time mine eye is my heart's guest,
And in his thoughts of love doth share a part:
So, either by thy picture or my love,
Thyself away art present still with me;
For thou not farther than my thoughts canst move,
And I am still with them, and they with thee;
Or if they sleep, thy picture in my sight
Awakes my heart to heart's and eye's delight.

XLVIII.

How careful was I when I took my way,
Each trifle under truest bars to thrust,
That, to my use it might unuséd stay
From hands of falsehood, in sure wards of trust!
But thou, to whom my jewels trifles are,
Most worthy comfort, now my greatest grief,
Thou, best of dearest, and mine only care,
Art left the prey of every vulgar thief.
Thee have I not locked up in any chest,
Save where thou art not, though I feel thou art,
Within the gentle closure of my breast,
From whence at pleasure thou may'st come and part;
And even thence thou wilt be stolen I fear,
For truth proves thievish for a prize so dear.[1]

XLIX.

Against that time, if ever that time come,
When I shall see thee frown on my defects,

[1] The same thought is in Venus and Adonis: —

"Rich preys make true men thieves."

Whenas[1] thy love hath cast his utmost sum,
Called to that audit by advised respects;
Against that time, when thou shalt strangely pass,
And scarcely greet me with that sun, thine eye,
When love, converted from the thing it was,
Shall reasons find of settled gravity;
Against that time do I ensconce[2] me here
Within the knowledge of mine own desert,
And this my hand against myself uprear,
To guard the lawful reasons on thy part:
To leave poor me thou hast the strength of laws,
Since, why to love, I can allege no cause.

L.

How heavy do I journey on the way,
When what I seek — my weary travel's end —
Doth teach that ease and that repose to say,
"Thus far the miles are measured from thy friend!"
The beast that bears me, tiréd with my woe,
Plods dully on to bear that weight in me,
As if by some instinct the wretch did know
His rider loved not speed, being made from thee:
The bloody spur cannot provoke him on
That sometimes anger thrusts into his hide,
Which heavily he answers with a groan,
More sharp to me than spurring to his side;
For that same groan doth put this in my mind,
My grief lies onward, and my joy behind.

[1] *Whenas*, when.
[2] *Ensconce*, fortify.

LI.

Thus can my love excuse the slow offence
Of my dull bearer, when from thee I speed:
From where thou art why should I haste me thence?
Till I return, of posting is no need.
O, what excuse will my poor beast then find,
When swift extremity can seem but slow?
Then should I spur, though mounted on the wind;
In wingéd speed no motion shall I know:
Then can no horse with my desire keep pace;
Therefore desire, of perfect love being made,
Shall neigh (no dull flesh) in his fiery race;
But love, for love, thus shall excuse my jade;
  Since from thee going he went wilful slow,
  Towards thee I'll run, and give him leave to go.

LII.

So am I as the rich, whose blesséd key
Can bring him to his sweet up-lockéd treasure,
The which he will not every hour survey,
For blunting the fine point of seldom pleasure.
Therefore are feasts so solemn and so rare,[1]
Since seldom coming, in the long year set,
Like stones of worth they thinly placéd are,
Or captain [2] jewels in the carcanet.[3]

1 There is a somewhat similar thought in Henry IV. Part I.: —

> "My state,
> Seldom but sumptuous, showed like a feast,
> And won by rareness much solemnity."

2 *Captain*, used adjectively for *chief*.
3 *Carcanet*, necklace.

So is the time that keeps you, as my chest,
Or as the wardrobe which the robe doth hide,
To make some special instant special-blest,
By new unfolding his imprisoned pride.
  Blessèd are you, whose worthiness gives scope,
  Being had, to triumph; being lacked, to hope.

LIII.

What is your substance, whereof are you made,
That millions of strange shadows on you tend?
Since every one hath, every one, one's shade,
And you, but one, can every shadow lend.
Describe Adonis, and the counterfeit[1]
Is poorly imitated after you;
On Helen's cheek all art of beauty set,
And you in Grecian tires are painted new:
Speak of the spring, and foizon of the year;[2]
The one doth shadow of your beauty show,
The other as your bounty doth appear,
And you in every blessèd shape we know.
  In all external grace you have some part,
  But you like none, none you, for constant heart.

LIV.

O, how much more doth beauty beauteous seem,
By that sweet ornament which truth doth give!
The rose looks fair, but fairer we it deem
For that sweet odor which doth in it live.

[1] *Counterfeit*, portrait.
[2] *Foizon* is plenty; and the *foizon of the year* is the autumn, or plentiful season.

The canker-blooms[1] have full as deep a dye
As the perfuméd tincture of the roses,
Hang on such thorns, and play as wantonly
When summer's breath their maskéd buds discloses:
But for their virtue only is their show,
They live unwooed, and unrespected fade;
Die to themselves. Sweet roses do not so;
Of their sweet deaths are sweetest odors made:
 And so of you, beauteous and lovely youth,
 When that shall fade, by[2] verse distils your truth.

LV.

Not marble, not the gilded monuments
Of princes, shall outlive this powerful rhyme;
But you shall shine more bright in these contents
Than unswept stone, besmeared with sluttish time.
When wasteful war shall statues overturn,
And broils root out the work of masonry,
Nor Mars his sword nor war's quick fire shall burn
The living record of your memory.
'Gainst death and all-oblivious enmity
Shall you pace forth; your praise shall still find room,
Even in the eyes of all posterity
That wear this world out to the ending doom.
 So, till the judgment that yourself arise,
 You live in this, and dwell in lovers' eyes.

LVI.

Sweet love, renew thy force; be it not said,
Thy edge should blunter be than appetite,

[1] *Canker-blooms*, the flowers of the canker or dog-rose.
[2] *By*. The word of the original is altered by Malone to ***my***. The change is certainly not wanted.

Which but to-day by feeding is allayed,
To-morrow sharpened in his former might:
So, love, be thou; although to-day thou fill
Thy hungry eyes, even till they wink with fulness,
To-morrow see again, and do not kill
The spirit of love with a perpetual dulness.
Let this sad interim like the ocean be
Which parts the shore, where two contracted-new
Come daily to the banks, that, when they see
Return of love, more blest may be the view;
Or call it winter, which, being full of care,
Makes summer's welcome thrice more wished, more rare.

LVII.

Being your slave, what should I do but tend
Upon the hours and times of your desire?
I have no precious time at all to spend,
Nor services to do, till you require.
Nor dare I chide the world-without-end hour,
Whilst I, my sovereign, watch the clock for you,
Nor think the bitterness of absence sour,
When you have bid your servant once adieu;
Nor dare I question with my jealous thought
Where you may be, or your affairs suppose,
But, like a sad slave, stay and think of nought,
Save, where you are how happy you make those:
So true a fool is love, that in your will
(Though you do any thing) he thinks no ill.

LVIII.

That God forbid, that made me first your slave,
I should in thought control your times of pleasure,

Or at your hand the account of hours to crave,
Being your vassal, bound to stay your leisure!
O, let me suffer (being at your beck)
The imprisoned absence of your liberty,
And patience, tame to sufferance, bide each check
Without accusing you of injury.
Be where you list; your charter is so strong,
That you yourself may privilege your time:
Do what you will, to you it doth belong
Yourself to pardon of self-doing crime.
  I am to wait, though waiting so be hell;
  Not blame your pleasure, be it ill or well.

LIX.

If there be nothing new, but that which is
Hath been before, how are our brains beguiled,
Which laboring for invention bear amiss
The second burthen of a former child!
O, that record could with a backward look,
Even of five hundred courses of the sun,
Show me your image in some antique book,
Since mind at first in character was done!
That I might see what the old world could say
To this composéd wonder of your frame;
Whether we are mended, or whe'r[1] better they,
Or whether revolution be the same.
  O! sure I am, the wits of former days
  To subjects worse have given admiring praise.

LX.

Like as the waves make towards the pebbled shore,
So do our minutes hasten to their end;

[1] *Whe'r*, whether.

Each changing place with that which goes before,
In sequent toil all forwards do contend.
Nativity, once in the main of light,[1]
Crawls to maturity, wherewith being crowned,
Crookéd eclipses 'gainst his glory fight,
And Time, that gave, doth now his gift confound.
Time doth transfix the flourish set on youth,
And delves the parallels[2] in beauty's brow;
Feeds on the rarities of nature's truth,
And nothing stands but for his scythe to mow.
  And yet, to times in hope, my verse shall stand,
  Praising thy worth, despite his cruel hand.

LXI.

Is it thy will thy image should keep open
My heavy eyelids to the weary night?
Dost thou desire my slumbers should be broken,
While shadows, like to thee, do mock my sight?
Is it thy spirit that thou send'st from thee
So far from home, into my deeds to pry;
To find out shames and idle hours in me,
The scope and tenor of thy jealousy?
O no! thy love, though much, is not so great;
It is my love that keeps mine eyé awake;
Mine own true love that doth my rest defeat,
To play the watchman ever for thy sake:
  For thee watch I, whilst thou dost wake elsewhere,
  From me far off, with others all-too-near.

1 *Main of light.* As the *main* of waters would signify the great body of waters, so the *main of light* signifies the mass or flood of light, into which a new-born child is launched.

2 *Parallels.* We have exactly the same idea in the 2d Sonnet:—

"When forty winters shall besiege thy brow,
And *dig* deep *trenches* in thy beauty's field."

LXII.

Sin of self-love possesseth all mine eye,
And all my soul, and all my every part;
And for this sin there is no remedy,
It is so grounded inward in my heart.
Methinks no face so gracious[1] is as mine,
No shape so true, no truth of such account,
And for myself mine own worth do define,
As I all other in all worths surmount.
But when my glass shows me myself indeed,
Beated[2] and chopped with tanned antiquity,
Mine own self-love quite contrary I read,
Self so self-loving were iniquity.
  'Tis thee (myself) that for myself I praise,
  Painting my age with beauty of thy days.

LXIII.

Against my love shall be, as I am now,
With Time's injurious hand crushed and o'erworn;
When hours have drained his blood, and filled his brow
With lines and wrinkles; when his youthful morn
Hath travelled on to age's steepy night;[3]
And all those beauties, whereof now he 's king,
Are vanishing or vanished out of sight,
Stealing away the treasure of his spring;

[1] *Gracious*, beautiful.

[2] *Beated*. So in the old copy; and it has been followed by Malone. He suggests that the true word may be *bated;* but he receives *beated* as the participle of the verb to *beat*.

[3] *Steepy night*. It has been proposed to read *sleepy night;* but in the 7th Sonnet we have the same notion of man climbing up the hill of age; and here the idea is also connected with the antithesis of *morn* and *night*.

For such a time do I now fortify
Against confounding age's cruel knife,
That he shall never cut from memory
My sweet love's beauty, though my lover's life.
  His beauty shall in these black lines be seen,
  And they shall live, and he in them, still green.

LXIV.

When I have seen by Time's fell hand defaced
The rich-proud cost of outworn buried age;
When sometime lofty towers I see down-rased,
And brass eternal, slave to mortal rage;
When I have seen the hungry ocean gain
Advantage on the kingdom of the shore,
And the firm soil win of the wat'ry main,
Increasing store with loss, and loss with store;
When I have seen such interchange of state,
Or state itself confounded to decay;
Ruin hath taught me thus to ruminate —
That time will come and take my love away.
  This thought is as a death, which cannot choose
  But weep to have that which it fears to lose.

LXV.

Since brass, nor stone, nor earth, nor boundless sea,
But sad mortality o'ersways their power,
How with this rage shall beauty hold a plea,
Whose action is no stronger than a flower?
O, how shall summer's honey breath hold out
Against the wreckful siege of battering days,
When rocks impregnable are not so stout,
Nor gates of steel so strong, but time decays?
O, fearful meditation! where, alack!

Shall Time's best jewel from Time's chest lie hid?[1]
Or what strong hand can hold his swift foot back?
Or who his spoil of beauty can forbid?
O, none, unless this miracle have might,
That in black ink my love may still shine bright.

LXVI.

Tired with all these, for restful death I cry, —
As, to behold desert a beggar born,
And needy nothing trimmed in jollity,
And purest faith unhappily forsworn,
And gilded honor shamefully misplaced,
And maiden virtue rudely strumpeted,
And right perfection wrongfully disgraced,
And strength by limping sway disabled,
And art made tongue-tied by authority,
And folly (doctor-like) controlling skill,
And simple truth miscalled simplicity,[2]
And captive good attending captain ill:
Tired with all these, from these would I begone,
Save that, to die, I leave my love alone.

LXVII.

Ah! wherefore with infection should he live,
And with his presence grace impiety,

[1] In Troilus and Cressida, Ulysses says, —

"Time hath, my lord, a *wallet* at his back,
In which he puts alms for oblivion."

Time's *chest* and Time's *wallet* are the same; they are the depositories of what was once great and beautiful, passed away, perished, and forgotten.

[2] *Simplicity* is here used for folly.

That sin by him advantage should achieve,
And lace[1] itself with his society?
Why should false painting imitate his cheek,
And steal dead seeing of his living hue?
Why should poor beauty indirectly seek
Roses of shadow, since his rose is true?
Why should he live now Nature bankrupt is,
Beggared of blood to blush through lively veins?
For she hath no exchequer now but his,
And, proud of many, lives upon his gains.
O, him she stores, to show what wealth she had
In days long since, before these last so bad.

LXVIII.

Thus is his cheek the map of days outworn,
When beauty lived and died as flowers do now,
Before these bastard signs of fair[2] were borne,
Or durst inhabit on a living brow;
Before the golden tresses of the dead,
The right of sepulchres, were shorn away,
To live a second life on second head,
Ere beauty's dead fleece made another gay:[3]
In him those holy antique hours are seen,
Without all ornament, itself, and true,
Making no summer of another's green,
Robbing no old to dress his beauty new;
And him as for a map doth Nature store,
To show false Art what beauty was of yore.

[1] *Lace*, embellish, ornament.
[2] *Fair*, beauty.
[3] See Merchant of Venice, Illustrations of Act III.

LXIX.

Those parts of thee that the world's eye doth view
Want nothing that the thought of hearts can mend:
All tongues (the voice of souls) give thee that due,[1]
Uttering bare truth, even so as foes commend.
Thine outward thus with outward praise is crowned;
But those same tongues that give thee so thine own,
In other accents do this praise confound,
By seeing farther than the eye hath shown.
They look into the beauty of thy mind,
And that, in guess, they measure by thy deeds;
Then (churls) their thoughts, although their eyes were kind,
To thy fair flower add the rank smell of weeds:
 But why thy odor matcheth not thy show,
 The solve[2] is this, — that thou dost common grow.

LXX.

That thou art blamed shall not be thy defect,
For slander's mark was ever yet the fair;

[1] *Due.* The original has *end.* Tyrwhitt sagaciously made the change, knowing that such a typographical error is not unfrequent. The separate letters drop out at the press; and the workman, who does not stand upon niceties, puts them together again after his own fashion. By the inversion of the *u* a pretty metamorphosis of *end* into *due* is made; and such feats of legerdemain are performed with a dexterity, which, however satisfactory to the operator, is not the most agreeable part of an author's experience, if he should ever indulge himself with the perusal of his own writings after they have passed the printer.

[2] *Solve.* The original has *solye.* Malone reads *solve* in the sense of *solution.* We have no parallel example of the use of *solve* as a noun.

The ornament of beauty is suspect,[1]
A crow that flies in heaven's sweetest air.
So thou be good, slander doth but approve
Thy worth the greater, being wooed of time;
For canker vice the sweetest buds doth love,
And thou present'st a pure, unstainéd prime.
Thou hast passed by the ambush of young days,
Either not assailed, or victor being charged;
Yet this thy praise cannot be so thy praise,
To tie up envy, evermore enlarged:
  If some suspect of ill masked not thy show,
  Then thou alone kingdoms of hearts shouldst owe.[2]

LXXI.

No longer mourn for me when I am dead
Than you shall hear the surly sullen bell
Give warning to the world that I am fled
From this vile world, with vilest worms to dwell:
Nay, if you read this line, remember not
The hand that writ it; for I love you so,
That I in your sweet thoughts would be forgot,
If thinking on me then should make you woe.
O, if (I say) you look upon this verse,
When I perhaps compounded am with clay,
Do not so much as my poor name rehearse;
But let your love even with my life decay:
  Lest the wise world should look into your moan,
  And mock you with me after I am gone.

1 *Suspect*, suspicion. So in King Henry IV. Part II.: —

"If my *suspect* be false, forgive me."

2 *Owe*, own.

LXXII.

O, lest the world should task you to recite
What merit lived in me that you should love
After my death, — dear love, forget me quite,
For you in me can nothing worthy prove;
Unless you would devise some virtuous lie,
To do more for me than mine own desert,
And hang more praise upon deceasèd I
Than niggard truth would willingly impart:
O, lest your true love may seem false in this,
That you for love speak well of me untrue,
My name be buried where my body is,
And live no more to shame nor me nor you.
For I am shamed by that which I bring forth,
And so should you to love things nothing worth.

LXXIII.

That time of year thou mayst in me behold
When yellow leaves, or none, or few, do hang
Upon those boughs which shake against the cold,
Bare ruined choirs, where late the sweet birds sang.
In me thou seest the twilight of such day
As after sunset fadeth in the west,
Which by and by black night doth take away,
Death's second self that seals up all in rest.
In me thou seest the glowing of such fire,
That on the ashes of his youth doth lie,
As the death-bed whereon it must expire,
Consumed with that which I was nourished by.
This thou perceiv'st, which makes thy love more strong,
To love that well which thou must leave ere long.

LXXIV.

But be contented: when that fell arrest
Without all bail shall carry me away,
My life hath in this line some interest,
Which for memorial still with thee shall stay.
When thou reviewest this, thou dost review
The very part was consecrate to thee.
The earth can have but earth, which is his due;
My spirit is thine, the better part of me:
So then thou hast but lost the dregs of life,
The prey of worms, my body being dead;
The coward conquest of a wretch's knife,
Too base of thee to be rememberéd.
  The worth of that, is that which it contains,
  And that is this, and this with thee remains.

LXXV.

So are you to my thoughts, as food to life,
Or as sweet-seasoned showers are to the ground;
And for the peace of you I hold such strife
As twixt a miser and his wealth is found:
Now proud as an enjoyer, and anon
Doubting the filching age will steal his treasure;
Now counting best to be with you alone,
Then bettered that the world may see my pleasure:
Sometime all full with feasting on your sight,
And by and by clean starvéd for a look;
Possessing or pursuing no delight,
Save what is had or must from you be took.
  Thus do I pine and surfeit day by day,
  Or gluttoning on all, or all away.

LXXVI.

Why is my verse so barren of new pride?
So far from variation or quick change?
Why, with the time, do I not glance aside
To new-found methods and to compounds strange?
Why write I still all one, ever the same,
And keep invention in a noted weed,[1]
That every word doth almost tell my name,
Showing their birth, and where they did proceed?
O know, sweet love, I always write of you,
And you and love are still my argument;
So all my best is dressing old words new,
Spending again what is already spent:
For as the sun is daily new and old,
So is my love still telling what is told.

LXXVII.

Thy glass will show thee how thy beauties wear,
Thy dial how thy precious minutes waste;
The vacant leaves thy mind's imprint will bear,
And of this book this learning mayst thou taste.
The wrinkles which thy glass will truly show,
Of mouthéd graves will give thee memory;
Thou by thy dial's shady stealth mayst know
Time's thievish progress to eternity.
Look what thy memory cannot contain,
Commit to these waste blanks, and thou shalt find
Those children nursed, delivered from thy brain,
To take a new acquaintance of thy mind.

[1] *A noted weed*, a dress known and familiar, through being always the same.

These offices, so oft as thou wilt look,
Shall profit thee, and much enrich thy book.

LXXVIII.

So oft have I invoked thee for my muse,
And found such fair assistance in my verse,
As every alien pen hath got my use,
And under thee their poesy disperse.
Thine eyes, that taught the dumb on high to sing,
And heavy ignorance aloft to fly,
Have added feathers to the learned's wing,
And given grace a double majesty.
Yet be most proud of that which I compile,
Whose influence is thine, and born of thee:
In others' works thou dost but mend the style,
And arts with thy sweet graces gracéd be,
But thou art all my art, and dost advance
As high as learning my rude ignorance.

LXXIX.

Whilst I alone did call upon thy aid,
My verse alone had all thy gentle grace,
But now my gracious numbers are decayed,
And my sick muse doth give another place.
I grant, sweet love, thy lovely argument
Deserves the travail of a worthier pen;
Yet what of thee thy poet doth invent,
He robs thee of, and pays it thee again.
He lends thee virtue, and he stole that word
From thy behavior; beauty doth he give,
And found it in thy cheek; he can afford
No praise to thee but what in thee doth live.

  Then thank him not for that which he doth say,
  Since what he owes thee thou thyself dost pay.

LXXX.

O, how I faint when I of you do write,
Knowing a better spirit doth use your name,
And in the praise thereof spends all his might,
To make me tongue-tied, speaking of your fame!
But since your worth (wide as the ocean is)
The humble as the proudest sail doth bear,
My saucy bark, inferior far to his,
On your broad main doth wilfully appear.
Your shallowest help will hold me up afloat,
Whilst he upon your soundless deep doth ride;
Or, being wrecked, I am a worthless boat,
He of tall building, and of goodly pride:
  Then if he thrive, and I be cast away,
  The worst was this; — my love was my decay.

LXXXI.

Or I shall live your epitaph to make,
Or you survive when I in earth am rotten;
From hence your memory death cannot take,
Although in me each part will be forgotten.
Your name from hence immortal life shall have,
Though I, once gone, to all the world must die:
The earth can yield me but a common grave,
When you entombéd in men's eyes shall lie.
Your monument shall be my gentle verse,
Which eyes not yet created shall o'er-read;
And tongues to be, your being shall rehearse,
When all the breathers of this world are dead;

You still shall live (such virtue hath my pen)
Where breath most breathes, — even in the mouths
of men.

LXXXII.

I grant thou wert not married to my muse,
And therefore mayst without attaint o'erlook
The dedicated words which writers use
Of their fair subject, blessing every book.
Thou art as fair in knowledge as in hue,
Finding thy worth a limit past my praise;
And therefore art enforced to seek anew
Some fresher stamp of the time-bettering days.
And do so, love; yet when they have devised
What strainéd touches rhetoric can lend,
Thou truly fair wert truly sympathized,
In true plain words, by thy true-telling friend;
And their gross painting might be better used
Where cheeks need blood; in thee it is abused.

LXXXIII.

I never saw that you did painting need,
And therefore to your fair no painting set.
I found, or thought I found, you did exceed
The barren tender of a poet's debt:
And therefore have I slept in your report,
That you yourself, being extant, well might show
How far a modern[1] quill doth come too short,
Speaking of worth, what worth in you doth grow.
This silence for my sin you did impute,
Which shall be most my glory, being dumb;

[1] *Modern*, trite; common.

For I impair not beauty being mute,
When others would give life, and bring a tomb.
There lives more life in one of your fair eyes
Than both your poets can in praise devise.

LXXXIV.

Who is it that says most? which can say more
Than this rich praise, — that you alone are you?
In whose confine immuréd is the store
Which should example where your equal grew?
Lean penury within that pen doth dwell,
That to his subject lends not some small glory;
But he that writes of you, if he can tell
That you are you, so dignifies his story,
Let him but copy what in you is writ,
Not making worse what nature made so clear,
And such a counterpart shall fame his wit,
Making his style admiréd every where.
You to your beauteous blessings add a curse,
Being fond on praise, which makes your praises worse.

LXXXV.

My tongue-tied muse in manners holds her still,
While comments of your praise, richly compiled,
Reserve[1] their character with golden quill,
And precious phrase by all the muses filed.
I think good thoughts, while others write good words,
And, like unlettered clerk, still cry "Amen'
To every hymn that able spirit affords,
In polished form of well-refinéd pen.

[1] *Reserve* is here again used for *preserve*.

Hearing you praised, I say, "'Tis so, 'tis true,"
And to the most of praise add something more;
But that is in my thought, whose love to you,
Though words come hindmost, holds his rank before.
  Then others for the breath of words respect,
  Me for my dumb thoughts, speaking in effect.

LXXXVI.

Was it the proud full sail of his great verse,
Bound for the prize of all-too-precious you,
That did my ripe thoughts in my brain inhearse,
Making their tomb the womb wherein they grew?
Was it his spirit, by spirits taught to write
Above a mortal pitch, that struck me dead?
No, neither he, nor his compeers by night
Giving him aid, my verse astonishéd.
He, nor that affable familiar ghost
Which nightly gulls him with intelligence,[1]
As victors, of my silence cannot boast;
I was not sick of any fear from thence.
  But when your countenance filed[2] up his line,
  Then lacked I matter; that enfeebled mine.

LXXXVII.

Farewell! thou art too dear for my possessing,
And like enough thou know'st thy estimate:
The charter of thy worth gives thee releasing;
My bonds in thee are all determinate.

1 Steevens conjectures that this is an allusion to Dr. Dee's pretended intercourse with a familiar spirit.

2 *Filed*, gave the last polish. Ben Jonson, in his verses on Shakspeare, speaks of his

"Well-turned and *true-filed* lines."

For how do I hold thee but by thy granting?
And for that riches where is my deserving?
The cause of this fair gift in me is wanting,
And so my patent back again is swerving.
Thyself thou gav'st, thy own worth then not knowing,
Or me, to whom thou gav'st it, else mistaking;
So thy great gift, upon misprision growing,
Comes home again, on better judgment making.
Thus have I had thee, as a dream doth flatter,
In sleep a king, but, waking, no such matter.

LXXXVIII.

When thou shalt be disposed to set me light,
And place my merit in the eye of Scorn,
Upon thy side against myself I'll fight,
And prove thee virtuous, though thou art forsworn.
With mine own weakness being best acquainted,
Upon thy part I can set down a story
Of faults concealed, wherein I am attainted;
That thou, in losing me, shalt win much glory:
And I by this will be a gainer too;
For bending all my loving thoughts on thee,
The injuries that to myself I do,
Doing thee vantage, double-vantage me.
Such is my love, to thee I so belong,
That for thy right myself will bear all wrong.

LXXXIX.

Say that thou didst forsake me for some fault,
And I will comment upon that offence:
Speak of my lameness, and I straight will halt;
Against thy reasons making no defence.

Thou canst not, love, disgrace me half so ill
To set a form upon desiréd change,
As I'll myself disgrace: knowing thy will,
I will acquaintance strangle,[1] and look strange;
Be absent from thy walks; and in my tongue
Thy sweet-belovéd name no more shall dwell;
Lest I (too much profane) should do it wrong,
And haply of our old acquaintance tell.
For thee, against myself I'll vow debate,
For I must ne'er love him whom thou dost hate.

XC.

Then hate me when thou wilt; if ever, now;
Now, while the world is bent my deeds to cross,
Join with the spite of fortune, make me bow,
And do not drop in for an after-loss:
Ah! do not, when my heart hath 'scaped this sorrow,
Come in the rearward of a conquered woe;
Give not a windy night a rainy morrow,
To linger out a purposed overthrow.
If thou wilt leave me, do not leave me last,
When other petty griefs have done their spite,
But in the onset come; so shall I taste
At first the very worst of fortune's might;
And other strains of woe, which now seem woe,
Compared with loss of thee will not seem so.

[1] *Strangle.* Malone gives several examples of the use of the verb; and Steevens adds, "This uncouth phrase seems to have been a favorite with Shakspeare." Why is any word called *uncouth* which expresses a meaning more clearly and forcibly than any other word? The miserable affectation of the last age, in rejecting words that in sound appeared not to harmonize with the mincing prettinesses of polite conversation, emasculated our language; and it will take some time to restore it to its ancient nervousness.

XCI.

Some glory in their birth, some in their skill,
Some in their wealth, some in their body's force;
Some in their garments, though new-fangled ill;
Some in their hawks and hounds, some in their horse;
And every humor hath his adjunct pleasure,
Wherein it finds a joy above the rest;
But these particulars are not my measure,
All these I better in one general best.
Thy love is better than high birth to me,
Richer than wealth, prouder than garments' cost,
Of more delight than hawks or horses be;
And, having thee, of all men's pride I boast.
  Wretched in this alone, that thou mayst take
  All this away, and me most wretched make.

XCII.

But do thy worst to steal thyself away,
For term of life thou art assuréd mine;
And life no longer than thy love will stay,
For it depends upon that love of thine.
Then need I not to fear the worst of wrongs,
When in the least of them my life hath end.
I see a better state to me belongs
Than that which on thy humor doth depend.
Thou canst not vex me with inconstant mind,
Since that my life on thy revolt doth lie.
O, what a happy title do I find,
Happy to have thy love, happy to die!
  But what's so blessed-fair that fears no blot?—
  Thou mayst be false, and yet I know it not.

XCIII.

So shall I live, supposing thou art true,
Like a deceivéd husband; so love's face
May still seem love to me, though altered-new;
Thy looks with me, thy heart in other place:
For there can live no hatred in thine eye,
Therefore in that I cannot know thy change.
In many's looks the false heart's history
Is writ, in moods and frowns and wrinkles strange;
But Heaven in thy creation did decree
That in thy face sweet love should ever dwell;
Whate'er thy thoughts or thy heart's workings be,
Thy looks should nothing thence but sweetness tell.
  How like Eve's apple doth thy beauty grow,
  If thy sweet virtue answer not thy show!

XCIV.

They that have power to hurt and will do none,
That do not do the thing they most do show,
Who, moving others, are themselves as stone,
Unmovéd, cold, and to temptation slow;
They rightly do inherit Heaven's graces,
And husband nature's riches from expense;
They are the lords and owners of their faces,
Others but stewards of their excellence.
The summer's flower is to the summer sweet,
Though to itself it only live and die;
But if that flower with base infection meet,
The basest weed outbraves his dignity;
  For sweetest things turn sourest by their deeds;
  Lilies that fester smell far worse than weeds.

XCV.

How sweet and lovely dost thou make the shame,
Which, like a canker in the fragrant rose,
Doth spot the beauty of thy budding name!
O, in what sweets dost thou thy sins enclose!
That tongue that tells the story of thy days,
Making lascivious comments on thy sport,
Cannot dispraise but in a kind of praise;
Naming thy name blesses an ill report.
O, what a mansion have those vices got
Which for their habitation chose out thee!
Where beauty's veil doth cover every blot,
And all things turn to fair, that eyes can see!
  Take heed, dear heart, of this large privilege;
  The hardest knife, ill used, doth lose his edge.

XCVI.

Some say, thy fault is youth, some wantonness;
Some say, thy grace is youth and gentle sport;
Both grace and faults are loved of more and less:
Thou mak'st faults graces that to thee resort.
As on the finger of a thronéd queen
The basest jewel will be well esteemed;
So are those errors that in thee are seen
To truths translated, and for true things deemed.
How many lambs might the stern wolf betray,
If like a lamb he could his looks translate!
How many gazers mightst thou lead away,
If thou wouldst use the strength of all thy state!
  But do not so; I love thee in such sort,
  As, thou being mine, mine is thy good report.

XCVII.

How like a winter hath my absence been
From thee, the pleasure of the fleeting year!
What freezings have I felt, what dark days seen!
What old December's bareness every where!
And yet this time removed[1] was summer's time;
The teeming autumn, big with rich increase,
Bearing the wanton burden of the prime,
Like widowed wombs after their lords' decease:
Yet this abundant issue seemed to me
But hope of orphans, and unfathered fruit;
For summer and his pleasures wait on thee,
And, thou away, the very birds are mute;
  Or, if they sing, 'tis with so dull a cheer,
  That leaves look pale, dreading the winter's near.

XCVIII.

From you have I been absent in the spring,
When proud-pied April, dressed in all his trim,
Hath put a spirit of youth in every thing,
That heavy Saturn laughed and leaped with him.
Yet nor the lays of birds, nor the sweet smell
Of different flowers in odor and in hue,
Could make me any summer's story tell,
Or from their proud lap pluck them where they grew:
Nor did I wonder at the lilies white,
Nor praise the deep vermilion in the rose;
They were but sweet, but figures of delight,
Drawn after you, you pattern of all those.

[1] Malone explains this as, "This time in which I was remote or absent from thee."

Yet seemed it winter still, and, you away,
As with your shadow I with these did play.

XCIX.

The forward violet thus did I chide; —
Sweet thief, whence didst thou steal thy sweet that smells,
If not from my love's breath? The purple pride
Which on thy soft cheek for complexion dwells,
In my love's veins thou hast too grossly dyed.
The lily I condemnéd for thy hand,
And buds of marjoram had stolen thy hair:
The roses fearfully on thorns did stand,
One blushing shame, another white despair;
A third, nor red nor white, had stolen of both,
And to his robbery had annexed thy breath:
But for his theft, in pride of all his growth
A vengeful canker eat him up to death.
More flowers I noted, yet I none could see,
But sweet or color it had stolen from thee.

C.

Where art thou, Muse, that thou forgett'st so long
To speak of that which gives thee all thy might?
Spend'st thou thy fury on some worthless song,
Darkening thy power, to lend base subjects light?
Return, forgetful Muse, and straight redeem
In gentle numbers time so idly spent;
Sing to the ear that doth thy lays esteem,
And gives thy pen both skill and argument.
Rise, restive Muse, my love's sweet face survey,
If Time have any wrinkle graven there;

If any, be a satire to decay,
And make Time's spoils despiséd every where.
  Give my love fame faster than Time wastes life;
  So thou prevent'st his scythe and crooked knife.

CI.

O truant Muse, what shall be thy amends
For thy neglect of truth in beauty dyed?
Both truth and beauty on my love depends;
So dost thou too, and therein dignified.
Make answer, Muse: wilt thou not haply say,
"Truth needs no color with his color fixed,
Beauty no pencil, beauty's truth to lay;
But best is best, if never intermixed?"—
Because he needs no praise, wilt thou be dumb?
Excuse not silence so; for it lies in thee
To make him much outlive a gilded tomb,
And to be praised of ages yet to be.
  Then do thy office, Muse; I teach thee how
  To make him seem long hence as he shows now.

CII.

My love is strengthened, though more weak in seeming;
I love not less, though less the show appear;
That love is merchandized, whose rich esteeming
The owner's tongue doth publish every where.
Our love was new, and then but in the spring,
When I was wont to greet it with my lays;
As Philomel in summer's front doth sing,
And stops his pipe in growth of riper days:
Not that the summer is less pleasant now
Than when her mournful hymns did hush the night,

But that wild music burthens every bough,
And sweets grown common lose their dear delight.
  Therefore, like her, I sometime hold my tongue,
  Because I would not dull you with my song.

CIII.

Alack! what poverty my muse brings forth,
That having such a scope to show her pride,
The argument, all bare, is of more worth
Than when it hath my added praise beside.
O, blame me not if I no more can write!
Look in your glass, and there appears a face
That over-goes my blunt invention quite,
Dulling my lines, and doing me disgrace.
Were it not sinful then, striving to mend,
To mar the subject that before was well?
For to no other pass my verses tend,
Than of your graces and your gifts to tell;
  And more, much more, than in my verse can sit,
  Your own glass shows you, when you look in it.

CIV.

To me, fair friend, you never can be old,
For as you were when first your eye I eyed,
Such seems your beauty still. Three winters' cold
Have from the forests shook three summers' pride;
Three beauteous springs to yellow autumn turned
In process of the seasons have I seen;
Three April perfumes in three hot Junes burned,
Since first I saw you fresh, which yet are green.
Ah! yet doth beauty, like a dial hand,
Steal from his figure, and no pace perceived;

So your sweet hue, which methinks still doth
stand,
Hath motion, and mine eye may be deceived.
For fear of which, hear this, thou age unbred,
Ere you were born, was beauty's summer dead.

CV.

Let not my love be called idolatry,
Nor my belovéd as an idol show,
Since all alike my songs and praises be,
To one, of one, still such, and ever so.
Kind is my love to-day, to-morrow kind,
Still constant in a wondrous excellence;
Therefore my verse, to constancy confined,
One thing expressing, leaves out difference.
Fair, kind, and true, is all my argument,
Fair, kind, and true, varying to other words;
And in this change is my invention spent,
Three themes in one, which wondrous scope affords.
Fair, kind, and true, have often lived alone,
Which three, till now, never kept seat in one.

CVI.

When in the chronicle of wasted time
I see descriptions of the fairest wights,
And beauty making beautiful old rhyme,
In praise of ladies dead and lovely knights,
Then in the blazon of sweet beauty's best,
Of hand, of foot, of lip, of eye, of brow,
I see their antique pen would have expressed
Even such a beauty as you master now.
So all their praises are but prophecies
Of this our time, all you prefiguring;

And, for they looked but with divining eyes,
They had not skill enough your worth to sing:
For we, which now behold these present days,
Have eyes to wonder, but lack tongues to praise.

CVII.

Not mine own fears, nor the prophetic soul
Of the wide world dreaming on things to come,
Can yet the lease of my true love control,
Supposed as forfeit to a cònfined doom.
The mortal moon hath her eclipse endured,
And the sad augurs mock their own presage;
Incertainties now crown themselves assured,
And peace proclaims olives of endless age.
Now with the drops of this most balmy time
My love looks fresh, and death to me subscribes,[1]
Since spite of him I'll live in this poor rhyme,
While he insults o'er dull and speechless tribes.
And thou in this shalt find thy monument,
When tyrants' crests and tombs of brass are spent.

CVIII.

What's in the brain that ink may character,
Which hath not figured to thee my true spirit?
What's new to speak, what now[2] to register,
That may express my love, or thy dear merit?
Nothing, sweet boy; but yet, like prayers divine,
I must each day say o'er the very same;
Counting no old thing old, thou mine, I thine,
Even as when first I hallowed thy fair name.

[1] *Subscribes*, submits; acknowledges as a superior.

[2] *Now*. So the original, but altered by Malone to *new*. We agree with Mr. Dyce in thinking the alteration unnecessary.

So that eternal love in love's fresh case
Weighs not the dust and injury of age,
Nor gives to necessary wrinkles place,
But makes antiquity for aye his page ;
  Finding the first conceit of love there bred,
  Where time and outward form would show it dead.

CIX.

O, never say that I was false of heart,
Though absence seemed my flame to qualify !
As easy might I from myself depart,
As from my soul, which in thy breast doth lie :
That is my home of love : if I have ranged,
Like him that travels, I return again ;
Just to the time, not with the time exchanged, —
So that myself bring water for my stain.
Never believe, though in my nature reigned
All frailties that besiege all kinds of blood,
That it could so preposterously be stained,
To leave for nothing all thy sum of good ;
  For nothing this wide universe I call,
  Save thou, my rose ; in it thou art my all.

CX.

Alas ! 'tis true, I have gone here and there,
And made myself a motley[1] to the view,
Gored[2] mine own thoughts, sold cheap what is most dear,
Made old offences of affections new.

[1] *Motley.* Jaques, in As You Like It, exclaims, "Invest me in my *motley.*" Motley was the dress of the domestic fool, or jester ; and thus the buffoon himself came to be called *a motley.* Jaques, addressing Touchstone, says, "Will you be married, *Motley ?*"

[2] *Gored*, wounded. In Hamlet we have, —

> "I have a voice and precedent of peace
> To keep my name *ungored.*"

Most true it is, that I have looked on truth
Askance and strangely ; but, by all above,
These blenches[1] gave my heart another youth,
And worse essays proved thee my best of love.
Now all is done, have[2] what shall have no end:
Mine appetite I never more will grind
On newer proof, to try an older friend,
A God in love, to whom I am confined.
Then give me welcome, next my heaven the best,
Even to thy pure and most most loving breast.

CXI.

O, for my sake do you with Fortune chide,
The guilty goddess of my harmful deeds,
That did not better for my life provide,
Than public means, which public manners breeds.
Thence comes it that my name receives a brand,
And almost thence my nature is subdued
To what it works in, like the dyer's hand:
Pity me then, and wish I were renewed;
Whilst, like a willing patient, I will drink
Potions of eysell[3] 'gainst my strong infection;
No bitterness that I will bitter think,
Nor double penance, to correct correction.

[1] *Blenches*, deviations.

[2] *Have.* This is the word of the old copy. The reading of all modern editions is,—

"Now all is done, *save* what shall have no end."

Malone says this is unintelligible. His conjectural reading, which Tyrwhitt recommended, appears to us more so. "Now all is done" clearly applies to the *blenches*, the *worse essays;* but the poet then adds, "*have* thou what shall have no end"—my constant affection, my undivided friendship.

[3] *Eysell*, vinegar.

Pity me then, dear friend, and I assure ye,
Even that your pity is enough to cure me.

CXII.

Your love and pity doth the impression fill
Which vulgar scandal stamped upon my brow;
For what care I who calls me well or ill,
So you o'ergreen my bad, my good allow?[1]
You are my all-the-world, and I must strive
To know my shames and praises from your tongue;
None else to me, nor I to none alive,
That my steeled sense or changes, right or wrong.[2]
In so profound abysm I throw all care
Of others' voices, that my adder's sense
To critic and to flatterer stoppéd are.
Mark how with my neglect I do dispense:—
You are so strongly in my purpose bred,
That all the world besides methinks are dead.[3]

[1] *Allow*, approve.

[2] This passage is obscure, and there is probably some slight misprint. Steevens says, with his usual amenity, "The meaning of this purblind and obscure stuff seems to be, 'You are the only person who has the power to change my stubborn resolution, *either* to what is right, or to what is wrong.'" We have little doubt that something like this is the meaning; but why has not this great conjectural critic, instead of calling out "purblind and obscure stuff," tried his hand at some slight emendation? He is venturous enough when the text is clear. We might read thus:—

"That my steeled sense *so* changes right or wrong;"

or we might read, as Malone has proposed, "*E'er* changes."

[3] This line presents in the old copy one of the many examples of how little the context was heeded. We there find,—

"That all the world *besides me thinks y' are* dead."

Malone changes this to—

"That all the world *besides methinks they are* dead."

We adopt Mr. Dyce's better reading.

CXIII.

Since I left you, mine eye is in my mind;
And that which governs me to go about
Doth part his function, and is partly blind,
Seems seeing, but effectually is out;
For it no form delivers to the heart
Of bird, of flower, or shape, which it doth latch;[1]
Of his quick objects hath the mind no part,
Nor his own vision holds what it doth catch;
For if it see the rud'st or gentlest sight,
The most sweet favor,[2] or deformed'st creature,
The mountain or the sea, the day or night,
The crow, or dove, it shapes them to your feature.
  Incapable of more, replete with you,
  My most true mind thus maketh mine untrue.[3]

CXIV.

Or whether doth my mind, being crowned with you,
Drink up the monarch's plague, this flattery,
Or whether shall I say mine eye saith true,
And that your love taught it this alchymy,
To make of monsters and things indigest
Such cherubins as your sweet self resemble,
Creating every bad a perfect best,
As fast as objects to his beams assemble?
O, 'tis the first; 'tis flattery in my seeing,
And my great mind most kingly drinks it up:

[1] *Latch.* The original has *lack.* Malone substituted *latch* which signifies to lay hold of.

[2] *Favor*, countenance.

[3] *Untrue* is here used as a substantive. So in Measure for Measure: —

"Say what you can, my false outweighs your *true.*"

Mine eye well knows what with his gust is 'greeing,
And to his palate doth prepare the cup.
  If it be poisoned, 'tis the lesser sin
  That mine eye loves it, and doth first begin.

CXV.

Those lines that I before have writ, do lie;
Even those that said I could not love you dearer;
Yet then my judgment knew no reason why
My most full flame should afterwards burn clearer.
But reckoning time, whose millioned accidents
Creep in 'twixt vows, and change decrees of kings,
Tan sacred beauty, blunt the sharp'st intents,
Divert strong minds to the course of altering things;
Alas! why, fearing of Time's tyranny,
Might I not then say, "Now I love you best,"
When I was certain o'er incertainty,
Crowning the present, doubting of the rest?
  Love is a babe; then might I not say so,
  To give full growth to that which still doth grow?

CXVI.

Let me not to the marriage of true minds
Admit impediments. Love is not love
Which alters when it alteration finds,
Or bends with the remover to remove:
O, no; it is an ever-fixéd mark,
That looks on tempests, and is never shaken;
It is the star to every wandering bark,
Whose worth 's unknown, although his height be taken.

Love 's not Time's fool, though rosy lips and cheeks
Within his bending sickle's compass come;
Love alters not with his brief hours and weeks,
But bears it out even to the edge of doom.
  If this be error, and upon me proved,
  I never writ, nor no man ever loved.

CXVII.

Accuse me thus; that I have scanted all
Wherein I should your great deserts repay;
Forgot upon your dearest love to call,
Whereto all bonds do tie me day by day;
That I have frequent been with unknown minds,
And given to time your own dear-purchased right;
That I have hoisted sail to all the winds
Which should transport me farthest from your sight.
Book both my wilfulness and errors down,
And on just proof surmise accumulate,
Bring me within the level of your frown,
But shoot not at me in your wakened hate:
  Since my appeal says, I did strive to prove
  The constancy and virtue of your love.

CXVIII.

Like as, to make our appetites more keen,
With eager[1] compounds we our palate urge;
As, to prevent our maladies unseen,
We sicken to shun sickness, when we purge;
Even so, being full of your ne'er-cloying sweetness,
To bitter sauces did I frame my feeding,

[1] *Eager*, sour; the French *aigre*.

And, sick of welfare, found a kind of meetness
To be diseased, ere that there was true needing.
Thus policy in love, to anticipate
The ills that were not, grew to faults assured,
And brought to medicine a healthful state,
Which, rank of goodness, would by ill be cured.
  But thence I learn, and find the lesson true,
  Drugs poison him that so fell sick of you.

CXIX.

What potions have I drunk of Siren tears,
Distilled from limbecs foul as hell within,
Applying fears to hopes, and hopes to fears,
Still losing when I saw myself to win!
What wretched errors hath my heart committed,
Whilst it hath thought itself so blessèd never!
How have mine eyes out of their spheres been fitted[1]
In the distraction of this madding fever!
O benefit of ill! now I find true
That better is by evil still made better;
And ruined love, when it is built anew,
Grows fairer than at first, more strong, far greater.
  So I return rebuked to my content,
  And gain by ill thrice more than I have spent.

CXX.

That you were once unkind, befriends me now,
And for that sorrow, which I then did feel,
Needs must I under my transgression bow,
Unless my nerves were brass or hammered steel.

[1] *Fitted*, subjected to fits.

For if you were by my unkindness shaken,
As I by yours, you 've passed a hell of time;
And I, a tyrant, have no leisure taken
To weigh how once I suffered in your crime.
O that our night of woe might have remembered[1]
My deepest sense, how hard true sorrow hits,
And soon to you, as you to me, then tendered
The humble salve which wounded bosoms fits!
  But that your trespass now becomes a fee:
  Mine ransoms yours, and yours must ransom me.

CXXI.

'Tis better to be vile than vile esteemed,
When not to be receives reproach of being,
And the just pleasure lost, which is so deemed
Not by our feeling, but by others' seeing.
For why should others' false adulterate eyes
Give salutation to my sportive blood?
Or on my frailties why are frailer spies,
Which in their wills count bad what I think good?
No. — I am that I am; and they that level
At my abuses, reckon up their own:
I may be straight, though they themselves be bevel;[2]
By their rank thoughts my deeds must not be shown;
  Unless this general evil they maintain, —
  All men are bad, and in their badness reign.

CXXII.

Thy gift, thy tables are within my brain
Full charactered with lasting memory,

[1] *Remembered*, reminded. [2] *Bevel*, bent in an angle.

Which shall above that idle rank remain,
Beyond all date, even to eternity:
Or at the least so long as brain and heart
Have faculty by nature to subsist;
Till each to razed oblivion yield his part
Of thee, thy record never can be missed.
That poor retention could not so much hold,[1]
Nor need I tallies thy dear love to score;
Therefore to give them from me was I bold,
To trust those tables that receive thee more:
  To keep an adjunct to remember thee,
  Were to import forgetfulness in me.

CXXIII.

No! Time, thou shalt not boast that I do change:
Thy pyramids built up with newer might
To me are nothing novel, nothing strange;
They are but dressings of a former sight.
Our dates are brief, and therefore we admire
What thou dost foist upon us that is old;
And rather make them born to our desire,
Than think that we before have heard them told.
Thy registers and thee I both defy,
Not wondering at the present nor the past;
For thy records and what we see do lie,
Made more or less by thy continual haste:
  This I do vow, and this shall ever be,
  I will be true, despite thy scythe and thee.

1 Malone says, " *That poor retention* is the table-book given to him by his friend, incapable of retaining, or rather of containing so much as the tablet of the brain."

CXXIV.

If my dear love were but the child of state,
It might for Fortune's bastard be unfathered,
As subject to Time's love, or to Time's hate,
Weeds among weeds, or flowers with flowers gathered.
No, it was builded far from accident;
It suffers not in smiling pomp, nor falls
Under the blow of thrallèd discontent,
Whereto the inviting time our fashion calls:
It fears not policy, that heretic,
Which works on leases of short-numbered hours,
But all alone stands hugely politic,
That it nor grows with heat, nor drowns with showers.
To this I witness call the fools of time,
Which die for goodness, who have lived for crime.

CXXV.

Were it aught to me I bore the canopy,
With my extern the outward honoring,
Or laid great bases for eternity,
Which prove more short than waste or ruining?
Have I not seen dwellers on form and favor
Lose all, and more, by paying too much rent,
For compound sweet foregoing simple savor,
Pitiful thrivers, in their gazing spent?
No; — let me be obsequious in thy heart,
And take thou my oblation, poor but free,
Which is not mixed with seconds,[1] knows no art,
But mutual render, only me for thee.

[1] *Seconds.* Mr. Dyce considers this word a misprint. The only note on the passage in the variorum editions is that of

Hence, thou suborned informer! a true soul,
When most impeached, stands least in thy control.

CXXVI.

O thou, my lovely boy, who in thy power
Dost hold Time's fickle glass, his sickle, hour;
Who hast by waning grown, and therein show'st
Thy lovers withering, as thy sweet self grow'st!
If Nature, sovereign mistress over wrack,
As thou go'st onwards, still will pluck thee back,
She keeps thee to this purpose, that her skill
May time disgrace, and wretched minutes kill.
Yet fear her, O thou minion of her pleasure;
She may detain, but not still keep her treasure:
Her audit, though delayed, answered must be,
And her quietus is to render thee.

CXXVII.

In tne old age black was not counted fair,
Or if it were, it bore not beauty's name;
But now is black beauty's successive heir,
And beauty slandered with a bastard shame:

Steevens: "I am just informed by an old lady that *seconds* is a provincial term for the *second kind of flour*, which is collected after the smaller bran is sifted. That our author's oblation was pure, *unmixed with baser matter*, is all that he meant to say." Mr. Dyce calls this note "preposterously absurd." Steevens, however, knew what he was doing. He mentions the flour, as in almost every other note upon the Sonnets, to throw discredit upon compositions with which he could not sympathize. He had a sharp, cunning, pettifogging mind; and he knew many prosaic things well enough. He knew that a *second* in a duel, a *seconder* in a debate, a *secondary* in ecclesiastical affairs, meant one next to the principal. The poet's friend has his chief oblation; no *seconds*, or inferior persons, are mixed up with his tribute of affection.

For since each hand hath put on nature's power,
Fairing the foul with art's false borrowed face,
Sweet beauty hath no name, no holy hour,
But is profaned, if not lives in disgrace.
Therefore my mistress' eyes are raven black,
Her eyes so suited; and they mourners seem
At such, who, not born fair, no beauty lack,
Slandering creation with a false esteem:
Yet so they mourn, becoming of their woe,
That every tongue says, beauty should look so.

CXXVIII.

How oft, when thou, my music, music play'st,
Upon that blessèd wood whose motion sounds
With thy sweet fingers, when thou gently sway'st
The wiry concord that mine ear confounds,
Do I envy' those jacks,[1] that nimble leap
To kiss the tender inward of thy hand,
Whilst my poor lips, which should that harvest reap,
At the wood's boldness by thee blushing stand!
To be so tickled, they would change their state
And situation with those dancing chips,
O'er whom thy fingers walk with gentle gait,
Making dead wood more blessed than living lips.
Since saucy jacks so happy are in this,
Give them thy fingers, me thy lips to kiss.

CXXIX.

The expense of spirit in a waste of shame
Is lust in action; and till action, lust

[1] *Jacks.* The small hammers, moved by the keys, which strike the strings of a virginal. In the comedy of "Ram Alley" we have, —

"Where be these rascals that skip up and down
Like *virginal jacks*?"

Is perjured, murderous, bloody, full of blame,
Savage, extreme, rude, cruel, not to trust;
Enjoyed no sooner, but despiséd straight;
Past reason hunted; and no sooner had,
Past reason hated, as a swallowed bait,
On purpose laid to make the taker mad:
Mad in pursuit, and in possession so;
Had, having, and in quest to have, extreme;
A bliss in proof, — and proved, a very woe;
Before, a joy proposed; behind, a dream:
  All this the world well knows; yet none knows well
  To shun the heaven that leads men to this hell.

CXXX.

My mistress' eyes are nothing like the sun;
Coral is far more red than her lips' red:
If snow be white, why then her breasts are dun;
If hairs be wires, black wires grow on her head.
I have seen roses damasked, red and white,
But no such roses see I in her cheeks;
And in some perfumes is there more delight
Than in the breath that from my mistress reeks
I love to hear her speak, — yet well I know
That music hath a far more pleasing sound;
I grant I never saw a goddess go, —
My mistress, when she walks, treads on the ground;
  And yet, by Heaven, I think my love as rare
  As any she belied with false compare.

CXXXI.

Thou art as tyrannous, so as thou art,
As those whose beauties proudly make them cruel;

For well thou know'st to my dear doting heart
Thou art the fairest and most precious jewel.
Yet, in good faith, some say that thee behold,
Thy face hath not the power to make love groan:
To say they err, I dare not be so bold,
Although I swear it to myself alone.
And, to be sure that is not false I swear,
A thousand groans, but thinking on thy face,
One on another's neck, do witness bear
Thy black is fairest in my judgment's place.
  In nothing art thou black, save in thy deeds,
  And thence this slander, as I think, proceeds.

CXXXII.

Thine eyes I love, and they, as pitying me,
Knowing thy heart, torment me with disdain;
Have put on black, and loving mourners be,
Looking with pretty ruth upon my pain.
And truly not the morning sun of heaven
Better becomes the gray cheeks of the east,
Nor that full star that ushers in the even
Doth half that glory to the sober west,
As those two mourning eyes become thy face:
O, let it then as well beseem thy heart
To mourn for me, since mourning doth thee grace,
And suit thy pity like in every part.
  Then will I swear beauty herself is black,
  And all they foul that thy complexion lack.

CXXXIII.

Beshrew that heart that makes my heart to groan
For that deep wound it gives my friend and me!

Is 't not enough to torture me alone,
But slave to slavery my sweet'st friend must be?
Me from myself thy cruel eye hath taken,
And my next self thou harder hast engrossed;
Of him, myself, and thee, I am forsaken;
A torment thrice threefold thus to be crossed.
Prison my heart in thy steel bosom's ward,
But then my friend's heart let my poor heart bail;
Who e'er keeps me, let my heart be his guard;
Thou canst not then use rigor in my jail:
  And yet thou wilt: for I, being pent in thee,
  Perforce am thine, and all that is in me.

CXXXIV.

So now I have confessed that he is thine,
And I myself am mortgaged to thy will;
Myself I'll forfeit, so that other mine
Thou wilt restore, to be my comfort still:
But thou wilt not, nor he will not be free,
For thou art covetous, and he is kind;
He learned but, surety-like, to write for me,
Under that bond that him as fast doth bind.
The statute[1] of thy beauty thou wilt take,
Thou usurer, that putt'st forth all to use,
And sue a friend, came debtor for my sake;
So him I lose through my unkind abuse.
  Him have I lost; thou hast both him and me,
  He pays the whole, and yet am I not free.

CXXXV.

Whoever hath her wish, thou hast thy will,
And will to boot, and will in overplus;

[1] *Statute*, security, or obligation.

More than enough am I that vex thee still,
To thy sweet will making addition thus.
Wilt thou, whose will is large and spacious,
Not once vouchsafe to hide my will in thine?
Shall will in others seem right gracious,
And in my will no fair acceptance shine?
The sea, all water, yet receives rain still,
And in abundance addeth to his store;
So thou, being rich in will, add to thy will
One will of mine, to make thy large will more
  Let no unkind, no fair beseechers kill;
  Think all but one, and me in that one *Will.*

CXXXVI.

If thy soul check thee that I come so near,
Swear to thy blind soul that I was thy *Will,*
And will, thy soul knows, is admitted there;
Thus far for love, my love-suit, sweet, fulfil.
Will will fulfil the treasure of thy love,
Ay, fill it full with wills, and my will one,
In things of great receipt with ease we prove;
Among a number one is reckoned none.
Then in the number let me pass untold,
Though in thy store's account I one must be;
For nothing hold me, so it please thee hold
That nothing me, a something sweet to thee:
  Make but my name thy love, and love that still,
  And then thou lov'st me,—for my name is *Will.*

CXXXVII.

Thou blind fool, Love, what dost thou to mine
    eyes,
That they behold, and see not what they see?

They know what beauty is, see where it lies,
Yet what the best is, take the worst to be.
If eyes, corrupt by over-partial looks,
Be anchored in the bay where all men ride,
Why of eyes' falsehood hast thou forgéd hooks,
Whereto the judgment of my heart is tied?
Why should my heart think that a several plot,[1]
Which my heart knows the wide world's common place?
Or mine eyes, seeing this, say this is not,
To put fair truth upon so foul a face?
In things right true my heart and eyes have erred,
And to this false plague are they now transferred.

CXXXVIII.

When my love swears that she is made of truth,
I do believe her, though I know she lies;
That she might think me some untutored youth,
Unlearnéd in the world's false subtleties,
Thus vainly thinking that she thinks me young,
Although she knows my days are past the best,
Simply I credit her false-speaking tongue;
On both sides thus is simple truth supprest.
But wherefore says she not she is unjust?
And wherefore say not I that I am old?
O, love's best habit is in seeming trust,
And age in love loves not to have years told:
Therefore I lie with her, and she with me,
And in our faults by lies we flattered be.[2]

1 See note on Love's Labor 's Lost, Act II. Sc. I.

2 There are many variations in the copy of this Sonnet as originally published in The Passionate Pilgrim. The differences are of that character which would lead us to believe that the author,

CXXXIX.

O, call not me to justify the wrong
That thy unkindness lays upon my heart;
Wound me not with thine eye, but with thy tongue;
Use power with power, and slay me not by art.
Tell me thou lov'st elsewhere; but in my sight,
Dear heart, forbear to glance thine eye aside.
What need'st thou wound with cunning, when thy might
Is more than my o'erpressed defence can 'bide?
Let me excuse thee: ah! my love well knows
Her pretty looks have been mine enemies;
And therefore from my face she turns my foes,
That they elsewhere might dart their injuries:
  Yet do not so; but since I am near slain,
  Kill me outright with looks, and rid my pain.

CXL.

Be wise as thou art cruel; do not press
My tongue-tied patience with too much disdain;

after the lapse of a few years, wrote it out a second time from memory. The variations are certainly not those of a transcriber: —

"When my love swears that she is made of truth,
I do believe her, though I know she lies,
That she might think me some untutored youth,
Unskilful in the world's false *forgeries*.
Thus vainly thinking that she thinks me young,
Although *I know* my *years be* past the best,
I smiling credit her false-speaking tongue,
Outfacing faults in love with love's ill rest.
But wherefore says *my love that* she is *young*?
And wherefore say not I that I am old?
O, love's best habit is *a soothing tongue*,
And age in love loves not to have years told.
  Therefore *I'll* lie with *love*, and *love* with me,
  Since that our faults *in love thus smothered be*."

Lest sorrow lend me words, and words express
The manner of my pity-wanting pain.
If I might teach thee wit, better it were,
Though not to love, yet, love, to tell me so;
(As testy sick men, when their deaths be near,
No news but health from their physicians know;)
For, if I should despair, I should grow mad,
And in my madness might speak ill of thee:
Now this ill-wresting world is grown so bad,
Mad slanderers by mad ears believéd be.
  That I may not be so, nor thou belied,
  Bear thine eyes straight, though thy proud heart go
      wide.

CXLI.

In faith I do not love thee with mine eyes,
For they in thee a thousand errors note;
But 'tis my heart that loves what they despise,
Who in despite of view is pleased to dote.
Nor are mine ears with thy tongue's tune delighted;
Nor tender feeling, to base touches prone,
Nor taste, nor smell, desire to be invited
To any sensual feast with thee alone:
But my five wits, nor my five senses can
Dissuade one foolish heart from serving thee,
Who leaves unswayed the likeness of a man,
Thy proud heart's slave and vassal wretch to be:
  Only my plague thus far I count my gain,
  That she that makes me sin, awards me pain.

CXLII.

Love is my sin, and thy dear virtue hate,
Hate of my sin, grounded on sinful loving:

O, but with mine compare thou thine own state,
And thou shalt find it merits not reproving;
Or, if it do, not from those lips of thine,
That have profaned their scarlet ornaments,
And sealed false bonds of love as oft as mine;
Robbed others' beds' revenues of their rents.
Be it lawful I love thee, as thou lov'st those
Whom thine eyes woo as mine impórtune thee:
Root pity in thy heart, that, when it grows,
Thy pity may deserve to pitied be.
  If thou dost seek to have what thou dost hide,
  By self-example mayst thou be denied!

CXLIII.

Lo, as a careful housewife runs to catch
One of her feathered creatures broke away,
Sets down her babe, and makes all swift despatch
In púrsuit of the thing she would have stay;
Whilst her neglected child holds her in chase,
Cries to catch her whose busy care is bent
To follow that which flies before her face,
Not prizing her poor infant's discontent;
So runn'st thou after that which flies from thee,
Whilst I thy babe chase thee afar behind;
But if thou catch thy hope, turn back to me,
And play the mother's part, kiss me, be kind:
  So will I pray that thou mayst have thy *Will*,
  If thou turn back, and my loud crying still.

CXLIV.

Two loves I have of comfort and despair,
Which like two spirits do suggest[1] me still;

[1] *Suggest*, tempt.

The better angel is a man right fair,
The worser spirit a woman, colored ill.
To win me soon to hell, my female evil
Tempteth my better angel from my side,
And would corrupt my saint to be a devil,
Wooing his purity with her foul pride.
And whether that my angel be turned fiend,
Suspect I may, yet not directly tell;
But being both from me, both to each friend,
I guess one angel in another's hell.
  Yet this shall I ne'er know, but live in doubt,
  Till my bad angel fire my good one out.[1]

CXLV.

Those lips that Love's own hand did make
Breathed forth the sound that said, "I hate,"
To me that languished for her sake:
But when she saw my woful state,
Straight in her heart did mercy come,
Chiding that tongue, that ever sweet
Was used in giving gentle doom;
And taught it thus anew to greet:
"I hate" she altered with an end,
That followed it as gentle day
Doth follow night, who like a fiend
From heaven to hell is flown away.
  "I hate" from hate away she threw,
  And saved my life, saying — "not you."

[1] The variations in the copy of this Sonnet in The Passionate Pilgrim are very slight. In the eighth line, instead of *foul pride*, we have *fair pride;* in the eleventh, instead of *from me*, we have *to me;* in the thirteenth, instead of *Yet this shall I ne'er know*, we have, *The truth I shall not know.*

CXLVI.

Poor soul, the centre of my sinful earth,
Fooled by those rebel powers that thee array,[1]
Why dost thou pine within, and suffer dearth,
Painting thy outward walls so costly gay?
Why so large cost, having so short a lease,
Dost thou upon thy fading mansion spend?
Shall worms, inheritors of this excess,
Eat up thy charge? Is this thy body's end?
Then, soul, live thou upon thy servant's loss,
And let that pine to aggravate thy store;
Buy terms divine in selling hours of dross;
Within be fed, without be rich no more:
  So shalt thou feed on Death, that feeds on men,
  And, Death once dead, there 's no more dying then.

CXLVII.

My love is as a fever, longing still
For that which longer nurseth the disease;
Feeding on that which doth preserve the ill,
The uncertain sickly appetite to please.
My reason, the physician to my love,
Angry that his prescriptions are not kept,
Hath left me, and I desperate now approve
Desire is death, which physic did except.

[1] In the original copy we have the following reading: —

"Poor soul, the centre of my sinful earth,
My sinful earth these rebel powers that thee array."

The received reading is a conjectural emendation by Malone. When the change in a text must rest wholly on conjecture, and some change is absolutely necessary, it appears to us that the change which has been established is in most cases better than any improvement.

Past cure I am, now reason is past care,
And frantic mad with evermore unrest;
My thoughts and my discourse as mad men's are,
At random from the truth vainly expressed;
  For I have sworn thee fair, and thought thee bright,
  Who art as black as hell, as dark as night.

CXLVIII.

O me! what eyes hath love put in my head,
Which have no correspondence with true sight!
Or, if they have, where is my judgment fled,
That censures[1] falsely what they see aright?
If that be fair whereon my false eyes dote,
What means the world to say it is not so?
If it be not, then love doth well denote
Love's eye is not so true as all men's; no,
How can it? O, how can Love's eye be true,
That is so vexed with watching and with tears?
No marvel then though I mistake my view;
The sun itself sees not, till heaven clears.
  O, cunning Love! with tears thou keep'st me blind,
  Lest eyes well-seeing thy foul faults should find.

CXLIX.

Canst thou, O cruel! say I love thee not,
When I, against myself, with thee partake?[2]
Do I not think on thee, when I forgot
Am of myself, all tyrant, for thy sake?
Who hateth thee that I do call my friend?
On whom frown'st thou that I do fawn upon?

[1] *Censures*, judges, estimates.
[2] *Partake*, take part. A partaker was a confederate.

Nay, if thou low'rst on me, do I not spend
Revenge upon myself with present moan?
What merit do I in myself respect,
That is so proud thy service to despise,
When all my best doth worship thy defect,
Commanded by the motion of thine eyes?
  But, love, hate on, for now I know thy mind;
  Those that can see thou lov'st, and I am blind.

CL.

O, from what power hast thou this powerful might,
With insufficiency my heart to sway?
To make me give the lie to my true sight,
And swear that brightness doth not grace the day?
Whence hast thou this becoming of things ill,
That in the very refuse of thy deeds
There is such strength and warrantise of skill,
That, in my mind, thy worst all best exceeds?
Who taught me how to love thee more,
The more I hear and see just cause of hate?
O, though I love what others do abhor,
With others thou shouldst not abhor my state;
  If thy unworthiness raised love in me,
  More worthy I to be beloved of thee.

CLI.

Love is too young to know what conscience is;
Yet who knows not, conscience is born of love?
Then, gentle cheater, urge not my amiss,[1]
Lest guilty of my faults, thy sweet self prove.
For thou betraying me, I do betray
My nobler part to my gross body's treason;

[1] *Amiss*, fault.

My soul doth tell my body that he may
Triumph in love; flesh stays no longer reason;
But rising at thy name, doth point out thee
As his triumphant prize. Proud of this pride,
He is contented thy poor drudge to be,
To stand in thy affairs, fall by thy side.
  No want of conscience hold it that I call
  Her love, for whose dear love I rise and fall.

CLII.

In loving thee thou know'st I am forsworn,
But thou art twice forsworn, to me love swearing;
In act thy bed-vow broke, and new faith torn,
In vowing new hate after new love bearing.
But why of two oaths' breach do I accuse thee,
When I break twenty? I am perjured most;
For all my vows are oaths but to misuse thee,
And all my honest faith in thee is lost:
For I have sworn deep oaths of thy deep kindness,
Oaths of thy love, thy truth, thy constancy;
And, to enlighten thee, gave eyes to blindness,
Or made them swear against the thing they see;
  For I have sworn thee fair: more perjured I,
  To swear, against the truth, so foul a lie!

CLIII.

Cupid laid by his brand, and fell asleep:
A maid of Dian's this advantage found,
And his love-kindling fire did quickly steep
In a cold valley-fountain of that ground;
Which borrowed from this holy fire of love
A dateless lively heat, still to endure,

And grew a seething bath, which yet men prove
Against strange maladies a sovereign cure.
But at my mistress' eye Love's brand new-fired,
The boy for trial needs would touch my breast;
I, sick withal, the help of bath desired,
And thither hied, a sad distempered guest,
  But found no cure: the bath for my help lies
  Where Cupid got new fire — my mistress' eyes.

CLIV.

The little love-god, lying once asleep,
Laid by his side his heart-inflaming brand,
Whilst many nymphs that vowed chaste life to keep
Came tripping by; but in her maiden hand
The fairest votary took up that fire
Which many legions of true hearts had warmed;
And so the general of hot desire
Was sleeping by a virgin hand disarmed.
This brand she quenchéd in a cool well by,
Which from Love's fire took heat perpetual,
Growing a bath and healthful remedy
For men diseased; but I, my mistress' thrall,
  Came there for cure, and this by that I prove,
  Love's fire heats water, water cools not love.

ILLUSTRATION OF THE SONNETS.

The original edition of this collection of poems bore the following title: "Shake-speare's Sonnets. Never before imprinted. At London, by G. Eld, for T. T., and are to be sold by John Wright, dwelling at Christ Church-gate. 1609." The volume is a small quarto. In addition to the Sonnets, it contains, at the end, "A Lover's Complaint. By William Shake-speare." In this collection the Sonnets are numbered from I. to CLIV., and they follow in their numerical order, as in the text we have presented to our readers. But, although this arrangement of the Sonnets is now the only one adopted in editions of Shakspeare's Poems, another occasionally prevailed up to the time of the publication of Steevens's fac-simile reprint of the Sonnets in 1766. An interval of thirty-one years elapsed between the publication of the volume by T. T. (Thomas Thorpe) in 1609, and the demand for a reprint of these remarkable Poems. In 1640 appeared "Poems, written by Wil. Shake-speare, Gent. Printed at London by Tho. Cotes, and are to be sold by John Benson." This volume, in duodecimo, contains the Sonnets, but in a totally different order, the original arrangement not only being departed from, but the lyrical poems of The Passionate Pilgrim scattered here and there, and sometimes a single Sonnet, sometimes two or three, and more rarely four or five, distinguished by some quaint title. No title includes more than five. In the editions of the Poems which appeared during a century afterwards, the original order of the Sonnets was adopted in some — that of the edition of 1640 in others. Lintot's, in 1709, for example, adheres to the original; Curll's, in 1710, follows the second edition. Cotes, the printer of the second edition, was also the printer of the second edition of the plays. That the principle of arrangement adopted in this edition was altogether arbitrary, and proceeded upon a false conception of many of these poems, we can have no hesitation in believing; but it is remarkable that within twenty-four years of Shakspeare's death an opinion should have existed that the original arrangement was also arbitrary, and that the Sonnets were essentially that collection of *fragments* which Meres described in 1598, when he wrote, "As the soul of Euphorbus was thought to live in Pythagoras, so the sweet witty soul of Ovid lives in mellifluous and honey-tongued Shakspeare: witness his Venus and Adonis, his Lucrece, his sugared Sonnets *among his private friends*." Upon the question of the *continuity* of the Sonnets depend many important considerations with reference to the life and personal character of the poet; and it is necessary, therefore, in this place, to examine that question with proportionate care.

The Sonnets of Shakspeare are distinguished from the general character of that class of poems by the continuity manifestly existing in many successive stanzas, which form, as it were, a group of flowers of the same hue and fragrance. Mr. Hallam has justly explained this peculiarity: —

"No one ever entered more fully than Shakspeare into the character of this species of poetry, which admits of no expletive imagery, no merely ornamental line. But, though each Sonnet has generally its proper unity, the sense — I do not mean the grammatical construction — will sometimes be found to spread from one to another, independently of that repetition of the leading idea, like variations of an air, which a series of them frequently exhibits, and on account of which they have latterly been reckoned by some rather an integral poem than a collection of Sonnets. But this is not uncommon among the Italians, and belongs, in fact, to those of Petrarch himself."

But, although a series may frequently exhibit a "repetition of the leading idea, like variations of an air," it by no means follows that they are to be therefore considered "rather an integral poem than a collection of Sonnets." In the edition of 1640 the "variations" were arbitrarily separated, in many cases, from the "air;" but, on the other hand, it is scarcely conceivable that in the earlier edition of 1609 these verses were intended to be presented as "an integral poem." Before we examine this matter, let us inquire into some of the circumstances connected with the original publication.

The first seventeen Sonnets contain a "leading idea" under every form of "variation." They are an exhortation to a friend, a male friend, to marry. Who this friend was has been the subject of infinite discussion. Chalmers maintains that it was Queen Elizabeth, and that there was no impropriety in Shakspeare addressing the queen by the masculine pronoun, because a queen is a prince; as we still say in the Liturgy, "our queen and *governor*." The reasoning of Chalmers on this subject, which may be found in his "Supplementary Apology," is one of the most amusing pieces of learned and ingenious nonsense that ever met our view. We believe that we must very summarily dismiss Queen Elizabeth. But Chalmers, with more reason, threw over the idea that the dedication of the bookseller to the edition of 1609 implied the person to whom the Sonnets were addressed. T. T., who dedicates, is, as we have mentioned, Thomas Thorpe, the publisher. W. H., to whom the dedication is addressed, was, according to the earlier critics, an humble person. He was either William Harte, the poet's nephew, or William Hews, some unknown individual; but Drake said, and said truly, that the person addressed in some of the Sonnets themselves was one of rank; and he maintained that it was Lord Southampton. "W. H.," he said, ought to have been H. W.—Henry Wriothesly. But Mr. Boaden and Mr. Brown have recently affirmed that "W. H." is William Herbert, Earl of Pembroke, who, in his youth and his rank, exactly corresponded with the person addressed by the poet. The words "begetter of these Sonnets," in the dedication, must mean, it is maintained, the person who was the immediate cause of their being written—to whom they were addressed. But *he* was "the *only* begetter of these Sonnets." The latter portion of the Sonnets are unquestionably addressed to a female, which at once disposes of the assertion that he was the *only* begetter, assuming the "begetter" to be used in the sense of *inspirer*. Chalmers disposes of this meaning of the word very cleverly: "W. H. was the bringer forth of the Sonnets. *Beget* is derived by Skinner from the Anglo-Saxon *begettan*, obtinere. Johnson adopts this derivation and sense; so that *begetter*, in the quaint language of Thorpe, the bookseller, Pistol, the ancient, and such affected persons, signified the *obtainer;* as to *get* and *getter*, in the present day, mean *obtain* and *obtainer*, or to procure and the procurer." But then, on the other hand, it is held, that when the bookseller wishes Mr. W. H. "that eternity promised by our ever-living poet," he means promised *him*. This inference, we must think, is somewhat strained. Be this as it may, the material question to examine is this: Are the greater portion of the Sonnets, putting aside those which manifestly apply to a female, or females, addressed to *one* male friend? Or are these the "sugared Sonnets" scattered among *many* "private friends"? When Meres printed his "Palladis Tamia," in 1598, there can be no doubt that Shakspeare's Sonnets, then existing only in manuscript, had obtained a reputation in the literary and courtly circles of that time. Probably the notoriety which Meres had given to the "sugared Sonnets" excited a publisher, in 1599, to produce something which should gratify the general curiosity. In that year appeared a collection of poems bearing the name of Shakspeare, and published by W. Jaggard, entitled "The Passionate Pilgrim." This little collection contains two Sonnets which are also given in the larger collection of 1609. They are those numbered CXXXVIII. and CXLIV. in that collection. In the modern reprints of The Passionate Pilgrim it is usual to omit these two Sonnets without explanation, because they have been previously given in the larger collection of Sonnets. But it is essential to bear in mind the fact, that in 1599 two of the Sonnets of the hundred and fifty-four published in 1609 were printed; and that one of them especially, that numbered CXLIV., has been held to form an important part of the supposed "integral poem." We may, therefore, conclude that the other Sonnets which appear to relate to the same persons as are referred to in the 144th Sonnet were also in existence. Further, the publication of these Sonnets in 1599 tends to remove the impression that might be derived from the tone of some of those in the larger collection of 1609 — that they were written when Shakspeare had passed the middle period of life. For example, in the 73d Sonnet the poet refers to the autumn of his years, the twilight of his day, the ashes of his youth. In the 138th, printed in 1599, he describes himself as "past the best" — as "old." He was then thirty-five. Dante was exactly this age when he described himself in "the midway of this our mortal life." In these remarkable particulars, therefore, — the mention of two persons, real or fictitious, who occupy an important position in the larger collection, and in the notice of the poet's age, — the two Sonnets of The Passionate Pilgrim are strictly connected with those published in 1609, of which they also form a part; and they lead to the conclusion that they were obtained for publication out of the scattered leaves floating about amongst "private friends." The publication of The Passionate Pilgrim was unquestionably unauthorized and piratical. The publisher got all he could which existed in manuscript; and he took two poems out of Love's Labour 's Lost, which was printed only the year before. In 1609, we have no hesitation in believing that the same process was repeated; that without the consent of the writer the hundred and fifty-four Sonnets — some forming a continuous poem, or poems; others isolated, in the subjects to which they relate, and the persons to whom they were addressed — were collected together without any key to their arrangement, and given to the public. Believing as we do that "W. H.," be he who he may, who put these poems in the hands of "T. T.," the publisher, arranged them in the most arbitrary manner, (of which there are many proofs,) we believe that the assumption of continuity, however ingeniously it may be maintained, is altogether fallacious. Where is the difficulty of imagining, with regard to poems of which each separate poem, sonnet, or stanza is either a "leading idea," or its "variation," that, picked up, as we think they were, from many quarters, the supposed connection must be in many respects fanciful, in some a result of chance, mixing what the poet wrote in his own person, either in moments of elation or depression, with other apparently continuous stanzas that painted an imaginary character, indulging in all the warmth of an exaggerated friendship, in the complaints of an abused confidence, in the pictures of an unhallowed and unhappy love; sometimes speaking with the real earnestness of true friendship and a modest estimation of his own merits; sometimes employing the language of an extravagant eulogy, and a more extravagant estimation of the powers of the man who was writing that eulogy? Suppose, for example, that in the leisure hours, we will say, of William Herbert, Earl of Pembroke, and William Shakspeare, the poet should have undertaken to address to the youth an argument why he should marry. Without believing the earl to be the W. H. of the Dedication, we know that he was a friend of Shakspeare. There is nothing in the first seventeen Sonnets which might not have been written in the artificial tone of the Italian poetry, in the working out of this scheme. Suppose, again, that in other Sonnets the poet, in the same artificial spirit, complains that the friend has robbed him of his mistress, and avows that he forgives the falsehood. There is nothing in all this which might not have been written essentially as a work of fiction, received as a work of fiction, handed about amongst "private friends" without the slightest apprehension that it would be regarded as an exposition of the private relations of two persons separated in rank as they probably were in their habitual intimacies — of very different ages, — the one an avowedly profligate boy, the other a matured man. But this supposition does not exclude the idea that the poet had also, at various times, composed, in the same measure, other poems, truly expressing his personal feelings, — with nothing inflated in their tone, perfectly simple and natural, offering praise, expressing love to his actual friends, (in the language of the time, "lovers,") showing regret in separation, dreading unkindness, hopeful of continued affection. These are also circulated amongst "private friends." Some "W. H." collects them together, ten, or twelve, or fifteen years after they have been written; and a publisher, of course, is found to give to the world any productions of a man so eminent as Shakspeare. But who arranged them? Certainly not the poet himself; for those who believe in their continuity must admit that there are portions which it is impossible to regard as continuous. In the same volume with these Sonnets was published a most exquisite narrative poem, A Lover's Complaint. The form of it entirely prevents any attempt to consider it autobiographical. The Sonnets, on the contrary, are personal in their form; but it is not therefore to be assumed that they are *all* personal in their relation to the author. It is impossible to be assumed that they could have been printed with the consent of the author as they now stand. If he had meant in all of them to express his actual feelings and position, the very slightest labor on his part — a few words of introduction, either in prose or verse — would have taken those parts which he would have naturally desired to appear like fiction, and which to us even now look like fiction, out of the possible range of reality. The same slight labor would, on the other hand, have classed amongst the real, apart from the artificial, those Sonnets which he would have desired to stand apart, and appear to us to stand apart, as the result of real moods of the poet's own mind.

It is our intention, without at all presuming to think that we have discovered any real order in which these extraordinary productions may be arranged, to offer them to the reader upon a principle of classification, which, on the one hand, does not attempt to reject the idea that a continuous poem, or rather several continuous poems, may be traced throughout the series, nor adopt the belief that the whole can be broken up into fragments; but which, on the other hand, does no violence to the meaning of the author by a pertinacious adherence to a principle of continuity, sometimes obvious enough, but at other times maintained by links as fragile as the harness of Queen Mab's chariot: —

"Her traces of the smallest spider's web,
Her collars of the moonshine's watery beams."

The reader will have the text of the first edition before him; and he will be enabled at every step to judge whether the original arrangement, to which we must constantly refer, was a systematic or an arbitrary one.

I.

The earliest productions of a youthful poet are commonly Love-Sonnets, or Elegies, as they were termed in Shakspeare's time. The next *age* to that of the schoolboy is that of

"the lover,
Sighing like furnace, with a woful ballad
Made to his mistress' eyebrow."

We commence our series with three Sonnets which certainly bear the marks of juvenility, when compared with others in this collection, as distinctly impressed upon them as the character of the poet's mind at different periods of his life is impressed upon Love's Labor 's Lost and Macbeth: —

Whoever hath her wish, thou hast thy will,
And will to boot, and will in overplus;
More than enough am I that vex thee still,
To thy sweet will making addition thus.
Wilt thou, whose will is large and spacious,
Not once vouchsafe to hide my will in thine?
Shall will in others seem right gracious,
And in thy will no fair acceptance shine?
The sea, all water, yet receives rain still,
And in abundance addeth to his store;
So thou, being rich in will, add to thy will
One will of mine, to make thy large will more.
Let no unkind, no fair beseechers kill;
Think all but one, and me in that one *Will*.

135.

If thy soul check thee that I come so near,
Swear to thy blind soul that I was thy *Will*,
And will, thy soul knows, is admitted there;
Thus far for love, my love-suit, sweet, fulfil.
Will will fulfil the treasure of thy love,
Ay, fill it full with wills, and my will one,
In things of great receipt with ease we prove;
Among a number one is reckoned none.
Then in the number let me pass untold,
Though in my stores' account I one must be;
For nothing hold me, so it please thee hold
That nothing me, a something sweet to thee:
  Make but my name thy love, and love that still,
  And then thou lov'st me — for my name is *Will*.

136.

Lo, as a careful housewife runs to catch
One of her feathered creatures broke away,
Sets down her babe, and makes all swift despatch
In púrsuit of the thing she would have stay;
Whilst her neglected child holds her in chase,
Cries to catch her whose busy care is bent
To follow that which flies before her face,
Not prizing her poor infant's discontent;
So runn'st thou after that which flies from thee,
Whilst I thy babe chase thee afar behind;
But if thou catch thy hope, turn back to me,
And play the mother's part, kiss me, be kind:
  So will I pray that thou mayst have thy *Will*,
  If thou turn back, and my loud crying still.

143.

The figures which we subjoin to each Sonnet show the place which it occupies in the collection of 1609. If the reader will turn to our reprint of that text, he will see where these Sonnets, through each of which the same play upon the poet's name is kept up with a boyish vivacity, are found. The two first follow one of those from which Mr. Brown derives the title of what he calls

"The Sixth Poem," being "To his Mistress on her Infidelity."* Mr. Brown, however, qualifies the dissimilarity of tone by the folling admission: "All the stanzas in the preceding poems (to Stanza 126) are retained in their original order; the printers, without disturbing the links, having done no worse than the joining together of five chains into one. But I suspect the same attention has not been paid to this address to his mistress. Indeed, I further suspect that some stanzas, irrelevant to the subject, have been introduced into the body of it." The stanzas to which Mr. Brown objects are the 135th and 136th, just given. But let us proceed. The poet now sings the praise of those eyes which so took his brother-poet, Phineas Fletcher:—

"But most I wonder how that *jetty* ray,
Which those two *blackest suns* do fair display,
Should shine so bright, and night should make so sweet a day."

We know not the color of Anne Hathaway's eyes; but how can we affirm that the following three Sonnets were not addressed to her?—

In the old age black was not counted fair,
Or, if it were, it bore not beauty's name;
But now is black beauty's successive heir,
And beauty slandered with a bastard shame:
For since each hand hath put on nature's power,
Fairing the foul with art's false borrowed face,
Sweet beauty hath no name, no holy hour,
But is profaned, if not lives in disgrace.
Therefore my mistress' eyes are raven black,
Her eyes so suited; and they mourners seem
At such, who, not born fair, no beauty lack,
Slandering creation with a false esteem:
Yet so they mourn, becoming of their woe,
That every tongue says beauty should look so.

127.

Thou art as tyrannous, so as thou art,
As those whose beauties proudly make them cruel:

* Shakspeare's Autobiographical Poems, p. 96.

For well thou know'st to my dear doting heart
Thou art the fairest and most precious jewel.
Yet, in good faith, some say that thee behold,
Thy face hath not the power to make love groan:
To say they err, I dare not be so bold,
Although I swear it to myself alone.
And, to be sure that is not false I swear,
A thousand groans, but thinking on thy face,
One on another's neck, do witness bear
Thy black is fairest in my judgment's place.
In nothing art thou black, save in thy deeds,
And thence this slander, as I think, proceeds.

131.

Thine eyes I love, and they, as pitying me,
Knowing thy heart, torment me with disdain;
Have put on black, and loving mourners be,
Looking with pretty ruth upon my pain.
And truly not the morning sun of heaven
Better becomes the gray cheeks of the east,
Nor that full star that ushers in the even,
Doth half that glory to the sober west,
As those two mourning eyes become thy face:
O, let it then as well beseem thy heart
To mourn for me, since mourning doth thee grace,
And suit thy pity like in every part.
Then will I swear beauty herself is black,
And all they foul that thy complexion lack.

132.

But the two last immediately precede the Sonnet beginning

"Beshrew that heart that makes my heart to groan
For that deep wound it gives my friend and me;" —

and so the lady of the "mourning eyes" is associated with a tale of treachery and sin. The line of the 131st Sonnet —

"In nothing art thou black, *save in thy deeds* —

may be held to imply something atrocious. The two first lines, however, show of what the poet-lover complains: —

"Thou art as *tyrannous*, so as thou art,
As those whose beauties proudly make them cruel."

The 128th Sonnet has never been exceeded in airy elegance, even by the professed writers of amatory poems: —

How oft, when thou, my music, music play'st
Upon that blessed wood whose motion sounds
With thy sweet fingers, when thou gently sway'st
The wiry concord that mine ear confounds,
Do I envy' those jacks, that nimble leap
To kiss the tender inward of thy hand,
Whilst my poor lips, which should that harvest reap,
At the wood's boldness by thee blushing stand!
To be so tickled, they would change their state
And situation with those dancing chips,
O'er whom thy fingers walk with gentle gait,
Making dead wood more blessed than living lips.
Since saucy jacks so happy are in this,
Give them thy fingers, me thy lips to kiss.

128.

The 130th, too, is one of the prettiest *vers de société* that a Suckling, or a Moore, could have produced: —

My mistress' eyes are nothing like the sun;
Coral is far more red than her lips' red:
If snow be white, why then her breasts are dun;
If hairs be wires, black wires grow on her head.
I have seen roses damasked, red and white,
But no such roses see I in her cheeks;
And in some perfumes is there more delight
Than in the breath that from my mistress reeks.
I love to hear her speak, — yet well I know
That music hath a far more pleasing sound;
I grant I never saw a goddess go, —
My mistress, when she walks, treads on the ground;
And yet, by Heaven, I think my love as rare
As any she belied with false compare.

130.

And of what character is the 129th Sonnet, which separates these two playful compositions? It is a solemn denunciation against unlicensed gratifications — a warning

"To shun the heaven that leads men to this hell."

If we are to bring those Sonnets in apposition where the "leading idea" is repeated, we shall have to go far back to find one that will accord with the 130th: —

So is it not with me as with that muse,
Stirred by a painted beauty to his verse;
Who heaven itself for ornament doth use,
And every fair with his fair doth rehearse;
Making a couplement of proud compare,
With sun and moon, with earth and sea's rich gems,
With April's first-born flowers, and all things rare
That heaven's air in his huge rondure hems.
O, let me, true in love, but truly write,
And then believe me, my love is as fair
As any mother's child, though not so bright
As those gold candles fixed in heaven's air:
Let them say more that like of hearsay well;
I will not praise, that purpose not to sell.
21.

This is the 21st Sonnet; and it has as much the character of a love-sonnet as any we have just given.

The *tyranny* of which the poet complains in the 131st Sonnet forms the subject of the three following: —

O, call not me to justify the wrong
That thy unkindness lays upon my heart;
Wound me not with thine eye, but with thy tongue;
Use power with power, and slay me not by art.
Tell me thou lov'st elsewhere; but in my sight,
Dear heart, forbear to glance thine eye aside.
What needst thou wound with cunning, when thy might
Is more than my o'erpressed defence can 'bide?
Let me excuse thee: ah! my love well knows
Her pretty looks have been my enemies;

And therefore from my face she turns my foes,
That they elsewhere might dart their injuries:
Yet do not so; but since I am near slain,
Kill me outright with looks, and rid my pain.

139.

Be wise as thou art cruel; do not press
My tongue-tied patience with too much disdain;
Lest sorrow lend me words, and words express
The manner of my pity-wanting pain.
If I might teach thee wit, better it were,
Though not to love, yet, love, to tell me so;
(As testy sick men, when their deaths be near,
No news but health from their physicians know;)
For, if I should despair, I should grow mad,
And in my madness might speak ill of thee:
Now this ill-wresting world is grown so bad,
Mad slanderers by mad ears believéd be.
That I may not be so, nor thou belied,
Bear thine eyes straight, though thy proud heart
go wide.

140.

Canst thou, O cruel! say I love thee not,
When I, against myself, with thee partake?
Do I not think on thee, when I forgot
Am of myself, all tyrant, for thy sake?
Who hateth thee that I do call my friend?
On whom frown'st thou that I do fawn upon?
Nay, if thou low'rst on me, do I not spend
Revenge upon myself with present moan?
What merit do I in myself respect,
That is so proud thy service to despise,
When all my best doth worship thy defect,
Commanded by the motion of thine eyes?
But, love, hate on, for now I know thy mind;
Those that can see thou lov'st, and I am blind.

149.

And yet the tyranny is meekly borne by the lover: —

Being your slave, what should I do but tend
Upon the hours and times of your desire?
I have no precious time at all to spend,
Nor services to do, till you require.
Nor dare I chide the world-without-end hour,
Whilst I, my sovereign, watch the clock for you,
Nor think the bitterness of absence sour,
When you have bid your servant once adieu;
Nor dare I question with my jealous thought
Where you may be, or your affairs suppose,
But, like a sad slave, stay and think of nought,
Save, where you are how happy you make those:
  So true a foot is love, that in your will
  (Though you do any thing) he thinks no ill.

57.

That God forbid, that made me first your slave,
I should in thought control your times of pleasure,
Or at your hand the account of hours to crave,
Being your vassal, bound to stay your leisure!
O, let me suffer (being at your beck)
The imprisoned absence of your liberty,
And patience, tame to sufferance, bide each check
Without accusing you of injury.
Be where you list; your charter is so strong,
That you yourself may privilege your time:
Do what you will, to you it doth belong
Yourself to pardon of self-doing crime.
  I am to wait, though waiting so be hell;
  Not blame your pleasure, be it ill or well.

58.

The Sonnets last given are the 57th and 58th. These are especially noticed by Mr. Brown as evidence that the person to whom he considers the Sonnets are addressed — W. H. — was "a man of rank." He adds, "Reproach is conveyed more forcibly, and, at the same time, with more kindness, in their strained humility, than it would have been by direct expostulation." The reproach, according to Mr. Brown, is for the "coldness" which the noble youth had evinced towards his friend. The "coldness" is implied in these stanzas, and in that which precedes them : —

Sweet love, renew thy force ; be it not said
Thy edge should blunter be than appetite,
Which but to-day by feeding is allayed,
To-morrow sharpened in his former might :
So, love, be thou ; although to-day thou fill
Thy hungry eyes, even till they wink with fulness,
To-morrow see again and do not kill
The spirit of love with a perpetual dulness.
Let this sad interim like the ocean be
Which parts the shore, where two contracted-new
Come daily to the banks, that, when they see
Return of love, more blessed may be the view ;
  Or call it winter, which, being full of care,
  Makes summer's welcome thrice more wished, more rare. 56.

We believe, on the contrary, that the three Sonnets are addressed to a female. It appears to us that a line in the 57th is decisive upon this :

"When you have bid your *servant* once adieu."

The lady was *the mistress*, the lover *the servant*, in the gallantry of Shakspeare's time. In Beaumont and Fletcher's "Scornful Lady" we have, "Was I not once your mistress, and you *my servant?*" The three stanzas, 56, 57, 58, are completely isolated from what precedes and what follows them ; and therefore we have no hesitation in transposing them to this class.

We are about to give a Sonnet which Mr. Brown thinks "should be expunged from the poem." We should regret to lose so pretty and playful a love-verse : —

Those lips that Love's own hand did make
Breathed forth the sound that said *I hate*,
To me that languished for her sake :
But when she saw my woful state,

Straight in her heart did mercy come,
Chiding that tongue, that ever sweet
Was used in giving gentle doom;
And taught it thus anew to greet:
I hate she altered with an end,
That followed it as gentle day
Doth follow night, who like a fiend
From heaven to hell is flown away.
I hate from hate away she threw,
And saved my life, saying — *not you.*

145.

It is, however, strangely opposed to the theory of continuity, for it occurs between the Sonnet which first appeared in The Passionate Pilgrim, —

"Two loves I have, of comfort and despair," —

and the magnificent lines beginning

"Poor soul, the centre of my sinful earth."

This sublime Sonnet Mr. Brown would also expunge. This is a hard sentence against it for being out of place. We shall endeavor to remove it to fitter company.

We have now very much reduced the number of stanzas which Mr Brown assigns to the Sixth Poem, entitled by him, "To his Mistress, on her Infidelity." There are only twenty-six stanzas in this division of Mr. Brown's Six Poems; for he rejects the Sonnets numbered 153 and 154, as belonging "to nothing but themselves." They belong, indeed, to the same class of poems as constitute the bulk of those printed in The Passionate Pilgrim. But, being printed in the collection of 1609, they offer very satisfactory evidence that "the begetter" of the Sonnets had no distinct principle of connection to work upon. He has printed, as already mentioned, two Sonnets which had previously appeared in The Passionate Pilgrim. But if they were taken out from the larger collection, no one could say that its continuity would be deranged. There are other Sonnets, properly so called, in The Passionate Pilgrim, which, if they were to be *added* to the larger collection, there would be no difficulty in inserting them, so as to be as continuous as the two which are common to both works. We have no objection to proceed with our analytical classification without including the two Sonnets on "the little love-god;" because, if we were attempting here to present all Shakspeare's love-verses which exist in print, not being in the plays, we should have to insert six other poems which are in The Passionate Pilgrim.

What, then, have we left of the Sonnets from the 127th to the 152d which may warrant those twenty-six stanzas being regarded (with two exceptions pointed out by Mr. Brown himself) as a continuous poem, to be entitled, "To his Mistress, on her Infidelity"? We have, indeed, a "leading idea," and a very distinct one, of some delusion, once cherished by the poet, against the power of which he struggles, and which his better reason finally rejects. But the complaint is not wholly that of the *infidelity* of a mistress; it is that the love which he bears towards her is incompatible with his sense of duty, and with that tranquility of mind which belongs to a pure and lawful affection. This "leading idea" is expressed in *ten* stanzas, which we print in the order in which they occur. They are more or less strong and direct in their allusions; but, whether the situation which the poet describes be real or imaginary — whether he speak from the depth of his own feelings, or with his wonderful dramatic power — there are no verses in our language more expressive of the torments of a passion based upon unlawfulness. Throes such as these were somewhat uncommon amongst the gallants of the days of Elizabeth: —

The expense of spirit in a waste of shame
Is lust in action; and till action, lust
Is perjured, murderous, bloody, full of blame,
Savage, extreme, rude, cruel, not to trust;
Enjoyed no sooner, but despiséd straight;
Past reason hunted; and no sooner had,
Past reason hated; as a swallowed bait,
On purpose laid to make the taker mad:
Mad in pursuit, and in possession so;
Had, having, and in quest to have, extreme;
A bliss in proof, — and proved, a very woe;
Before, a joy proposed; behind, a dream;
All this the world well knows; yet none knows well
To shun the heaven that leads men to this hell.

129.

Thou blind fool, Love, what dost thou to mine eyes,
That they behold, and see not what they see?
They know what beauty is, see where it lies,
Yet what the best is, take the worst to be.
If eyes, corrupt by over-partial looks,
Be anchored in the bay where all men ride,
Why of eyes, falsehood hast thou forgéd hooks,
Whereto the judgment of my heart is tied?
Why should my heart think that a several plot
Which my heart knows that wide world's common
place?
Or mine eyes, seeing this, say this is not,
To put fair truth upon so foul a face?
  In things right true my heart and eyes have erred,
  And to this false plague are they now transferred.

137.

When my love swears that she is made of truth,
I do believe her, though I know she lies;
That she might think me some untutored youth,
Unlearned in the world's false subtleties.
Thus vainly thinking that she thinks me young,
Although she knows my days are past the best,
Simply I credit her false-speaking tongue;
On both sides thus is simple truth suppressed.
But wherefore says she not she is unjust?
And wherefore say not I that I am old?
O, love's best habit is in seeming trust,
And age in love loves not to have age told:
  Therefore I lie with her, and she with me,
  And in our faults by lies we flattered be.

138.

In faith I do not love thee with mine eyes,
For they in thee a thousand errors note;
But 'tis my heart that loves what they despise,
Who in despite of view is pleased to dote.
Nor are mine ears with thy tongues tune delighted;
Nor tender feeling, to base touches prone,

Nor taste nor smell, desire to be invited
To any sensual feast with thee alone :
But my five wits, nor my five senses can
Dissuade one foolish heart from serving thee,
Who leaves unswayed the likeness of a man,
Thy proud heart's slave and vassal wretch to be:
Only my plague thus far I count my gain,
That she that makes me sin awards me pain.

141.

Love is my sin, and my dear virtue hate,
Hate of my sin, grounded on sinful loving :
O, but with mine compare thou thine own state,
And thou shalt find it merits not reproving ;
Or if it do, not from these lips of thine,
That have profaned their scarlet ornaments,
And sealed false bonds of love as oft as mine ;
Robbed others' beds' revenues of their rents.
Be it lawful I love thee, as thou lov'st those
Whom thine eyes woo as mine impórtune thee :
Root pity in thy heart, that when it grows,
Thy pity may deserve to pitied be.
If thou dost seek to have what thou dost hide,
By self-example mayst thou be denied !

142.

My love is as a fever, longing still
For that which longer nurseth the disease ;
Feeding on that which doth preserve the ill,
The uncertain sickly appetite to please.
My reason, the physician to my love,
Angry that his prescriptions are not kept,
Hath left me, and I desperate now approve,
Desire is death, which physic did except.
Past cure I am, now reason is past care,
And frantic mad with evermore unrest ;
My thoughts and my discourse as madmen's are,
At random from the truth vainly expressed ;

For I have sworn thee fair, and thought thee bright,
Who art as black as hell, as dark as night.

147.

O me! what eyes hath love put in my head,
Which have no correspondence with true sight?
Or, if they have, where is my judgment fled,
That censures falsely what they see aright?
If that be fair whereon my false eyes dote,
What means the world to say it is not so?
If it be not, then love doth well denote
Love's eye is not so true as all men's: no,
How can it? O, how can Love's eye be true,
That is so vexed with watching and with tears?
No marvel then though I mistake my view;
The sun itself sees not till heaven clears.
O, cunning Love! with tears thou keepst me blind,
Lest eyes well-seeing thy foul faults should find.

148.

O, from what power hast thou this powerful might,
With insufficiency my heart to sway?
To make me give the lie to my true sight,
And swear that brightness doth not grace the day?
Whence hast thou this becoming of things ill,
That in the very refuse of thy deeds
There is such strength and warrantise of skill,
That in my mind thy worst all best exceeds?
Who taught thee how to make me love thee more,
The more I hear and see just cause of hate?
O, though I love what others do abhor,
With others thou shouldst not abhor my state;
If thy unworthiness raised love in me,
More worthy I to be beloved of thee.

150.

Love is too young to know what conscience is;
Yet who knows not conscience is born of love?

Then, gentle cheater, urge not my amiss,
Lest guilty of my faults thy sweet self prove.
For thou betraying me, I do betray
My nobler part to my gross body's treason;
My soul doth tell my body that he may
Triumph in love; flesh stays no further reason,
But, rising at thy name, doth point out thee
As his triumphant prize. Proud of this pride,
He is contented thy poor drudge to be,
To stand in thy affairs, fall by thy side.
No want of conscience hold it that I call
Her love, for whose dear love I rise and fall.

151.

In loving thee thou know'st I am forsworn,
But thou art twice forsworn, to me love swearing;
In act thy bed-vow broke, and new faith torn,
In vowing new hate after new love bearing.
But why of two oath's breach do I accuse thee,
When I break twenty? I am perjured most;
For all my vows are oaths but to misuse thee,
And all my honest faith in thee is lost:
For I have sworn deep oaths of thy deep kindness,
Oaths of thy love, thy truth, thy constancy;
And, to enlighten thee, gave eyes to blindness,
Or made them swear against the thing they see;
For I have sworn thee fair: more perjured I,
To swear against the truth, so foul a lie!

152.

We have only three Sonnets left, out of the twenty-six stanzas, in which we may find any allusion to the "infidelity" of the poet's 'mistress." They are these: —

Beshrew that heart that makes my heart to groan
For that deep wound it gives my friend and me!
Is 't not enough to torture me alone,
But slave to slavery my sweet'st friend must be?

Me from myself thy cruel eye hath taken,
And my next self thou harder hast engrossed;
Of him, myself, and thee, I am forsaken;
A torment thrice threefold thus to be crossed.
Prison my heart in thy steel bosom's ward,
But then my friend's heart let my poor heart bail;
Who e'er keeps me, let my heart be his guard;
Thou can'st not then use rigor in my jail:
And yet thou wilt; for I, being pent in thee,
Perforce am thine, and all that is in me.

133.

So now I have confessed that he is thine,
And I myself am mortgaged to thy will;
Myself I'll forfeit, so that other mine
Thou wilt restore, to be my comfort still:
But thou wilt not, nor he will not be free,
For thou art covetous, and he is kind;
He learned but, surety-like, to write for me,
Under that bond that him as fast doth bind.
The statute of thy beauty thou wilt take,
Thou usurer, that putt'st forth all to use,
And sue a friend, came debtor for my sake;
So him I lose through my unkind abuse.
Him have I lost; thou hast both him and me;
He pays the whole, and yet am I not free.

134.

Two loves I have of comfort and despair,
Which like two spirits do suggest me still;
The better angel is a man right fair,
The worser spirit a woman, colored ill.
To win me soon to hell, my female evil
Tempteth my better angel from my side,
And would corrupt my saint to be a devil,
Wooing his purity with her foul pride.
And whether that my angel be turned fiend,
Suspect I may, but not directly tell;

But being both from me, both to each friend,
I guess one angel in another's hell.
  Yet this shall I ne'er know, but live in doubt,
  Till my bad angel fire my good one out.

144.

The 144th, we must again point out, was printed in The Passionate Pilgrim in 1599. This Sonnet, then, referring, as it appears to do, to private circumstances of considerable delicacy, was public enough to fall into the hands of a piratical bookseller, ten years before the larger collection in which it a second time appears was printed. But in that larger collection the poet accuses the friend as well as the mistress. We have no means of knowing whether the six Sonnets, in which this accusation appears, existed in 1599, or what was the extent of their publicity; but by their publication in 1609 we are enabled to compare "the better angel" with "the worser spirit": —

Full many a glorious morning have I seen
Flatter the mountain-tops with sovereign eye,
Kissing with golden face the meadows green,
Gilding pale streams with heavenly alchymy;
Anon permit the basest clouds to ride
With ugly rack on his celestial face,
And from the forlorn world his visage hide,
Stealing unseen to west with this disgrace:
Even so my sun one early morn did shine,
With all triumphant splendor on my brow;
But out! alack! he was but one hour mine,
The region cloud hath masked him from me now.
  Yet him for this my love no whit disdaineth;
  Suns of the world may stain, when heaven's sun
      staineth.

33.

Why didst thou promise such a beauteous day,
And make me travel forth without my cloak,
To let base clouds o'ertake me in my way,
Hiding thy bravery in their rotten smoke?
'Tis not enough that through the cloud thou break,
To dry the rain on my storm-beaten face,

For no man well of such a salve can speak,
That heals the wound, and cures not the disgrace:
Nor can thy shame give physic to my grief;
Though thou repent, yet I have still the loss:
The offender's sorrow lends but weak relief
To him that bears the strong offence's cross.
  Ah! but those tears are pearl which thy love
      sheds,
  And they are rich, and ransom all ill deeds.

34.

No more be grieved at that which thou hast done:
Roses have thorns, and silver fountains mud;
Clouds and eclipses stain both moon and sun,
And loathsome canker lives in sweetest bud.
All men make faults, and even I in this,
Authórizing thy trespass with compare,
Myself corrupting, salving thy amiss,
Excusing thy sins more than thy sins are:
For to thy sensual fault I bring in sense,
(Thy adverse party is thy advocate,)
And 'gainst myself a lawful plea commence:
Such civil war is in my love and hate
  That I an accessory needs must be
  To that sweet thief which sourly robs from me.

35.

Take all my loves, my love, yea, take them all;
What hast thou then more than thou hadst before?
No love, my love, that thou mayst true love call;
All mine was thine before thou hadst this more.
Then if for my love thou my love receivest,
I cannot blame thee, for my love thou usest;
But yet be blamed, if thou thyself deceivest
By wilful taste of what thyself refusest.
I do forgive thy robbery, gentle thief,
Although thou steal thee all my poverty;
And yet, love knows, it is a greater grief
To bear love's wrong than hate's known injury.

Lascivious grace, in whom all ill well shows,
Kill me with spites; yet we must not be foes.

40.

Those pretty wrongs that liberty commits,
When I am sometime absent from thy heart,
Thy beauty and thy years full well befits,
For still temptation follows where thou art.
Gentle thou art, and therefore to be won;
Beauteous thou art, therefore to be assailed;
And when a woman woos, what woman's son
Will sourly leave her till she have prevailed?
Ah, me! but yet thou mightst my seat forbear,
And chide thy beauty and thy straying youth,
Who lead thee in their riot even there
Where thou art forced to break a twofold truth;
Hers, by thy beauty tempting her to thee;
Thine, by thy beauty being false to me.

41.

That thou hast her, it is not all my grief.
And yet it may be said I loved her dearly;
That she hath thee, is of my wailing chief,
A loss in love that touches me more nearly.
Loving offenders, thus I will excuse ye:—
Thou dost love her, because thou knew'st I love her;
And for my sake even so doth she abuse me,
Suffering my friend for my sake to approve her.
If I lose thee, my loss is my love's gain,
And, losing her, my friend hath found that loss;
Both find each other, and I lose both twain,
And both for my sake lay on me this cross:
But here 's the joy; my friend and I are one;
Sweet flattery! then she loves but me alone.

42.

It is probably to the same friend that the following mild reflections upon the general faults of his character are addressed:—

They that have power to hurt and will do none,
That do not do the thing they most do show,
Who, moving others, are themselves as stone,
Unmovéd, cold, and to temptation slow;
They rightly do inherit heaven's graces,
And husband nature's riches from expense;
They are the lords and owners of their faces,
Others but stewards of their excellence.
The summer's flower is to the summer sweet,
Though to itself it only live and die;
But if that flower with base infection meet,
The basest weed outbraves his dignity:
  For sweetest things turn sourest by their deeds;
  Lilies that fester smell far worse than weeds.

94.

How sweet and lovely dost thou make the shame,
Which, like a canker in the fragrant rose,
Doth spot the beauty of thy budding name!
O, in what sweets dost thou thy sins enclose!
That tongue that tells the story of thy days,
Making lascivious comments on thy sport,
Cannot dispraise but in a kind of praise;
Naming thy name blesses an ill report.
O, what a mansion have those vices got,
Which for their habitation chose out thee!
Where beauty's veil doth cover every blot,
And all things turn to fair that eyes can see!
  Take heed, dear heart, of this large privilege;
  The hardest knife ill used doth lose his edge.

95.

Some say, thy fault is youth, some wantonness;
Some say, thy grace is youth and gentle sport;
Both grace and faults are loved of more and less:
Thou mak'st faults graces that to thee resort.
As on the finger of a thronéd queen
The basest jewel will be well esteemed;

So are those errors that in thee are seen
To truths translated, and for true things deemed.
How many lambs might the stern wolf betray,
If like a lamb he could his looks translate!
How many gazers mightst thou lead away,
If thou wouldst use the strength of all thy state!
But do not so; I love thee in such sort,
As, thou being mine, mine is thy good report.

96.

But the poet, true to his general principle of morals, holds that forgiveness should follow upon repented transgressions: —

Like as, to make our appetites more keen,
With eager compounds we our palate urge:
As, to prevent our maladies unseen,
We sicken to shun sickness, when we purge;
Even so, being full of your ne'er-cloying sweetness,
To bitter sauces did I frame my feeling,
And, sick of welfare, found a kind of meetness
To be diseased ere that there was true needing.
Thus policy in love, to anticipate
The ills that were not, grew to faults assured,
And brought to medicine a healthful state,
Which, rank of goodness, would by ill be cured.
But thence I learn, and find the lesson true,
Drugs poison him that so fell sick of you.

118.

What potions have I drunk of Siren tears,
Distilled from limbecs foul as hell within,
Applying fears to hopes, and hopes to fears,
Still losing when I saw myself to win!
What wretched errors hath my heart committed,
Whilst it hath thought itself so blessèd never!
How have mine eyes out of their spheres been fitted,
In the distraction of this madding fever!
O, benefit of ill! now I find true
That better is by evil still made better;

And ruined love, when it is built anew,
Grows fairer than at first, more strong, far greater.
So I return rebuked to my content,
And gain by ill thrice more than I have spent.

119.

That you were once unkind, befriends me now,
And for that sorrow, which I then did feel,
Needs must I under my transgression bow,
Unless my nerves were brass or hammered steel.
For if you were by my unkindness shaken,
As I by yours, you have passed a hell of time:
And I, a tyrant, have no leisure taken
To weigh how once I suffered in your crime.
O that our night of woe might have remembered
My deepest sense, how hard true sorrow hits,
And soon to you, as you to me, then tendered
The humble salve which wounded bosoms fits!
But that your trespass now becomes a fee;
Mine ransoms yours, and yours must ransom me.

120.

II.

We have thus selected all the Sonnets, or stanzas, that appear to have reference to the subject of love, — whether those which express the light playfulness of affection, the abiding confidence, the distracting doubts, the reproaches for pride or neglect, the fierce jealousies, the complaints that another is preferred. Much of this may be real, much merely dramatic. But it appears to us that it would have been quite impossible to have maintained that these fragments relate to a particular incident of the poet's life — the indulgence of an illicit love, with which the equally illicit attachment of a youthful friend interfered — unless there had been a forced association of the whole series of Sonnets with that youthful friend to whom the first seventeen Sonnets are clearly addressed. Mr. Brown groups the Sonnets from the 27th to the 55th as the "Second Poem," which he entitles, "To his Friend — who had robbed him of his mistress — forgiving him." Now, literally, the Sonnets we have already given, the 33d, 34th, 35th, 40th, 41st, and 42d, are all that within these limits can be held to have reference to such a subject. The 27th and 28th Sonnets have not the slightest allusion to this supposed injury; and we shall presently endeavor to show that they have been wrested from their proper place. The 29th, 30th, 31st, and 32d are Sonnets of the most confiding friendship, full of the simplest and therefore the deepest pathos, and which we have no hesitation in classing amongst those which are strictly personal — those to which the lines of Wordsworth apply: —

> "Scorn not the Sonnet: Critic, you have frowned
> Mindless of its just honors. With this key
> Shakspeare unlocked his heart."

The following exquisite lines are familiar to most poetical students: —

When in disgrace with fortune and men's eyes,
I all alone beweep my outcast state,
And trouble deaf Heaven with my bootless cries,
And look upon myself, and curse my fate,
Wishing me like to one more rich in hope,
Featured like him, like him with friends possessed,
Desiring this man's art, and that man's scope,
With what I most enjoy contended least;
Yet in these thoughts myself almost despising,
Haply I think on thee, — and then my state
(Like to the lark at break of day arising
From sullen earth) sings hymns at heaven's gate;
For thy sweet love remembered, such wealth brings
That then I scorn to change my state with kings.

29.

When to the sessions of sweet silent thought
I summon up remembrance of things past,
I sigh the lack of many a thing I sought,
And with old woes new wail my dear times' waste:
Then can I drown an eye, unused to flow,
For precious friends hid in death's dateless night.

And weep afresh love's long-since cancelled woe,
And moan the expense of many a vanished sight.
Then can I grieve at grievances foregone,
And heavily from woe to woe tell o'er
The sad account of fore-bemoanéd moan,
Which I new pay as if not paid before.
  But if the while I think on thee, dear friend,
  All losses are restored, and sorrows end.

30.

Thy bosom is endearéd with all hearts,
Which I by lacking have supposéd dead;
And there reigns love and all love's loving parts,
And all those friends which I thought buriéd.
How many a holy and obsequious tear
Hath dear religious love stolen from mine eye,
As interest of the dead which now appear
But things removed, that hidden in thee lie?
Thou art the grave where buried love doth live,
Hung with the trophies of my lovers gone,
Who all their parts of me to thee did give;
That due of many now is thine alone:
  Their images I loved I view in thee,
  And thou (all they) hast all the all of me.

31.

If thou survive my well-contented day,
When that churl Death my bones with dust shall cover,
And shalt by fortune once more resurvey
These poor rude lines of thy deceaséd lover,
Compare them with the bettering of the time;
And though they be outstripped by every pen,
Reserve them for my love, not for their rhyme,
Exceeded by the height of happier men.
O then vouchsafe me but this loving thought!
Had my friend's muse grown with this growing age,
A dearer birth than this his love had brought,
To march in ranks of better equipage:

But since he died, and poets better prove,
Theirs for their style I'll read, his for his love.

32.

Immediately succeeding these are the three stanzas we have already quoted, in which the poet is held to accuse his friend of having robbed him of his mistress. In these stanzas the friend is spoken of in connection with a "sensual fault," a "trespass," &c. But in those which follow, the "bewailed guilt" belongs to the poet — the "worth and truth" to his friend. Surely these are not continuous. In the 36th, 37th, 38th, and 39th Sonnets, we have the expression of that deep humility which may be traced through many of these remarkable compositions, and of which we find the first sound in the 29th Sonnet: —

Let me confess that we two must be twain,
Although our undivided loves are one;
So shall those blots that do with me remain,
Without thy help, by me be borne alone.
In our two loves there is but one respect,
Though in our lives a separable spite,
Which, though it alter not love's sole effect,
Yet doth it steal sweet hours from love's delight.
I may not evermore acknowledge thee,
Lest my bewailéd guilt should do thee shame;
Nor thou with public kindness honor me,
Unless thou take that honor from thy name:
But do not so; I love thee in such sort,
As, thou being mine, mine is thy good report.

36.

As a decrepit father takes delight
To see his active child do deeds of youth,
So I, made lame by fortune's dearest spite,
Take all my comfort of thy worth and truth;
For whether beauty, birth, or wealth, or wit,
Or any of these all, or all, or more,
Entitled in thy parts do crownéd sit,
I make my love engrafted to this store:

So then I am not lame, poor, nor despised,
Whilst that this shadow doth such substance give,
That I in thy abundance am sufficed,
And by a part of all thy glory live.
  Look what is best, that best I wish in thee ;
  This wish I have ; then ten times happy me !

37.

How can my muse want subject to invent,
While thou dost breathe, that pour'st into my verse
Thine own sweet argument, too excellent
For every vulgar paper to rehearse ?
O, give thyself the thanks, if aught in me
Worthy perusal stand against thy sight ;
For who 's so dumb that cannot write to thee,
When thou thyself dost give invention light ?
Be thou the tenth muse, ten times more in worth
Than those old nine which rhymers invocate ;
And he that calls on thee, let him bring forth
Eternal numbers to outlive long date.
  If my slight muse do please these curious days,
  The pain be mine, but thine shall be the praise.

38.

O, how thy worth with manners may I sing,
When thou art all the better part of me ?
What can mine own praise to mine own self bring ?
And what is 't but mine own, when I praise thee ?
Even for this let us divided live,
And our dear love lose name of single one,
That by this separation I may give
That due to thee which thou deserv'st alone.
O absence, what a torment wouldst thou prove,
Were it not thy sour leisure gave sweet leave
To entertain the time with thoughts of love,
(Which time and thoughts so sweetly doth deceive,)
  And that thou teachest how to make one twain,
  By praising him here, who doth hence remain !

39.

The 40th, 41st, and 42d Sonnets return to the complaint of his friend's faithlessness. Surely, then, the Sonnets we have just quoted must be interpolated. The 43d is entirely isolated from what precedes and what follows. But in the 39th we have allusions to "separation" and "absence;" and in the 44th we return to the subject of "injurious distance." With some alterations of arrangement we can group nine Sonnets together, which form a connected epistle to an absent friend, and which convey those sentiments of real affection which can only be adequately transmitted in language and imagery, possessing, as these portions do, the charm of nature and simplicity. The tone of truth and reality is remarkably contrasted with those artificial passages which have imparted their character to the whole series in the estimation of many:—

How heavy do I journey on the way,
When what I seek — my weary travel's end —
Doth teach that ease and that repose to say,
"Thus far the miles are measured from thy friend!"
The beast that bears me, tirèd with my woe,
Plods dully on, to bear that weight in me,
As if by some instinct the wretch did know
His rider loved not speed, being made from thee:
The bloody spur cannot provoke him on
That sometimes anger thrusts into his hide;
Which heavily he answers with a groan,
More sharp to me than spurring to his side;
For that same groan doth put this in my mind,
My grief lies onward, and my joy behind.

50.

Thus can my love excuse the slow offence
Of my dull bearer, when from thee I speed:
From where thou art why should I haste me thence?
Till I return, of posting is no need.
O, what excuse will my poor beast then find,
When swift extremity can seem but slow?
Then should I spur, though mounted on the wind;
In wingèd speed no motion shall I know:
Then can no horse with my desire keep pace:
Therefore desire, of perfect love being made,

Shall neigh (no dull flesh) in his fiery race ;
But love, for love, thus shall excuse my jade ;
  Since from thee going he went wilful slow,
  Towards thee I'll run, and give him leave to
      go.
51.

So am I as the rich, whose blesséd key
Can bring him to his sweet up-lockéd treasure,
The which he will not every hour survey,
For blunting the fine point of seldom pleasure.
Therefore are feasts so solemn and so rare,
Since seldom coming, in the long year set,
Like stones of worth they thinly placéd are,
Or captain jewels in the carcanet.
So is the time that keeps you as my chest,
Or as the wardrobe which the robe doth hide,
To make some special instant special-blest,
By new unfolding his imprisoned pride.
  Blesséd are you, whose worthiness gives scope,
  Being had, to triumph, being lacked, to hope.
52.

Weary with toil, I haste me to my bed,
The dear repose for limbs with travel tired ;
But then begins a journey in my head,
To work my mind, when body's work 's expired:
For then my thoughts (from far where I abide)
Intend a zealous pilgrimage to thee,
And keep my drooping eyelids open wide,
Looking on darkness which the blind do see ;
Save that my soul's imaginary sight
Presents thy shadow to my sightless view,
Which, like a jewel hung in ghastly night,
Makes black night beauteous, and her old face
      new.
  Lo, thus, by day my limbs, by night my mind,
  For thee, and for myself, no quiet find.
27.

How can I then return in happy plight,
That am debarred the benefit of rest?
When day's oppression is not eased by night,
But day by day and night by day oppressed?
And each, though enemies to either's reign,
Do in consent shake hands to torture me,
The one by toil, the other to complain
How far I toil, still farther off from thee.
I tell the day, to please him, thou art bright,
And dost him grace when clouds do blot the heaven:
So flatter I the swart-complexioned night;
When sparkling stars twire not, thou gild'st the even.
  But day doth daily draw my sorrows longer,
  And night doth nightly make grief's length seem stronger.

28.

Is it thy will thy image should keep open
My heavy eyelids to the weary night?
Dost thou desire my slumbers should be broken,
While shadows, like to thee, do mock my sight?
Is it thy spirit that thou send'st from thee
So far from home, into my deeds to pry;
To find out shames and idle hours in me,
The scope and tenor of thy jealousy?
O no! thy love, though much, is not so great;
It is my love that keeps mine eye awake;
Mine own true love that doth my rest defeat,
To play the watchman ever for thy sake:
  For thee watch I, whilst thou dost wake elsewhere
  From me far off, with others all-to-near.

61.

When most I wink, then do mine eyes best see,
For all the day they view things unrespected:
But when I sleep, in dreams they look on thee,
And darkly bright, are bright in dark directed;
Then thou whose shadow shadows doth make bright,
How would thy shadow's form from happy show

To the clear day with thy much clearer light,
When to unseeing eyes thy shade shines so?
How would (I say) mine eyes be blessèd made
By looking on thee in the living day,
When in dead night thy fair, imperfect shade
Through heavy sleep on sightless eyes doth stay?
All days are nights to see, till I see thee,
And nights, bright days, when dreams do show thee me.

43.

If the dull substance of my flesh were thought,
Injurious distance should not stop my way;
For then, despite of space, I would be brought
From limits far remote, where thou dost stay.
No matter then, although my foot did stand
Upon the farthest earth removed from thee,
For nimble thought can jump both sea and land,
As soon as think the place where he would be.
But ah! thought kills me, that I am not thought,
To leap large lengths of miles when thou art gone,
But that, so much of earth and water wrought,
I must attend time's leisure with my moan;
Receiving nought by elements so slow
But heavy tears, badges of either's woe:—

44.

The other two, slight air and purging fire,
Are both with thee, wherever I abide;
The first my thought, the other my desire,
These present-absent with swift motion slide.
For when these quicker elements are gone
In tender embassy of love to thee,
My life, being made of four, with two alone,
Sinks down to death, oppressed with melancholy;
Until life's composition be recurred
By those swift messengers returned from thee,
Who even but now come back again, assured
Of thy fair health, recounting it to me:

This told, I joy; but then no longer glad,
I send them back again, and straight grow sad.

45.

The transpositions we have made in the arrangement are justified by the consideration that in the original text the 50th, 51st, and 52d Sonnets are entirely isolated; that the 27th and 28th are also perfectly unconnected with what precedes and what follows; that the 61st stands equally alone; and that the 43d, 44th, and 45th are in a similar position. We have now a perfect little poem describing the journey — the restless pilgrimage of thought — the desire for return.

The thoughts of a temporary separation lead to the fear that absence may produce estrangement: —

How careful was I, when I took my way,
Each trifle under truest bars to thrust,
That, to my use, it might unusèd stay
From hands of falsehood, in sure wards of trust!
But thou to whom my jewels trifles are,
Most worthy comfort, now my greatest grief,
Thou, best of dearest, and mine only care,
Art left the prey of every vulgar thief.
Thee have I not locked up in any chest,
Save where thou art not, though I feel thou art,
Within the gentle closure of my breast,
From whence at pleasure thou mayst come and part;
And even thence thou wilt be stolen I fear,
For truth proves thievish for a prize so dear.

48.

The sentiment is somewhat differently repeated in a Sonnet which is entirely isolated in the place where it stands in the original: —

So are you to my thoughts, as food to life,
Or as sweet-seasoned showers are to the ground;
And for the peace of you I hold such strife
As 'twixt a miser and his wealth is found:
Now proud as an enjoyer, and anon
Doubting the filching age will steal his treasure;

Now counting best to be with you alone,
Then bettered that the world may see my pleasure:
Sometime, all full with feasting on your sight,
And by and by clean starvéd for a look;
Possessing or pursuing no delight,
Save what is had or must from you be took.
Thus do I pine and surfeit day by day,
Or gluttoning on all, or all away.

75.

But the 49th Sonnet carries forward the dread expressed in the 48th that his friend will "be stolen," into the apprehension that coldness, and neglect, and desertion may one day ensue:—

Against that time, if ever that time come,
When I shall see thee frown on my defects,
Whenas thy love hath cast his utmost sum,
Called to that audit by advised respects;
Against that time, when thou shalt strangely pass,
And scarcely greet me with that sun, thine eye,
When love, converted from the thing it was,
Shall reasons find of settled gravity;
Against that time do I ensconce me here
Within the knowledge of mine own desert,
And this my hand against myself uprear,
To guard the lawful reasons on thy part:
To leave poor me thou hast the strength of laws,
Since, why to love, I can allege no cause.

49.

This Sonnet is also completely isolated; but much farther on, according to the original arrangement, we find the idea here conveyed of that self-sacrificing humility which will endure unkindness without complaint, worked out with exquisite tenderness:—

When thou shalt be disposed to set me light,
And place my merit in the eye of Scorn,
Upon thy side against myself I'll fight,
And prove thee virtuous, though thou art forsworn,

With mine own weakness being best acquainted,
Upon thy part I can set down a story
Of faults concealed, wherein I am attainted;
That thou, in losing me, shalt win much glory:
And I by this will be a gainer too;
For bending all my loving thoughts on thee,
The injuries that to myself I do,
Doing thee vantage, double-vantage me.
  Such is my love, to thee I so belong,
  That for thy right myself will bear all wrong.

88.

Say that thou didst forsake me for some fault,
And I will comment upon that offence:
Speak of my lameness, and I straight will halt;
Against thy reasons making no defence.
Thou canst not, love, disgrace me half so ill,
To set a form upon desired change,
As I 'll myself disgrace: knowing thy will,
I will acquaintance strangle, and look strange;
Be absent from thy walks; and in my tongue
Thy sweet belovéd name no more shall dwell;
Lest I (too much profane) should do it wrong,
And haply of our old acquaintance tell.
  For thee, against myself, I 'll vow debate,
  For I must ne'er love him whom thou dost hate.

89.

Then hate me when thou wilt; if ever, now;
Now, while the world is bent my deeds to cross,
Joir with the spite of fortune, make me bow,
And do not drop in for an after loss:
Ah! do not, when my heart hath 'scaped this sorrow,
Come in the rearward of a conquered woe;
Give not a windy night a rainy morrow,
To linger out a purposed overthrow.
If thou wilt leave me, do not leave me last,
When other petty griefs have done their spite,

But in the onset come; so shall I taste
At first the very worst of fortunes's might;
  And other strains of woe, which now seem woe,
  Compared with loss of thee will not seem so.

90.

Some glory in their birth, some in their skill,
Some in their wealth, some in their body's force;
Some in their garments, though new-fangled ill;
Some in their hawks and hounds, some in their horse;
And every humor hath his adjunct pleasure,
Wherein it finds a joy above the rest;
But these particulars are not my measure,
All these I better in one general best.
Thy love is better than high birth to me,
Richer than wealth, prouder than garments' cost,
Of more delight than hawks or horses be;
And having thee, of all men's pride I boast.
  Wretched in this alone, that thou mayst take
  All this away, and me most wretched make.

91.

But do thy worst to steal thyself away,
For term of life thou art assuréd mine;
And life no longer than thy love will stay,
For it depends upon that love of thine.
Then need I not to fear the worst of wrongs,
When in the least of them my life hath end.
I see a better state to me belongs
Than that which on thy humor doth depend.
Thou canst not vex me with inconstant mind,
Since that my life on thy revolt doth lie.
O, what a happy title do I find,
Happy to have thy love, happy to die!
  But what 's so blesséd-fair that fears no blot?—
  Thou mayst be false, and yet I know it not:—

92.

So shall I live, supposing thou art true,
Like a deceivėd husband; so love's face
May still seem love to me, though altered-new;
Thy looks with me, thy heart in other place:
For there can live no hatred in thine eye,
Therefore in that I cannot know thy change.
In many's looks the false heart's history
Is writ, in moods and frowns and wrinkles strange;
But Heaven in thy creation did decree
That in thy face sweet love should ever dwell;
Whate'er thy thoughts or thy heart's workings be,
Thy looks should nothing thence but sweetness tell.
How like Eve's apple doth thy beauty grow,
If thy sweet virtue answer not thy show!

93.

Separated from the preceding stanzas by three Sonnets, the 94th, 95th, and 96th, which we have already given — (they are those in which a friend is mildly upbraided for the defects in his character) — we have a second little poem on Absence. It would be difficult to find any thing more perfect in our own or any other language: —

How like a winter hath my absence been
From thee, the pleasure of the fleeting year!
What freezings have I felt, what dark days seen!
What old December's bareness every where!
And yet this time removed was summer's time;
The teeming autumn, big with rich increase,
Bearing the wanton burden of the prime,
Like widowed wombs after their lord's decease:
Yet this abundant issue seemed to me
But hope of orphans, and unfathered fruit;
For summer and his pleasures wait on thee,
And, thou away, the very birds are mute;
Or, if they sing, 'tis with so dull a cheer,
That leaves look pale, dreading the winter 's near.

97.

From you have I been absent in the spring,
When proud-pied April, dressed in all his trim,
Hath put a spirit of youth in every thing
That heavy Saturn laughed and leaped with him.
Yet nor the lays of birds, nor the sweet smell
Of different flowers in odor and in hue,
Could make me any summer's story tell,
Or from their proud lap pluck them where they grew:
Nor did I wonder at the lilies white,
Nor praise the deep vermilion in the rose;
They were but sweet, but figures of delight,
Drawn after you, you pattern of all those.
  Yet seemed it winter still, and, you away,
  As with your shadow I with these did play:—

98.

The forward violet thus did I chide:—
Sweet thief, whence didst thou steal thy sweet that
    smells,
If not from my love's breath? The purple pride
Which on thy soft cheek for complexion dwells,
In my love's veins thou hast too grossly died.
The lily I condemnéd for thy hand,
And buds of marjoram had stolen thy hair:
The roses fearfully on thorns did stand,
One blushing shame, another white despair;
A third, nor red nor white, had stolen of both,
And to his robbery had annexed thy breath;
But for his theft, in pride of all his growth
A vengeful canker ate him up to death.
  More flowers I noted, yet I none could see,
  But sweet or color it had stolen from thee.

99.

But this poem is quite unconnected with what precedes it. It is placed where it is upon no principle of continuity. Are we then to infer that the friend whose "shame" is "like a canker in the budding rose" is the person who is immediately afterwards addressed as one from whom every flower had stolen "sweet or color?" If we read these three stanzas without any impression of their connection with something that has gone before, we shall irresistibly feel that they are addressed to a female. They point at repeated absences; and why may they not then be addressed to the poet's first love? The Earl of Southampton, or the Earl of Pembroke, to whom the series of Sonnets are held all to refer, except when they especially address a dark-haired lady of questionable character, would not have been greatly pleased to have been complimented on the sweetness of his breath, or the whiteness of his hand. The Sonnets which are unquestionably addressed to a male, although they employ the term "beauty" in a way which we cannot easily comprehend in our own days, have always reference to *manly* beauty. The comparisons in the above Sonnets as clearly relate to *female* beauty. They are precisely the same as Spencer uses in one of his Amoretti, — the 64th; which thus concludes: —

> "Such fragrant flowers do give most odorous smell,
> But her sweet odor did them all excel."

It appears to us that in both the poems on Absence, in the stanzas which anticipate neglect and coldness, and in others which we have given and are about to give, we must not be too ready to connect their images with the person who is addressed in the first seventeen Sonnets; or be always prepared to "seize a clew which *innumerable* passages give us," according to Mr. Hallam, "and suppose that they allude to a youth of high rank as well as personal beauty and accomplishment." * The chief characteristic of those passages which clearly apply to that "unknown youth" is, as it appears to us, extravagance of admiration conveyed in very hyperbolical language. Much that we have quoted offers no example of the justice of Mr. Hallam's complaint against these productions: "There is a weakness and folly in all excessive and misplaced affection, which is not redeemed by the touches of nobler sentiments that abound in this long series of Sonnets." It would be difficult, we think, to find more forcible thoughts expressed in more simple, and therefore touching language, than in the following continuous verses. They comprise all the Sonnets numbered from 109 to 125, with the exception of 118, 119, 120, 121, three of which we have already printed as belonging to another subject than the poet's constancy of affection; and one of which we shall give as an isolated fragment: —

* Literature of Europe, vol. iii. p. 503.

O, never say that I was false of heart,
Though absence seemed my flame to qualify!
As easy might I from myself depart,
As from my soul which in thy breast doth lie:
That is my home of love; if I have ranged,
Like him that travels, I return again;
Just to the time, not with the time exchanged,—
So that myself bring water for my slain.
Never believe, though in my nature reigned
All frailties that besiege all kinds of blood,
That it could so preposterously be stained,
To leave for nothing all thy sum of good;
For nothing this wide universe I call,
Save thou, my rose; in it thou art my all.

109.

Alas, 'tis true, I have gone here and there,
And made myself a motley to the view,
Gored mine own thoughts, sold cheap what is most dear,
Made old offences of affections new.
Most true it is that I have looked on truth
Askance and strangely; but, by all above,
These blenches give my heart another youth,
And worse essays proved thee my best of love.
Now all is done, save what shall have no end:
Mine appetite I never more will grind
On newer proof, to try an older friend,
A God in love, to whom I am confined.
Then give me welcome, next my heaven the best,
Even to thy pure and most, most loving breast.

110.

O, for my sake do you with fortune chide,
The guilty goddess of my harmful deeds,
That did not better for my life provide,
Than public means, which public manners breeds.
Thence comes it that my name receives a brand,
And almost thence my nature is subdued

To what it works in, like the dyer's hand :
Pity me, then, and wish I were renewed ;
Whilst, like a willing patient, I will drink
Potions of eysell, 'gainst my strong infection ;
No bitterness that I will bitter think,
Nor double penance, to correct correction.
Pity me then, dear friend, and I assure ye,
Even that your pity is enough to cure me.

111.

Your love and pity doth the impression fill
Which vulgar scandal stamped upon my brow ;
For what care I who calls me well or ill,
So you o'er-green my bad, my good allow ?
You are my all-the-world, and I must strive
To know my shames and praises from your tongue ;
None else to me, nor I to none alive,
That my steeled sense or changes, right or wrong.
In so profound abysm I throw all care
Of other's voices, that my adder's sense
To critic and to flatterer stoppéd are.
Mark how with my neglect I do dispense : —
You are so strongly in my purpose bred,
That all the world besides methinks are dead.

112.

Since I left you, mine eye is in my mind ;
And that which governs me to go about
Doth part his function, and is partly blind,
Seems seeing, but effectually is out ;
For it no form delivers to the heart ;
Of bird, of flower, or shape, which it doth latch ;
Of his quick objects hath the mind no part,
Nor his own vision holds what it doth catch ;
For if it see the rud'st or gentlest sight,
The most sweet favor, or deformed'st creature,
The mountain or the sea, the day or night,
The crow, or dove, it shapes them to your feature.

Incapable of more, replete with you,
My most true mind thus maketh mine untrue.

113.

Or whether doth my mind, being crowned with you,
Drink up the monarch's plague, this flattery,
Or whether shall I say mine eye saith true,
And that your love taught it this alchymy,
To make of monsters and things indigest
Such cherubims as your sweet self resemble,
Creating every bad a perfect best,
As fast as objects to his beams assemble?
O, 'tis the first; 'tis flattery in my seeing,
And my great mind most kingly drinks it up:
Mine eye well knows what with his gust is 'greeing,
And to his palate doth prepare the cup:
If it be poisoned, 'tis the lesser sin
That mine eye loves it, and doth first begin.

114.

Those lines that I before have writ, do lie,
Even those that said I could not love you dearer;
Yet then my judgment knew no reason why
My most full flame should afterwards burn clearer.
But reckoning time, whose millioned accidents
Creep in 'twixt vows, and change decrees of kings,
Tan sacred beauty, blunt the sharp'st intents,
Divert strong minds to the course of altering things;
Alas! why, fearing of time's tyranny,
Might I not say, "Now I love you best,"
When I was certain o'er incertainty,
Crowning the present, doubting of the rest?
Love is a babe; then might I not say so,
To give full growth to that which still doth grow?

115.

Let me not to the marriage of true minds
Admit impediments. Love is not love

Which alters when it alteration finds,
Or bends with the remover to remove;
O, no; it is an ever-fixéd mark,
That looks on tempests, and is never shaken;
It is the star to every wandering bark,
Whose worth 's unknown, although his height be taken.
Love 's not Time's fool, though rosy lips and cheeks
Within his bending sickle's compass come;
Love alters not, with his brief hours and weeks,
But bears it out even to the edge of doom.
If this be error, and upon me proved,
I never writ, nor no man ever loved.

116.

Accuse me thus; that I have scanted all
Wherein I should your great deserts repay;
Forgot upon your dearest love to call,
Whereto all bonds do tie me day by day;
That I have frequent been with unknown minds,
And given to time your own dear purchased right;
That I have hoisted sail to all the winds
Which should transport me farthest from your sight.
Book both my wilfulness and errors down,
And on just proof, surmise accumulate,
Bring me within the level of your frown,
But shoot not at me in your wakened hate:
Since my appeal says, I did strive to prove
The constancy and virtue of your love.

117.

Thy gift, thy tables, are within my brain
Full charactered with lasting memory,
Which shall above that idle rank remain
Beyond all date, even to eternity:
Or at the least so long as brain and heart
Have faculty by nature to subsist;
Till each to razed oblivion yield his part
Of thee, thy record never can be missed.

That poor retention could not so much hold,
Nor need I tallies thy dear love to score;
Therefore to give them from me was I bold,
To trust those tables that receive thee more:
  To keep an adjunct to remember thee,
  Were to import forgetfulness in me.

122.

No! Time, thou shalt not boast that I do change·
Thy pyramids built up with newer might
To me are nothing novel, nothing strange;
They are but blessings of a former sight.
Our dates are brief, and therefore we admire
What thou dost foist upon us that is old;
And rather make them born to our desire,
Than think that we before have heard them told.
Thy registers and thee I both defy,
Not wondering at the present nor the past;
For thy recórds and what we see do lie,
Made more or less by thy continual haste;
  This I do vow, and this shall ever be,
  I will be true, despite thy scythe and thee:—

123.

If my dear love were but the child of state,
It might for fortune's bastard be unfathered,
As subject to time's love, or to time's hate,
Weeds among weeds, or flowers with flowers gathered.
No, it was builded far from accident;
It suffers not in smiling pomp, nor falls
Under the blow of thrallèd discontent,
Whereto the inviting time our fashion calls.
It fears not policy, that heretic,
Which works on leases of short-numbered hours,
But all alone stands hugely politic,
That it nor grows with heat, nor drowns with showers.

To this I witness call the fools of time,
Which die for goodness, who have lived for crime.

124.

Were it aught to me I bore the canopy,
With my extern the outward honoring,
Or laid great bases for eternity,
Which prove more short than waste or ruining?
Have I not seen dwellers on form and favor
Lose all, and more, by paying too much rent,
For compound sweet foregoing simple savor,
Pitiful thrivers, in their gazing spent?
No; let me be obsequious in thy heart,
And take thou my oblation, poor but free,
Which is not mixed with seconds, knows no art,
But mutual render, only me for thee.
Hence, thou suborned informer! a true soul,
When most impeached, stands least in thy control.

125.

Dr. Drake, in maintaining that the Sonnets, from the 1st to the 126th, were addressed to Lord Southampton, has alleged, as "one of the most striking proofs of this position," the fact "that the language of the Dedication to the Rape of Lucrece, and that of the 26th Sonnet, are almost precisely the same." If the reader will turn to this Dedication, he will at once see the resemblance. "The *love* I dedicate to your lordship is without end," shows that in the Sonnets, as in the works of contemporary writers, the perpetually recurring terms of *love* and *lover* were meant to convey the most profound respect as well as the strongest affection. In that age, friendship was not considered as a mere conventional intercourse for social gratification. There was depth and strength in it. It partook of the spiritual energy which belonged to a higher philosophy of the affections than now presides over clubs and dinner-parties. "My friend," or "my lover," meant something more than one who is ordinarily civil, returns our calls, and shakes hands upon great occasions. Lord Southampton, in a letter of introduction to a grave Lord Chancellor, calls Shakspeare "my especial friend." To Lord Southampton Shakspeare dedicates "love without end." This 26th Sonnet, we have little doubt, is *also* a dedication, accompanying some new production of the mighty dramatist, in accordance with his declaration, "What I have done is yours, what I have to do is yours, being part in all I have devoted yours:" —

Lord of my love, to whom in vassalage
Thy merit hath my duty strongly knit,
To thee I send this written embassage,
To witness duty, not to show my wit.
Duty so great, which wit so poor as mine
May make seem bare, in wanting words to show it;
But that I hope some good conceit of thine
In thy soul's thought, all naked, will bestow it:
Till whatsoever star that guides by moving,
Points on me graciously with fair aspéct,
And puts apparel on my tattered loving,
To show me worthy of thy sweet respect:
Then may I dare to boast how I do love thee,
Till then, not show my head where thou may'st prove me.

26.

The Sonnet which precedes this has also the marked character of the same respectful affection; and, like the 26th, in all probability accompanied some offering of friendship: —

Let those who are in favor with their stars
Of public honor and proud titles boast,
Whilst I, whom fortune of such triumph bars,
Unlooked for joy in that I honor most.
Great princes' favorites their fair leaves spread,
But as the marigold at the sun's eye;
And in themselves their pride lies buriéd,
For at a frown they in their glory die.
The painful warrior famouséd for fight,
After a thousand victories once foiled,
Is from the book of honor razéd quite,
And all the rest forgot for which he toiled:
Then happy I, that love and am beloved,
Where I may not remove, nor be removed.

25.

Again: the 23d Sonnet is precisely of the same character. All these appear to us wholly unconnected with the poems which surround them — little gems, perfect in themselves, and wanting no setting to add to their beauty: —

As an unperfect actor on the stage,
Who with his fear is put besides his part,
Or some fierce thing replete with too much rage,
Whose strength's abundance weakens his own heart;
So I, for fear of trust, forget to say
The perfect ceremony of love's rite,
And in mine own love's strength seem to decay,
O'ercharged with burthen of mine own love's might.
O, let my books be then the eloquence
And dumb presages of my speaking breast;
Who plead for love, and look for recompence,
More than that tongue that more hath more expressed.
O, learn to read what silent love hath writ:
To hear with eyes belongs to love's fine wit.

23.

Between the 23d and 25th Sonnets, which we have just given, — remarkable as they are for the most exquisite simplicity of thought and diction, — occurs the following *conceit:* —

Mine eye hath played the painter, and hath stelled
Thy beauty's form in table of my heart;
My body is the frame wherein 'tis held,
And perspective it is best painter's art.
For through the painter must you see his skill,
To find where your true image pictured lies,
Which in my bosom's shop is hanging still,
That hath his windows glazéd with thine eyes.
Now see what good turns eyes for eyes have done;
Mine eyes have drawn thy shape, and thine for me
Are windows to my breast, where-through the sun
Delights to peep, to gaze therein on thee;
Yet eyes this cunning want to grace their art,
They draw but what they see, know not the heart.

24.

But, separated by a long interval, we find two variations of the air, entirely out of place where they occur. Can we doubt that these three form one little poem of themselves ? —

Mine eye and heart are at a mortal war,
How to divide the conquest of thy sight;
Mine eye my heart thy picture's sight would bar,
My heart mine eye the freedom of that right.
My heart doth plead, that thou in him dost lie,
(A closet never pierced with crystal eyes,)
But the defendant doth that plea deny,
And says in him thy fair appearance lies.
To 'cide this title is impannellèd
A quest of thoughts, all tenants to the heart;
And by their verdict is determinèd
The clear eye's moiety, and the dear heart's part:
As thus; mine eye's due is thine outward part,
And my heart's right thine inward love of heart.

46.

Betwixt mine eye and heart a league is took,
And each doth good turns now unto the other:
When that mine eye is famished for a look,
Or heart in love with sighs himself doth smother,
With my love's picture then my eye doth feast,
And to the painted banquet bids my heart:
Another time mine eye is my heart's guest,
And in his thoughts of love doth share a part:
So, either by thy picture or my love,
Thyself away art present still with me;
For thou not farther than my thoughts canst move,
And I am still with them, and they with thee;
Or if they sleep, thy picture in my sight
Awakes my heart to heart's and eye's delight.

47.

The 77th Sonnet interrupts the continuity of a poem which we shall presently give, in which the writer refers, with some appearance of jealousy, to an " alien pen." There can be no doubt that this Sonnet is completely isolated. It is clearly intended to accompany the present of a note-book: —

Thy glass will show thee how thy beauties wear,
Thy dial how thy precious minutes waste;
The vacant leaves thy mind's imprint will bear,
And of this book this learning mayst thou taste.
The wrinkles which thy glass will truly show,
Of mouthèd graves will give thee memory;
Thou by thy dial's shady stealth mayst know
Time's thievish progress to eternity.
Look, what thy memory cannot contain,
Commit to these waste blanks, and thou shalt find
Those children nursed, delivered from thy brain,
To take a new acquaintance of thy mind.
These offices, so oft as thou wilt look,
Shall profit thee, and much enrich thy book.

77.

The 76th to the 87th Sonnets (omitting the 77th and 81st) have been held to refer to a particular event in the poetical career of Shakspeare. He expresses something like jealousy of a rival poet — "a better spirit." By some, Spenser is supposed to be alluded to; by others, Daniel. But we do not accept these stanzas as a proof that William Herbert is the person always addressed in these Sonnets, for the alleged reason that Daniel was patronized by the Pembroke family, and that, in 1601, he dedicated a book to William Herbert, to which Shakspeare is held to allude in the 82d Sonnet, by the expression "dedicated words." This is Mr. Boaden's theory. One of the Sonnets supposed also to refer to William Herbert as "a man right fair" was published in 1599, when the young nobleman was only 19 years of age. But in the stanzas which relate to some poetical rivalry, real or imaginary, the person addressed has

"added feathers to the learned's wing,
And given grace a double majesty."

He is

"as fair in knowledge as in hue."

The praises of the "lovely boy," be he William Herbert or not, are always confined to his personal appearance and his good nature. There is a quiet tone about the following, which separates them from the Sonnets addressed to that "unknown youth;" and yet they may be as unreal as we believe most of those to be: —

Why is my verse so barren of new pride?
So far from variation or quick change?
Why, with the time, do I not glance aside
To new-found methods and to compounds strange?
Why write I still all one, ever the same,
And keep invention in a noted weed,
That every word doth almost tell my name,
Showing their birth, and where they did proceed?
O, know, sweet love, I always write of you,
And you and love are still my argument;
So all my best is dressing old words new,
Spending again what is already spent:
For as the sun is daily new and old,
So is my love still telling what is told.

76.

So oft have I invoked thee for my muse,
And found such fair assistance in my verse,
As every alien pen hath got my use,
And under thee their poesy disperse.
Thine eyes, that taught the dumb on high to sing,
And heavy ignorance aloft to fly,
Have added feathers to the learned's wing,
And given grace a double majesty.
Yet be most proud of that which I compile,
Whose influence is thine, and born of thee:
In others' works thou dost but mend the style,
And arts with thy sweet graces gracéd be;
But thou art all my art, and dost advance
As high as learning my rude ignorance.

78.

Whilst I alone did call upon thy aid,
My verse alone had all thy gentle grace;

But now my gracious numbers are decayed,
And my sick muse doth give another place.
I grant, sweet love, thy lovely argument
Deserves the travail of a worthier pen;
Yet what of thee thy poet doth invent,
He robs thee of, and pays it thee again.
He lends thee virtue, and he stole that word
From thy behavior; beauty doth he give,
And found it in thy cheek; he can afford
No praise to thee but what in thee doth live.
  Then thank him not for that which he doth say,
  Since what he owes thee thou thyself dost pay.

79.

O, how I faint when I of you do write,
Knowing a better spirit doth use your name,
And in the praise thereof spends all his might,
To make me tongue-tied, speaking of your fame!
But since your worth (wide as the ocean is)
The humble as the proudest sail doth bear,
My saucy bark, inferior far to his,
On your broad main doth wilfully appear.
Your shallowed help will hold me up afloat,
Whilst he upon your soundless deep doth ride;
Or, being wrecked, I am a worthless boat,
He of tall building, and of goodly pride:
  Then if he thrive, and I be cast away,
  The worst was this — my love was my decay.

80.

I grant thou wert not married to my muse,
And therefore mayst without attaint o'erlook
The dedicated words which writers use
Of their fair subject, blessing every book.
Thou art as fair in knowledge as in hue,
Finding thy worth a limit past my praise;
And therefore art enforced to seek anew
Some fresher stamp of the time-bettering days.

And do so, love; yet when they have devised
What strainéd touches rhetoric can lend,
Thou truly fair wert truly sympathized
In true plain words, by thy true-telling friend;
And their gross painting might be better used
Where cheeks need blood; in thee it is abused.

82.

I never saw that you did painting need,
And therefore to your fair no painting set.
I found, or thought I found, you did exceed
The barren tender of a poet's debt:
And therefore have I slept in your report,
That you yourself, being extant, well might show
How far a modern quill doth come too short,
Speaking of worth, what worth in you doth grow.
This silence for my sin you did impute,
Which shall be most my glory, being dumb;
For I impair not beauty being mute,
When others would give life, and bring a tomb.
There lives more life in one of your fair eyes
Than both your poets can in praise devise.

83.

Who is it that says most? which can say more
Than this rich praise,—that you alone are you?
In whose confine immuréd is the store
Which should example where your equal grew.
Lean penury within that pen doth dwell,
That to his subject lends not some small glory;
But he that writes of you, if he can tell
That you are you, so dignifies his story,
Let him but copy what in you is writ,
Not making worse what nature made so clear,
And such a counterpart shall fame his wit,
Making his style admiréd every where.
You to your beauteous blessings add a curse,
Being fond on praise, which makes your praises worse.

84.

My tongue-tied muse in manners holds her still,
While comments of your praise, richly compiled,
Reserve their character with golden quill,
And precious phrase by all the muses filed.
I think good thoughts, while others write good words,
And, like unlettered clerk, still cry "Amen"
To every hymn that able spirit affords,
In polished form of well-refinéd pen.
Hearing you praised, I say, "'Tis so, 'tis true,"
And to the most of praise add something more;
But that is in my thought, whose love to you,
Though words come hindmost, holds his rank before.
  Then others for the breath of words respect,
  Me for my dumb thoughts, speaking in effect.

85.

Was it the proud full sail of his great verse,
Bound for the prize of all-to-precious you,
That did my ripe thoughts in my brain inhearse,
Making their tomb the womb wherein they grew?
Was it his spirit, by spirits taught to write
Above a mortal pitch, that struck me dead?
No, neither he, nor his compeers by night
Giving him aid, my verse astonishéd.
He, nor that affable familiar ghost
Which nightly gulls him with intelligence,
As victors of my silence cannot boast;
I was not sick of any fear from thence.
  But when your countenance filed up his line,
  Then lacked I matter — that enfeebled mine.

86.

Farewell! thou art too dear for my possessing,
And like enough thou know'st thy estimate;
The charter of thy worth gives thee releasing;
My bonds in thee are all determinate.
For how do I hold thee but by thy granting?
And for that riches where is my deserving?

The cause of this fair gift in me is wanting,
And so my patent back again is swerving.
Thyself thou gav'st, thy own worth then not knowing,
Or me, to whom thou gav'st it, else mistaking;
So thy great gift, upon misprision growing,
Comes home again, on better judgment making.
Thus have I had thee, as a dream doth flatter,
In sleep a king, but waking no such matter.

87.

We cannot trace the connection of the 121st Sonnet with what precedes and what follows it. It may stand alone — a somewhat impatient expression of contempt for the opinion of the world, which too often galls those most, who, in the consciousness of right, ought to be best prepared to be indifferent to it: —

'Tis better to be vile, than vile esteemed,
When not to be receives reproach of being,
And the just pleasure lost, which is so deemed
Not by our feeling, but by others' seeing.
For why should others' false adulterate eyes
Give salutation to my sportive blood?
Or on my frailties why are frailer spies,
Which in their wills count bad what I think good?
No. — I am that I am; and they that level
At my abuses, reckon up their own:
I may be straight, though they themselves be bevel;
By their rank thoughts my deeds must not be shown;
Unless this general evil they maintain, —
All men are bad, and in their badness reign.

121.

Lastly, of the Sonnets entirely independent of the other portions of the series, the following, already mentioned, furnishes one of the many proofs which we have endeavored to produce that the original arrangement was in many respects an arbitrary one: —

Poor soul, the centre of my sinful earth,
Fooled by those rebel powers that thee array,

Why dost thou pine within, and suffer dearth,
Painting thy outward walls so costly gay?
Why so large cost, having so short a lease,
Dost thou upon thy fading mansion spend?
Shall worms, inheritors of this excess,
Eat up thy charge? Is this thy body's end?
Then, soul, live thou upon thy servant's loss,
And let that pine to aggravate thy store;
Buy terms divine in selling hours of dross;
Within be fed, without be rich no more:
So shalt thou feed on death, that feeds on men,
And, death once dead, there 's no more dying then.

146.

III.

We have thus, with a labor which we fear may be disproportionate to the results, separated those parts of this series of poems which appeared to be manifestly complete in themselves, or not essentially connected with what has been supposed to be the "leading idea" which prevails throughout the collection. It has been said, with great eloquence, "It is true, that, in the poetry as well as in the fictions of early ages, we find a more ardent tone of affection in the language of friendship than has since been usual; and yet no instance has been adduced of such rapturous devotedness, such an idolatry of admiring love, as the greatest being whom Nature ever produced in the human form pours forth to some unknown youth in the majority of these Sonnets." * The same accomplished critic further speaks of the strangeness of "Shakspeare's humiliation in addressing him (the youth) as a being before whose feet he crouched, whose frown he feared, whose injuries, and those of the most insulting kind, — the seduction of the mistress to whom we have alluded, — he felt and bewailed without resenting." We should agree with Mr. Hallam, *if these circumstances were manifest*, that, notwithstanding the fre-

* Hallam, Literature of Europe, vol. iii. p. 502.

quent beauties of these Sonnets, the pleasure of their perusal would be much diminished. But we believe that these impressions have been in a great degree produced by regarding the original arrangement as the natural and proper one — as one suggested by the dependence of one part upon another, in a poem essentially continuous. Mr. Hallam, with these impressions, adds, somewhat strongly, " It is impossible not to wish that Shakspeare had never written them." Let us, however, analyze what we have presented to the reader in a different order than that of the original edition : —

I.

Will,	3 Sonnets.	
Black eyes,	3 "	
The virginal,	1 "	
False compare,	2 "	
Tyranny,	3 "	
Slavery,	2 "	
Coldness,	1 "	
I hate not you,	1 "	
The little love-god, (not reprinted,)	2 "	
Love and hatred,	10 "	
Infidelity,	3 "	
Injury,	6 "	
A friend's faults,	3 "	
Forgiveness,	3 "	
		— 43

II.

Confiding friendship,	4 "	
Humility,	4 "	
Absence,	9 "	
Estrangement,	9 "	
A second absence,	3 "	
Fidelity,	13 "	
Dedications,	3 "	
The picture,	3 "	
The note-book,	1 "	
Rivalry,	10 "	
Reputation,	1 "	
The soul,	1 "	
		— 61

We have thus as many as 104 Sonnets, which, if they had been differently arranged upon their original publication, might have been read with undiminished pleasure, as far as regards the strangeness of their author's humiliation before one unknown youth, and have, therefore, left us no regret that he had written them. If we are to regard a few of these as real disclosures, with reference to a " dark-haired lady whom the poet loved, but over whose relations to him there is thrown a veil of mystery, allowing us to see little except the feeling of the parties, — that their love was guilt," — we are to consider, what is so justly added by the writer from whom we quote, that " much that is most unpleasing in the circumstances connected with those magnificent lyrics is removed by the air of despondency and remorse which breathes through those which come most closely on the facts." * But it must not be forgotten, that in an age when the Italian models of poetry were so diligently cultivated, imaginary loves and imaginary jealousies were freely admitted into verses which appeared to address themselves to the reader in the personal character of the poet. Regarding a poem, whether a sonnet or an epic, essentially as a work of *art*, the artist was not careful to separate his own identity from the sentiments and situations which he delineated — any more than the pastoral poets of the next century were solicitous to tell their readers that their Corydons and Phyllises were not absolutely themselves and their mistresses. The " Amoretti " of Spenser, for example, consisting of eighty-eight Sonnets, is also a puzzle to all those who regard such productions as necessarily autobiographical. These poems were published in 1596; in several passages a date is tolerably distinctly marked, for there are lines which refer to the completion of the first six Books of the " Fairy Queen," and to Spenser's appointment to the laureatship, — " the badge which I do bear." And yet they are full of the complaints of an unrequited love, and of a disdainful mistress, at a period when Spenser was married, and settled with his family in Ireland. Chalmers is here again ready with his solution of the difficulty. They were addressed, as well as Shakspeare's Sonnets, to Queen Elizabeth. We believe that, taken as works of art, having a certain degree of continuity, the Sonnets of Spenser, of Daniel, of Drayton, of Shakspeare, although in many instances they might shadow forth real feelings, and be outpourings of the inmost heart, were presented to the world as exercises of fancy, and were received by the world as such. The most usual form which such compositions assumed was that of love-verses. Spenser's " Amoretti "

* Edinburgh Review, vol. lxxi. p. 466.

are entirely of this character, as their name implies. Daniel's, which are fifty-seven in number, are all addressed "To Delia;" Drayton's, which he calls "Ideas," are somewhat more miscellaneous in their character. These were the three great poets of Shakspeare's days. Spenser's "Amoretti" was first printed in 1595; Daniel's "Delia" in 1592; Drayton's "Ideas" in 1594. This was about the period of the publication of the Venus and Adonis and the Lucrece, when Shakspeare had taken his rank amongst the poets of his time — independent of his dramatic rank. He chose a new subject for a series of Sonnets; he addressed them to some youth, some imaginary person, as we conceive; he made this fiction the vehicle for stringing together a succession of brilliant images, exhausting every artifice of language to present one idea under a thousand different forms —

"varying to other words;
And in this change is my invention spent."

Coleridge, with his usual critical discrimination, speaking of the Italian poets of the fifteenth and sixteenth centuries, and glancing also at our own of the same period, says, "In opposition to the present age, and perhaps in as faulty an extreme, they placed the essence of poetry in the *art*. The excellence at which they aimed consisted in the exquisite polish of the diction, combined with perfect simplicity." * This, we apprehend, is the characteristic excellence of Shakspeare's Sonnets; displaying, to the careful reader, "the studied position of words and phrases, so that not only each part should be melodious in itself, but contribute to the harmony of the whole." He sought for a canvas in which this elaborate coloring, this skilful management of light and shade, might be attempted, in an address to a young man, instead of a scornful Delia or a proud Daphne; and he commenced with an exhortation to that young man to marry. To allow of that energy of language which would result from the assumption of strong feeling, THE POET links himself with the young man's happiness by the strongest expressions of friendship — in the common language of that day, love. We say, advisedly, *the poet;* for it is in this character that the connection between the two friends is preserved throughout; and it is in this character that the personal beauty of the young man is made a constantly recurring theme.

* Biographia Literaria, vol. ii. p. 27.

With these imperfect observations, we present the continuous poem which appears in the first nineteen Sonnets : —

From fairest creatures we desire increase,
That thereby beauty's rose might never die,
But as the riper should by time decease,
His tender heir might bear his memory:
But thou, contracted to thine own bright eyes,
Feed'st thy light's flame with self-substantial fuel,
Making a famine where abundance lies,
Thyself thy foe, to thy sweet self too cruel.
Thou that art now the world's fresh ornament,
And only herald to the gaudy spring,
Within thine own bud buriest thy content,
And, tender churl, mak'st waste in niggarding.
Pity the world, or else this glutton be,
To eat the world's due, by the grave and thee.

1.

When forty winters shall besiege thy brow,
And dig deep trenches in thy beauty's field,
Thy youth's proud livery, so gazed on now,
Will be a tattered weed, of small worth held:
Then being asked where all thy beauty lies,
Where all the treasure of thy lusty days;
To say, within thine own deep sunken eyes,
Were an all-eating shame, and thriftless praise.
How much more praise deserved thy beauty's use,
If thou couldst answer — "This fair child of mine
Shall sum my count, and make my old excuse —"
Proving his beauty by succession thine!
This were to be new-made when thou art old,
And see thy blood warm when thou feel'st it cold.

2.

Look in thy glass, and tell the face thou viewest,
Now is the time that face should form another;
Whose fresh repair if now thou not renewest,
Thou dost beguile the world, unbless some mother.

For where is she so fair, whose uneared womb,
Disdains the tillage of thy husbandry?
Or who is he so fond will be the tomb
Of his self-love, to stop posterity?
Thou art thy mother's glass, and she in thee
Calls back the lovely April of her prime:
So thou through windows of thine age shalt see,
Despite of wrinkles, this thy golden time.
  But if thou live, remembered not to be,
  Die single, and thine image dies with thee.

3.

Unthrifty loveliness, why dost thou spend
Upon thyself thy beauty's legacy?
Nature's bequest gives nothing, but doth lend,
And, being frank, she lends to those are free.
Then, beauteous niggard, why dost thou abuse
The bounteous largess given thee to give?
Profitless usurer, why dost thou use
So great a sum of sums, yet canst not live?
For having traffic with thyself alone,
Thou of thyself thy sweet self dost deceive.
Then how, when nature calls thee to be gone,
What acceptable audit canst thou leave?
  Thy unused beauty must be tombed with thee,
  Which, used, lives thy executor to be.

4.

Those hours, that with gentle work did frame
The lovely gaze where every eye doth dwell,
Will play the tyrants to the very same,
And that unfair which fairly doth excel;
For never-resting time leads summer on
To hideous winter, and confounds him there;
Sap checked with frost, and lusty leaves quit gone,
Beauty o'ersnowed, and bareness every where;
Then, were not summer's distillation left,
A liquid prisoner pent in walls of glass,

Beauty's effect with beauty were bereft,
Nor it, nor no remembrance what it was.
  But flowers distilled, though they with winter meet,
  Leese but their show; their substance still lives sweet.

5.

Then let not winter's ragged hand deface
In thee thy summer, ere thou be distilled;
Make sweet some phial; treasure thou some place
With beauty's treasure, ere it be self-killed.
That use is not forbidden usury,
Which happies those that pay the willing loan;
That 's for thyself to breed another thee,
Or ten times happier, be it ten for one;
Ten times thyself were happier than thou art,
If ten of thine ten times refigured thee:
Then, what could Death do if thou should'st depart,
Leaving the living in posterity?
  Be not self-willed, for thou art much too fair
  To be Death's conquest, and make worms thine heir.

6.

Lo, in the orient when the gracious light
Lifts up his burning head, each under eye
Doth homage to his new-appearing sight,
Serving with looks his sacred majesty;
And having climbed the steep-up heavenly hill,
Resembling strong youth in his middle age,
Yet mortal looks adore his beauty still,
Attending on his golden pilgrimage;
But when from high-most pitch, with weary car,
Like feeble age, he reeleth from the day,
The eyes, 'fore duteous, now converted are
From his low tract, and look another way:
  So thou, thyself outgoing in thy noon,
  Unlooked on diest, unless thou get a son.

7.

Music to hear, why hear'st thou music sadly?
Sweets with sweets war not, joy delights in joy.
Why lov'st thou that which thou receiv'st not gladly?
Or else receiv'st with pleasure thine annoy?
If the true concord of well-tunéd sounds,
By unions married, do offend thine ear,
They do but sweetly chide thee, who confounds
In singleness the parts that thou shouldst bear.
Mark how one string, sweet husband to another,
Strikes each in each by mutual ordering;
Resembling sire and child and happy mother,
Who all in one, one pleasing note do sing:
  Whose speechless song, being many, seeming one,
  Sings this to thee, "Thou single wilt prove none."

8.

Is it for fear to wet a widow's eye,
That thou consum'st thyself in single life?
Ah! if thou issueless shalt hap to die,
The world will wail thee like a makeless wife;
The world will be thy widow, and still weep,
That thou no form of thee hast left behind,
When every private widow well may keep,
By children's eyes, her husband's shape in mind.
Look, what an unthrift in the world doth spend,
Shifts but his place, for still the world enjoys it:
But beauty's waste hath in the world an end,
And kept unused, the user so destroys it.
  No love toward others in that bosom sits,
  That on himself such murderous shame commits.

9.

For shame! deny that thou bear'st love to any,
Who for thyself art so unprovident.
Grant, if thou wilt, thou art beloved of many,
But that thou none lov'st is most evident;
For thou art so possessed with murderous hate,
That 'gainst thyself thou stick'st not to conspire;

Seeking that beauteous roof to ruinate,
Which to repair should be thy chief desire.
O, change thy thought, that I may change my mind!
Shall hate be fairer lodged than gentle love?
Be as thy presence is, gracious and kind,
Or to thyself, at least, kind-hearted prove;
  Make thee another self, for love of me,
  That beauty still may live in thine or thee.

10.

As fast as thou shalt wane, so fast thou grow'st
In one of thine, from that which thou departest;
And that fresh blood which youngly thou bestow'st,
Thou mayst call thine, when thou from youth convertest.
Herein lives wisdom, beauty, and increase;
Without this, folly, age, and cold decay:
If all were minded so, the times should cease,
And threescore years would make the world away.
Let those whom Nature hath not made for store,
Harsh, featureless, and rude, barrenly perish:
Look, whom she best endowed, she gave thee more;
Which bounteous gift thou shouldst in bounty cherish:
  She carved thee for her seal, aud meant thereby
  Thou shouldst print more, nor let that copy die.

11.

When I do count the clock that tells the time,
And see the brave day sunk in hideous night;
When I behold the violet past prime,
And sable curls all silvered o'er with white;
When lofty trees I see barren of leaves,
Which erst from heat did canopy the herd,
And summer's green all girded up in sheaves,
Borne on the bier with white and bristly beard;
Then of thy beauty do I question make,
That thou among the wastes of time must go,

Since sweets and beauties do themselves forsake,
And die as fast as they see others grow;
And nothing 'gainst Time's scythe can make defence,
Save breed, to brave him when he takes thee hence.

12.

O that you were yourself! but, love, you are
No longer yours than you yourself here live:
Against this coming end you should prepare,
And your sweet semblance to some other give.
So should that beauty which you hold in lease
Find no determination: then you were
Yourself again, after yourself's decease,
When your sweet issue your sweet form should bear.
Who lets so fair a house fall to decay,
Which husbandry in honor might uphold
Against the stormy gusts of winter's day,
And barren rage of death's eternal cold?
O! none but unthrifts:—Dear my love, you know
You had a father; let your son say so.

13.

Not from the stars do I my judgment pluck;
And yet methinks I have astronomy,
But not to tell of good or evil luck,
Of plagues, of deaths, or season's quality:
Nor can I fortune to brief minutes tell,
Pointing to each his thunder, rain, and wind,
Or say, with princes if it shall go well,
By oft predict that I in heaven find;
But from thine eyes my knowledge I derive,
And (constant stars) in them I read such art,
As truth and beauty shall together thrive,
If from thyself to store thou wouldst convert:
Or else of thee this I prognosticate,
Thy end is truth's and beauty's doom and date.

14.

When I consider every thing that grows
Holds in perfection but a little moment,
That this huge state presenteth nought but shows
Whereon the stars in secret influence comment;
When I perceive that men as plants increase,
Cheered and checked ever by the selfsame sky;
Vaunt in their youthful sap, at height decrease,
And wear their brave state out of memory;
Then the conceit of this inconstant stay
Sets you most rich in youth before my sight,
Where wasteful time debaseth with decay,
To change your day of youth to sullied night;
  And, all in war with time, for love of you,
  As he takes from you, I engraft you new.

15.

But wherefore do not you a mightier way
Make war upon this bloody tyrant, Time?
And fortify yourself in your decay
With means more blessèd than my barren rhyme?
Now stand you on the top of happy hours;
And many maiden gardens, yet unset,
With virtuous wish would bear you living flowers,
Much liker than your painted counterfeit;
So should the lines of life that life repair,
Which this, Time's pencil, or my pupil pen,
Neither in inward worth, nor outward fair,
Can make you live yourself in eyes of men.
  To give away yourself, keeps yourself still;
  And you must live, drawn by your own sweet skill.

16.

Who will believe my verse in time to come,
If it were filled with your most high deserts?
Though yet Heaven knows it is but as a tomb
Which hides your life, and shows not half your parts.
If I could write the beauty of your eyes,
And in fresh numbers number all your graces,

The age to come would say, this poet lies,
Such heavenly touches ne'er touched earthly faces.
So should my papers, yellowed with their age,
Be scorned, like old men of less truth than tongue;
And your true rights be termed a poet's rage,
And stretchéd metre of an antique song:
But were some child of yours alive that time,
You should live twice; — in it, and in my rhyme.

17.

Shall I compare thee to a summer's day?
Thou art more lovely and more temperate:
Rough winds do shake the darling buds of May,
And summer's lease hath all too short a date:
Sometime too hot the eye of heaven shines,
And often is his gold complexion dimmed;
And every fair from fair sometime declines,
By chance, or nature's changing course, untrimmed;
But thy eternal summer shall not fade,
Nor lose possession of that fair thou owest;
Nor shall Death brag thou wanderest in his shade,
When in eternal lines to time thou growest;
So long as men can breathe, or eyes can see,
So long lives this, and this gives life to thee.

18.

Devouring Time, blunt thou the lion's paws,
And make the earth devour her own sweet brood;
Pluck the keen teeth from the fierce tiger's jaws,
And burn the long-lived phœnix in her blood;
Make glad and sorry seasons, as thou fleets,
And do whate'er thou wilt, swift-footed Time,
To the wide world, and all her fading sweets;
But I forbid thee one most heinous crime:
O, carve not with thy hours my love's fair brow,
Nor draw no lines there with thine antique pen;
Him in thy course untainted do allow,
For beauty's pattern to succeeding men.

Yet, do thy worst, old Time: despite thy wrong,
My love shall in my verse ever live young.
19.

That this series of Sonnets, powerful as they are, displaying not only the most abundant variety of imagery, but the greatest felicity in making the whole harmonious, constitutes a poem ambitious only of the honors of a work of Art, is, we think, manifest. If it had been addressed to a real person, no other object could have been proposed than a display of the most brilliant ingenuity. In the next age it would have been called an exquisite "copy of verses." But in the next age, probably, — certainly in our own, — the author would have been pronounced arrogant beyond measure in the anticipation of the immortality of his rhymes. There is a show of modesty, indeed, in the expressions "barren rhyme" and "pupil pen;" but that is speedily cast off, and "eternal summer" is promised through "eternal lines;" and

"So long as men can breathe, or eyes can see,
So long lives this, and this gives life to thee."

Regarding these nineteen Sonnets as a continuous poem, wound up to the climax of a hyperbolical promise of immortality to the object whom it addresses, we receive the 20th Sonnet as the commencement of another poem in which the same idea is retained. The poet is bound to the youth by ties of strong affection; but nature has called upon the possessor of that beauty

"Which steals men's eyes, and women's souls amazeth,"

to cultivate closer ties. This Sonnet, through an utter misconception of the language of Shakspeare's time, has produced a comment sufficiently odious to throw an unpleasant shade over much which follows. The idea which it contains is continued in the 53d Sonnet; and we give the two in connection: —

A woman's face, with nature's own hand painted,
Hast thou, the master-mistress of my passion;
A woman's gentle heart, but not acquainted
With shifting change, as is false woman's fashion
An eye more bright than theirs, less false in rolling,
Gilding the object whereupon it gazeth;

A man in hue, all hues in his controlling,
Which steals men's eyes, and women's souls amazeth.
And for a woman wert thou first created;
Till Nature, as she wrought thee, fell a-doting,
And by addition me of thee defeated,
By adding one thing to my purpose nothing.
But since she pricked thee out for women's pleasure,
Mine be thy love, and thy love's use their treasure.

20.

What is your substance, whereof are you made,
That millions of strange shadows on you tend?
Since every one hath, every one, one's shade,
And you, but one, can every shadow lend.
Describe Adonis, and the counterfeit
Is poorly imitated after you;
On Helen's cheek all art of beauty set,
And you in Grecian tires are painted new:
Speak of the spring, and foizon of the year;
The one doth shadow of your beauty show,
The other as your bounty doth appear,
And you in every blessèd shape we know.
In all external grace you have some part,
But you like none, none you, for constant heart.

53.

Between the 20th Sonnet and the 53d occur, as it appears to us, a number of fragments which we have variously classified, and which seem to have no relation to the praises of that "unknown youth" who has been supposed to preside over five sixths of the entire series of verses. We have little doubt that the "begetter" of the Sonnets was not able to beget, or obtain all; and that there is a considerable hiatus between the 20th Sonnet and the second hyperbolical close, which he filled up as well as he could, from other "sugared sonnets amongst private friends:" —

O, how much more doth beauty beauteous seem,
By that sweet ornament which truth doth give!
The rose looks fair, but fairer we it deem
For that sweet odor which doth in it live.

The canker-blooms have full as deep a dye
As the perfumèd tincture of the roses,
Hang on such thorns, and play as wantonly
When summer's breath their maskèd buds discloses:
But, for their virtue only is their show,
They live unwooed, and unrespected fade;
Die to themselves. Sweet roses do not so;
Of their sweet deaths are sweetest odors made:
And so of you, beauteous and lovely youth,
When that shall fade, by verse distils your truth.

54.

Not marble, not the gilded monuments
Of princes, shall outlive this powerful rhyme;
But you shall shine more bright in these contents
Than unswept stone, besmeared with sluttish time.
When wasteful war shall statues overturn,
And broils root out the work of masonry,
Nor Mars his sword nor war's quick fire shall burn
The living record of your memory.
'Gainst death and all oblivious enmity
Shall you pace forth; your praise shall still find room,
Even in the eyes of all posterity
That wear this world out to the ending doom.
So till the judgment that yourself arise,
You live in this, and dwell in lovers' eyes.

55.

Wherever we meet with these magnificent promises of the immortality which the poet's verses are to bestow, we find them associated with that personage, the representative at once of "Adonis" and of "Helen," who presents himself to us as the unreal coinage of the fancy. In many of the lines which we have given in the second division of this inquiry, the reader will have noticed the affecting modesty, the humility without abasement, of the great poet comparing himself with others. Here Shakspeare indeed speaks. For example, take the whole of the 32d Sonnet. We should scarcely imagine, if the poem were continuous as Mr.

Brown believes, that the last stanza of the second portion of it in his classification would conclude with these lines: —

"Not marble, not the gilded monuments
Of princes, shall outlive *this powerful rhyme*."

They contrast remarkably with the tone of the 32d Sonnet, —

"These *poor rude lines* of thy deceasèd lover."

Meres has a passage: "As Ovid saith of his works, —

'Jamque opus exegi quod nec Jovis ira, nec ignis,
Nec poterit ferrum, nec edax abolere vetustas;'

and as Horace saith of his,—

'Exegi monumentum ære perennius,' &c.;

so say *I* severally of Sir Philip Sidney's, Spenser's, Daniel's, Drayton's, *Shakspeare's*, and Warner's works." What Ovid and Horace said is imitated in the 55th Sonnet. But we greatly doubt if what Meres would have said of Shakspeare *he* would have said of himself, except in some assumed character, to which we have not the key. Ben Jonson, to whom a boastful spirit has with some justice been objected, never said any thing so strong of his own writings; and he wrote with too much reliance, in this and other particulars, upon classical examples. But Jonson was not a writer of Sonnets, which, pitched in an artificial key, made this boastful tone a constituent part of the whole performance. The *man*, who never once speaks of his own merits in the greatest productions of the human intellect, when he put on the imaginary character in which a *poet* is weaving a fiction out of his supposed personal relations, did not hesitate to conform himself to the practice of other masters of the art. Shakspeare here adopted the tone which Spenser, Daniel, and Drayton had adopted. The parallel appears to us very remarkable; and we must beg the indulgence of our readers while we present them a few passages from each of these writers.

And first of Spenser. His 27th Sonnet will furnish an adequate notion of the general tone of his "Amoretti," and of the self-exultation which appears to belong to this species of poem: —

"Fair proud! now tell me, why should fair be proud,
Sith all world's glory is but dross unclean,

And in the shade of death itself shall shroud,
However now thereof ye little ween!
That goodly idol, now so gay beseen,
Shall doff her flesh's borrowed fair attire;
And be forgot as it had never been;
That many now much worship and admire!
Ne any then shall after it inquire,
Ne any mention shall thereof remain,
But what this verse, that never shall expire,
Shall to you purchase with her thankless pain!
Fair! be no longer proud of that shall perish,
But that, which shall you make immortal, cherish."

And the 69th Sonnet is still more like the model upon which Shakspeare formed his 55th: —

"The famous warriors of the antique world
Used trophies to erect in stately wise,
In which they would the records have enrolled
Of their great deeds and valorous emprise.
What trophy then shall I most fit devise,
In which I may record the memory
Of my love's conquest, peerless beauty's prize,
Adorned with honor, love, and chastity?
Even this verse, vowed to eternity,
Shall be thereof immortal monument;
And tell her praise to all posterity,
That may admire such worlds rare wonderment;
The happy purchase of my glorious spoil,
Gotten at last with labor and long toil."

Spenser's 75th Sonnet also thus closes: —

"My verse your virtues rare shall éternize,
And in the heavens write your glorious name,
Where, when as Death shall all the world subdue,
Our love shall live, and later life renew."

Of Daniel's Sonnets, the 41st and 42d furnish examples of the same tone, though somewhat more subdued than in Shakspeare or Spenser: —

"Be not displeased that these my papers should
Bewray unto the world how fair thou art;
Or that my wits have showed the best they could,
(The chastest flame that ever warméd heart!)
Think not, sweet Delia, this shall be thy shame,
My muse should sound thy praise with mournful warble;
How many live, the glory of whose name
Shall rest in ice, when thine is graved in marble!

Thou mayst in after ages live esteemed,
Unburied in these lines, reserved in pureness;
These shall entomb those eyes, that have redeemed
Me from the vulgar, thee from all obscureness.
Although my careful accents never moved thee,
Yet count it no disgrace that I have loved thee."

"Delia, these eyes, that so admire thine,
Have seen those walls which proud ambition reared
To check the world; how they entombed have lien
Within themselves, and on them ploughs have eared.
Yet never found that barbarous hand attained
The spoil of fame deserved by virtuous men;
Whose glorious actions luckily had gained
The eternal annals of a happy pen.
And therefore grieve not if thy beauties die;
Though time do spoil thee of the fairest veil
That ever yet covered mortality;
And must enstar the needle and the rail.
That grace which doth more than enwoman thee,
Lives in my lines, and must eternal be."

But Drayton, if he displayed not the energy of Shakspeare, the fancy of Spenser, or the sweetness of Daniel, is not behind either in the extravagance of his admiration, or his confidence in his own power. The 6th and the 44th "Ideas" are sufficient examples:—

"How many paltry, foolish, painted things,
That now in coaches trouble every street,
Shall be forgotten, whom no poet sings,
Ere they be well wrapped in their winding-sheet!
When I to thee eternity shall give,
When nothing else remaineth of these days,
And queens hereafter shall be glad to live
Upon the alms of thy superfluous praise;
Virgins and matrons reading these my rhymes,
Shall be so much delighted with thy story,
That they shall grieve they lived not in these times,
To have seen thee, their sex's only glory:
So thou shalt fly above the vulgar throng,
Still to survive in my immortal song."

"Whilst thus my pen strives to eternize thee,
Age rules my lines with wrinkles in my face,
Where, in the map of all my misery,
Is modelled out the world of my disgrace;
Whilst, in despite of tyrannizing rhymes,
Medea-like, I make thee young again,

Proudly thou scorn'st my world-outwearing rhymes,
And murther'st virtue with thy coy disdain;
And though in youth my youth untimely perish,
To keep thee from oblivion and the grave,
Ensuing ages yet my rhymes shall cherish,
Where I entombed my better part shall save;
  And though this earthly body fade and die,
  My name shall mount upon eternity."

We now proceed to what appears another continuous poem amongst Shakspeare's Sonnets, addressed to the same object as the first nineteen stanzas were addressed to, and devoted to the same admiration of his personal beauty. The leading idea is now that of the spoils of Time, to be repaired only by the immortality of verse:—

Where art thou, Muse, that thou forgett'st so long
To speak of that which gives thee all thy might?
Spend'st thou thy fury on some worthless song?
Darkening thy power, to lend base subjects light?
Return, forgetful Muse, and straight redeem
In gentle numbers time so idly spent;
Sing to the ear that doth thy lays esteem,
And gives thy pen both skill and argument.
Rise, restive Muse, my love's sweet face survey,
If Time have any wrinkle graven there;
If any, be a satire to decay,
And make Time's spoils despiséd every where.
  Give my love fame faster than Time wastes life;
  So thou prevent'st his scythe and crooked knife.

100.

O, truant Muse, what shall be thy amends,
For thy neglect of truth in beauty dyed?
Both truth and beauty on my love depends;
So dost thou too, and therein dignified.
Make answer, Muse; wilt thou not haply say,
"Truth needs no color with his color fixed,
Beauty no pencil, beauty's truth to lay;
But best is best, if never intermixed"?—
Because he needs no praise, wilt thou be dumb?
Excuse not silence so; for it lies in thee

To make him much outlive a gilded tomb,
And to be praised of ages yet to be.
 Then do thy office, Muse; I teach thee how
 To make him seem long hence as he shows now.

101.

My love is strengthened, though more weak in seeming:
I love not less, though less the show appear;
That love is merchandised whose rich esteeming
The owner's tongue doth publish every where.
Our love was new, and then but in the spring,
When I was wont to greet it with my lays;
As Philomel in summer's front doth sing,
And stops his pipe in growth of riper days;
Not that the summer is less pleasant now
Than when her mournful hymns did hush the night,
But that wild music burthens every bough,
And sweets grown common lose their dear delight.
 Therefore, like her, I sometime hold my tongue,
 Because I would not dull you with my song.

102.

Alack! what poverty my muse brings forth,
That having such a scope to show her pride,
The argument, all bare, is of more worth,
Than when it hath my added praise beside.
O, blame me not if I no more can write!
Look in your glass, and there appears a face
That overgoes my blunt invention quite,
Dulling my lines, and doing me disgrace.
Were it not sinful then, striving to mend,
To mar the subject that before was well?
For to no other pass my verses tend,
Than of your graces and your gifts to tell;
 And more, much more, than in my verse can sit,
 Your own glass shows you, when you look in it.

103.

To me, fair friend, you never can be old,
For as you were when first your eye I eyed,
Such seems your beauty still. Three winters' cold
Have from the forest shook three summers' pride;
Three beauteous springs to yellow autumn turned,
In process of the seasons have I seen,
Three April perfumes in three hot Junes burned,
Since first I saw you fresh which yet are green.
Ah! yet doth beauty, like a dial hand,
Steal from his figure, and no pace perceived;
So your sweet hue, which methinks still doth stand,
Hath motion, and mine eye may be deceived.
For fear of which, hear this, thou age unbred,
Ere you were born, was beauty's summer dead.

104

Let not my love be called idolatry,
Nor my belovéd as an idol show,
Since all alike my songs and praises be,
To one, of one, still such, and ever so.
Kind is my love to-day, to-morrow kind,
Still constant in a wondrous excellence;
Therefore my verse, to constancy confined,
One thing expressing, leaves out difference.
Fair, kind, and true, is all my argument,
Fair, kind, and true, varying to other words;
And in this change is my invention spent,
Three themes in one, which wondrous scope affords.
Fair, kind, and true, have often lived alone,
Which three, till now, never kept seat in one.

105.

When in the chronicle of wasted time
I see descriptions of the fairest wights,
And beauty making beautiful old rhyme,
In praise of ladies dead and lovely knights,
Then in the blazon of sweet beauty's best,
Of hand, of foot, of lip, of eye, of brow,

I see their antique pen would have expressed
Even such a beauty as you master now.
So all their praises are but prophecies
Of this our time, all you prefiguring;
And for they looked but with divining eyes,
They had not skill enough your worth to sing:
  For we, which now behold these present days,
  Have eyes to wonder, but lack tongues to praise.
106.

Not mine own fears, nor the prophetic soul
Of the wide world dreaming on things to come,
Can yet the lease of my true love control,
Supposed as forfeit to a cónfined doom.
The mortal moon hath her eclipse endured,
And the sad augurs mock their own presage;
Incertainties now crown themselves assured,
And peace proclaims olives of endless age.
Now with the drops of this most balmy time
My love looks fresh, and Death to me subscribes,
Since spite of him I 'll live in this poor rhyme,
While he insults o'er dull and speechless tribes.
  And thou in this shalt find thy monument,
  When tyrants' crests and tombs of brass are spent.
107.

What 's in the brain that ink may character,
Which hath not figured to thee my true spirit?
What 's new to speak, what now to register,
That may express my love, or thy dear merit?
Nothing, sweet boy; but yet, like prayers divine,
I must each day say o'er the very same;
Counting no old thing old, thou mine, I thine,
Even as when first I hallowed thy fair name.
So that eternal love in love's fresh case
Weighs not the dust and injury of age,
Nor gives to necessary wrinkles place,
But makes antiquity for aye his page;

Finding the first conceit of love there bred,
Where time and outward form would show it dead.

108.

If there be nothing new, but that which is
Hath been before, how are our brains beguiled,
Which, laboring for invention, bear amiss
The second burthen of a former child!
O, that record could with a backward look,
Even of five hundred courses of the sun,
Show me your image in some antique book,
Since mind at first in character was done!
That I might see what the old world could say
To this composéd wonder of your frame;
Whether we are mended, or whe'r better they,
Or whether revolution be the same.
O! sure I am, the wits of former days
To subjects worse have given admiring praise.

59.

Like as the waves make towards the pebbled shore,
So do our minutes hasten to their end;
Each changing place with that which goes before,
In sequent toil all forwards do contend.
Nativity, once in the main of light,
Crawls to maturity, wherewith being crowned,
Crooked eclipses 'gainst his glory fight,
And Time, that gave, doth now his gift confound.
Time doth transfix the flourish set on youth,
And delves the parallels in beauty's brow;
Feeds on the rarities of nature's truth,
And nothing stands but for his scythe to mow.
And yet, to times in hope, my verse shall stand,
Praising thy worth, despite his cruel hand.

60.

Of these eleven stanzas nine are consecutive in the original, being numbered 100 to 108. The other two, the 59th and 60th, are certainly isolated in the first arrangement; but the idea of the

108th glides into the 59th, and closes appropriately with the 60th. But there is a short poem which stands completely alone in the original edition, the 126th; and it is remarkable for being of a different metrical character, wanting the distinguishing feature of the Sonnet in its number of lines. Its general tendency, however, connects it with those which we have just given:—

O thou, my lovely boy, who in thy power
Dost hold Time's fickle glass, his sickle, hour;
Who hast by waning grown, and therein show'st
Thy lovers withering, as thy sweet self grow'st!
If Nature, sovereign mistress over wrack,
As thou goest onwards, still will pluck thee back,
She keeps thee to this purpose, that her skill
May time disgrace, and wretched minutes kill.
Yet fear her, O thou minion of her pleasure;
She may detain, but not still keep her treasure:
Her audit, though delayed, answered must be,
And her quietus is to render thee.

126.

There is an enemy as potent as Time, who cuts down the pride of youth as the flower of the field. That enemy is Death; and the poet most skilfully presents the images of mortality to his "lovely boy" in connection with the decay of the elder friend. In this portion of the poem there is a touching simplicity, which, however, is intermingled with passages which, denoting that the *Poet* is still speaking in character, take the stanzas, in some degree, out of the range of the real:—

My glass shall not persuade me I am old,
So long as youth and thou are of one date;
But when in thee Time's furrows I behold,
Then look I death my days should expiate.
For all that beauty that doth cover thee
Is but the seemly raiment of my heart,
Which in thy breast doth live, as thine in me;
How can I then be elder than thou art?
O, therefore, love, be of thyself so wary,
As I not for myself but for thee will;

Bearing thy heart, which I will keep so chary
As tender nurse her babe from faring ill.
Presume not on thy heart when mine is slain;
Thou gav'st me thine, not to give back again.

22.

Sin of self-love possesseth all mine eye,
And all my soul, and all my every part;
And for this sin there is no remedy,
It is so grounded inward in my heart.
Methinks no face so gracious is as mine,
No shape so true, no truth of such account,
And for myself mine own worth do define,
As I all other in all worths surmount.
But when my glass shows me myself indeed,
Beated and chopped with tanned antiquity,
Mine own self-love quite contrary I read,
Self so self-loving were iniquity.
'Tis thee (myself) that for myself I praise,
Painting my age with beauty of thy days.

62.

Against my love shall be, as I am now,
With Time's injurious hand crushed and o'erworn;
When hours have drained his blood, and filled his brow
With lines and wrinkles; when his youthful morn
Hath travelled on to age's steepy night;
And all those beauties, whereof now he 's king,
Are vanishing or vanished out of sight,
Stealing away the treasure of his spring;
For such a time do I now fortify
Against confounding age's cruel knife,
That he shall never cut from memory
My sweet love's beauty, though my lover's life.
His beauty shall in these black lines be seen,
And they shall live, and he in them, still green.

63.

When I have seen by Time's fell hand defaced
The rich-proud cost of outworn buried age;
When sometime lofty towers I see down razed,
And brass eternal, slave to mortal rage;
When I have seen the hungry ocean gain
Advantage on the kingdom of the shore,
And the firm soil win of the wat'ry main,
Increasing store with loss, and loss with store;
When I have seen such interchange of state,
Or state itself confounded to decay;
Ruin hath taught me thus to ruminate —
That time will come and take my love away.
  This thought is as a death, which cannot choose
  But weep to have that which it fears to lose.

64.

Since brass, nor stone, nor earth, nor boundless sea,
But sad mortality o'ersways their power,
How with this rage shall beauty hold a plea,
Whose action is no stronger than a flower?
O, how shall summer's honey breath hold out
Against the wreckful siege of battering days,
When rocks impregnable are not so stout,
Nor gates of steel so strong, but time decays?
O, fearful meditation! where, alack!
Shall Time's best jewel from Time's chest lie hid?
Or what strong hand can hold his swift foot back?
Or who his spoil of beauty can forbid?
  O, none, unless this miracle have might,
  That in black ink my love may still shine bright.

65

Tired with all these, for restful death I cry, —
As, to behold desert a beggar born,
And needy nothing trimmed in jollity,
And purest faith unhappily forsworn,
And gilded honor shamefully misplaced,
And maiden virtue rudely strumpeted,

And right perfection wrongfully disgraced,
And strength by limping sway disablèd,
And art made tongue-tied by authority,
And folly (doctor-like) controlling skill,
And simple truth miscalled simplicity,
And captive good attending captain ill:
Tired with all these, from these would I be gone,
Save that, to die, I leave my love alone.

66.

Ah! wherefore with infection should he live,
And with his presence grace impiety,
That sin by him advantage should achieve,
And lace itself with his society?
Why should false painting imitate his cheek,
And steal dead seeing of his living hue?
Why should poor beauty indirectly seek
Roses of shadow, since his rose is true?
Why should he live now Nature bankrupt is,
Beggared of blood to blush through lively veins?
For she hath no exchequer now but his,
And, proud of many, lives upon his gains.
O, him she stores, to show what wealth she had,
In days long since, before these last so bad.

67.

Thus is his cheek the map of days outworn,
When beauty lived and died as flowers do now,
Before these bastard signs of fair were borne,
Or durst inhabit on a living brow;
Before the golden tresses of the dead,
The right of sepulchres, were shorn away,
To live a second life on second head,
Ere beauty's dead fleece made another gay:
In him those holy antique hours are seen,
Without all ornament, itself, and true,
Making no summer of another's green,
Robbing no old to dress his beauty new;

And him as for a map doth Nature store,
To show false art what beauty was of yore.

68.

Those parts of thee that the world's eye doth view
Want nothing that the thought of hearts can mend:
All tongues (the voice of souls) give thee that due,
Uttering bare truth, even so as foes commend.
Thine outward thus with outward praise is crowned;
But those same tongues that give thee so thine own,
In other accents do this praise confound,
By seeing farther than the eye hath shown.
They look into the beauty of thy mind,
And that, in guess, they measure by thy deeds;
Then (churls) their thoughts, although their eyes were kind,
To thy fair flower add the rank smell of weeds:
But why thy odor matcheth not thy show,
The solve is this, — that thou dost common grow.

69.

That thou art blamed shall not be thy defect,
For slander's mark was ever yet the fair;
The ornament of beauty is suspect,
A crow that flies in heaven's sweetest air.
So thou be good, slander doth but approve
Thy worth the greater, being wooed of time:
For canker vice the sweetest buds doth love,
And thou present'st a pure, unstainéd prime.
Thou hast passed by the ambush of young days,
Either not assailed, or victor being charged;
Yet this thy praise cannot be so thy praise,
To tie up envy, evermore enlarged:
If some suspect of ill masked not thy show,
Then thou alone kingdoms of hearts shouldst owe.

70.

No longer mourn for me when I am dead
Than you shall hear the surly, sullen bell

Give warning to the world that I am fled
From this vile world, with vilest worms to dwell:
Nay, if you read this line, remember not
The hand that writ it; for I love you so,
That I in your sweet thoughts would be forgot,
If thinking on me then should make you woe.
O, if (I say) you look upon this verse,
When I perhaps compounded am with clay,
Do not so much as my poor name rehearse;
But let your love even with my life decay:
  Lest the wise world should look into your moan,
  And mock you with me after I am gone.

71.

O, lest the world should task you to recite
What merit lived in me, that you should love
After my death,—dear love, forget me quite,
For you in me can nothing worthy prove;
Unless you would devise some virtuous lie,
To do more for me than mine own desert,
And hang more praise upon deceasèd I
Than niggard truth would willingly impart:
O, lest your true love may seem false in this,
That you for love speak well of me untrue,
My name be buried where my body is,
And live no more to shame nor me nor you.
  For I am shamed by that which I bring forth,
  And so should you, to love things nothing worth.

72.

That time of year thou mayst in me behold
When yellow leaves, or none, or few, do hang
Upon those boughs which shake against the cold,
Bare ruined choirs, where late the sweet birds sang.
In me thou seest the twilight of such day
As after sunset fadeth in the west,
Which by and by black night doth take away,
Death's second self that seals up all in rest.

In me thou seest the glowing of such fire
That on the ashes of his youth doth lie,
As the death-bed whereon it must expire,
Consumed with that which it was nourished by.
  This thou perceiv'st, which makes thy love more strong
  To love that well which thou must leave ere long.

73.

But be contented: when that fell arrest
Without all bail shall carry me away,
My life hath in this line some interest,
Which for memorial still with thee shall stay.
When thou reviewest this, thou dost review
The very part was consecrate to thee.
The earth can have but earth, which is his due;
My spirit is thine, the better part of me:
So then thou hast but lost the dregs of life,
The prey of worms, my body being dead;
The coward conquest of a wretch's knife,
Too base of thee to be rememberéd.
  The worth of that, is that which it contains,
  And that is this, and this with thee remains.

74.

Or I shall live your epitaph to make,
Or you survive when I in earth am rotten;
From hence your memory death cannot take,
Although in me each part will be forgotten.
Your name from hence immortal life shall have,
Though I, once gone, to all the world must die:
The earth can yield me but a common grave,
When you entombéd in men's eyes shall lie.
Your monument shall be my gentle verse,
Which eyes not yet created shall o'er-read:
And tongues to be, your being shall rehearse,
When all the breathers of this world are dead;

You still shall live (such virtue hath my pen)
Where breath most breathes, — even in the mouths
of men. 81.

Thirteen of these stanzas, the 62d to the 74th, follow in their original order. The first of the fifteen, the 22d Sonnet, stands quite alone, although its idea is continued in the 62d. The last of the series, the 81st, not only stands alone, but actually cuts off the undoubted connection between the 80th and the 82d Sonnets. The 71st to the 74th Sonnets seem bursting from a heart oppressed with a sense of its own unworthiness, and surrendered to some overwhelming misery. There is a line in the 74th which points at suicide. We cling to the belief that the sentiments here expressed are essentially dramatic. In the 32d Sonnet, where we recognize the man Shakspeare speaking in his own modest and cheerful spirit, death is to come across his " *well-contented* day." The opinion which we have endeavored to sustain of the probable admixture of the artificial and the real in the Sonnets, arising from their supposed original fragmentary state, necessarily leads to the belief that some are accurate illustrations of the poet's situation and feelings. It is collected from these Sonnets, for example, that his profession as a player was disagreeable to him; and this complaint is found amongst those portions which we have separated from the series of verses which appear to us to be written in an artificial character; it might be addressed to any one of his family, or some honored friend, such as Lord Southampton: —

"O, for my sake do you with Fortune chide,
The guilty goddess of my harmful deeds,
That did not better for my life provide
Than public means, which public manners breeds.
Thence comes it that my name receives a brand,
And almost thence my nature is subdued
To what it works in, like the dyer's hand."

But if from his professional occupation his nature was felt by him to be subdued to what it worked in, — if thence his name received a brand, — if vulgar scandal sometimes assailed him, — he had high thoughts to console him, such as were never before imparted to mortal. This was probably written in some period of dejection, when his heart was ill at ease, and he looked upon the world with a slight tinge of indifference, if not of dislike. Every man of high genius has felt something of this. It was reserved for the highest to throw it off, "like dew-drops from the lion's mane." But the profound self-abasement and despondency of the 74th Sonnet, exquisite as the diction is, appear to us unreal, as a representation of the mental state of William Shakspeare; written, as it most probably was, at a period of his life when he revels and luxuriates (in the comedies which belong to the close of the sixteenth century) in the spirit of enjoyment, gushing from a heart full of love for his species, at peace with itself and with all the world.

We have thus, if we have not been led away by imaginary associations, connected the verses addressed to

"the world's fresh ornament,
And only herald to the gaudy spring."

in a poem, or poems, of fifty stanzas, written upon a plan by which it is obviously presented as a work of fiction, in which the poet displays his art in a style accordant with the existing fashion and the example of other poets. The theme is the personal beauty of a wonderful youth, and the strong affection of a poet. Beauty is to be perpetuated by marriage, and to be immortalized in the poet's verses. Beauty is gradually to fade before Time, but is to be still immortalized. Beauty is to yield to Death, as the poet himself yields, but its memory is to endure in "eternal lines." Separating from this somewhat monotonous theme those portions of a hundred and fifty-four Sonnets which do not appear essentially to belong to it, we separate, as we believe, more or less, what has a personal interest in these compositions from what is meant to be dramatic — the real from the fictitious. Our theory, we well know, is liable to many objections; but it is based upon the unquestionable fact that these one hundred and fifty-four Sonnets cannot be received as a continuous poem upon any other principle than that the author had written them continuously. If there are some parts which are acknowledged interpolations, may there not be other parts that are open to the same belief? If there are parts entirely different in their tone from the bulk of these Sonnets, may we not consider that one portion was meant to be artificial and another real, — that the poet sometimes spoke in an assumed character, sometimes in a natural one? This theory we know could not hold if the poet had himself arranged the sequence of these verses; but as it is manifest that two stanzas have been introduced from a poem printed ten years earlier, — that others are acknowledged to be out of order, and others positively dragged in without the slightest connection, — may we not carry the separation still farther, and, believing that the "begetter" — the *getter-up* — of these Sonnets had levied contributions upon all Shakspeare's "private friends," — assume that he was indifferent to any arrangement which might make each portion of the poem tell its own history? There is one decided advantage in the separation which we have proposed — the idea with which the series opens, and which is carried, *here and there*, in the original, through the first hundred and twenty-six Sonnets, does not now over-ride the whole of the series. The separate parts may be read with more pleasure when they are relieved from this strained and exaggerated association.

There are three points connected with the opinion we have formed with regard to the entire series of Sonnets, which we must briefly notice before we leave the subject. The first is, the inconsistencies which obviously present themselves in adopting the theory that the series of Sonnets — or at least the first hundred and twenty-six Sonnets — are addressed to *one* person. It is not our intention to discuss the question *to whom* they were addressed, which question depends upon the adoption of the theory that they are addressed *to one.* Drake's opinion that they were addressed to Lord Southampton rests upon the belief that Shakspeare looked up to some friend to whom they point, "with reverence and homage." The latter theory, that William Herbert, Earl of Pembroke, was their object, is supported by the facts, derived from Clarendon and others, that he was "a man of noble and gallant character, though always of a licentious life." W. H. is held to be William Herbert; and Mr. Hallam says, "Proofs of the low moral character of 'W. H.' are continual." We venture to think that the term "continual" is somewhat loosely applied. The one "sensual fault," of which the poet complains, is obscurely hinted at in the 33d, 34th, 35th, 40th, 41st, and 42d stanzas; and the general faults of his friend's character, from which the injury proceeded, are summed up in the 94th, 95th, and 96th. We shall search in vain throughout the hundred and fifty-four Sonnets for any similar indications of the "low moral character" of the person addressed.

But the supposed continuity of the poem implies arrangement, and therefore consistency in the author. In the 41st stanza the *one* friend, according to this theory, is reproached for the treachery which is involved in the indulgence of his passions. The poet says "thou mightst

> "chide thy beauty and thy *straying youth,*
> Who lead thee in *their riot* even there
> Where thou art forced to break a twofold truth."

Again, in the 95th stanza we have these lines : —

> "How sweet and lovely dost thou make *the shame,*
> Which, like a canker in the fragrant rose,
> Doth spot the beauty of thy *budding* name ! "

And, —

> "O, what a mansion have those *vices* got,
> Which for their habitation chose out thee ! "

Here are not only secret "vices," but "shame," defacing the character. "Tongues" make "lascivious comments" on the story of his days. Is it to this person that in the 69th Sonnet we have these lines addressed ? —

> "Those parts of thee that the world's eye doth view
> Want nothing that the thought of hearts can mend."

Is it to this person that the 70th Sonnet is devoted, in which are these remarkable words ? —

> "Thou present'st *a pure, unstainèd prime.*
> Thou hast passed by *the ambush of young days,*
> *Either not assailed, or victor* being charged."

These lines, be it remembered, occur *between* the first reproof for licentiousness in the 41st stanza, and the repetition of the blame in the 95th. Surely, if the poem is to be taken as continuous, and as addressed to *one* person, such contradictions would make us believe that the whole is based on unreality, and that the poet was satisfied to utter the wildest inconsistencies, merely to produce verses of exquisite beauty, but of "true no-meaning."

The second point to which we would briefly request attention is the supposed date of the series of Sonnets. The date must, it is evident, be settled in some measure according to the presiding belief in the person to whom they are held to be addressed. Mr. Hallam, who thinks the hypothesis of William Herbert sufficiently proved to demand our assent, says, "Pembroke succeeded to his father in 1601. I incline to think that the Sonnets were written about that time, some probably earlier, some later." Pembroke was born in 1580. Now, in the earlier Sonnets, according to the hypothesis, he might be called "beauteous and lovely youth," or "sweet boy;" but Southampton could not be so addressed, unless the earlier Sonnets were written even before the dedication of the Venus and Adonis to him, in 1593; for Southampton was born in 1573. Further, it is said that, whilst the person addressed was one who stood "on the top of happy hours," the poet who addressed him was

"Beated and chopped with tanned antiquity,"

as in the 62d Sonnet,—

"With Time's injurious hand crushed and o'erworn,"

as in the 63d; and approaching the termination of his career, as so exquisitely described in the 73d:—

"That time of year thou may'st in me behold
When yellow leaves, or none, or few, do hang
Upon those boughs which shake against the cold,
Bare ruined choirs, where late the sweet birds sang.
In me thou seest the twilight of such day
As after sunset fadeth in the west,
Which by and by black night doth take away,
Death's second self, that seals up all in rest.
In me thou seest the glowing of such fire
That on the ashes of his youth doth lie,
As the death-bed whereon it must expire,
Consumed by that which it was nourished by.
This thou perceiv'st, which makes my love more strong
To love that well which thou must leave, ere long."

Most distinctly in this particular portion of the Sonnets the extreme youth of the person addressed is steadily kept in view. But some are written earlier, some later; time is going on. In the 104th Sonnet the poet says that three winters, three springs, and three summers have passed

"Since first I saw you fresh, which yet are green."

But, carrying on the principle of continuity, we find that in the 138th Sonnet the poet's "days are past the best;" and he adds,—

"And wherefore say not I that I am *old?*"

That Sonnet, we have here to repeat, was published in The Passionate Pilgrim when the poet was thirty-five. But let us endeavor to find one more gleam of light amidst this obscurity. In one of the Sonnets in which the poet upbraids his friend with his licentiousness, the 94th, we have these lines:—

"The summer's flower is to the summer sweet,
Though to itself it only live and die;
But if that flower with base infection meet,
The basest weed outbraves his dignity:
For sweetest things turn sourest by their deeds;
Lilies that fester smell far worse than weeds."

The thought is here quite perfect, and the image of the last line is continued from the 11th and 12th, ending in a natural climax. But we have precisely the same line as the last in a play of Shakspeare's age, one, indeed, which has been attributed to himself, "The Reign of King Edward III." Let us transcribe the passage where it occurs, in the scene where Warwick exhorts his daughter to resist the dangerous addresses of the King:—

"That sin doth ten times aggravate itself
That is committed in a holy place:
An evil deed done by authority
Is sin and subornation. Deck an ape
In tissue, and the beauty of his robe
Adds but the greater scorn unto the beast.
A spacious field of reasons could I urge
Between his glory, daughter, and thy shame;
That, poison shows worst in a golden cup;
Dark night seems darker by the lightning flash;
Lilies that fester smell worse than weeds;
And every glory that inclines to sin,
The shame is treble by the opposite."

We doubt, exceedingly, whether the author of the 94th Sonnet, where the image of the festering lilies is a portion of the thought which has preceded it, would have transplanted it from the play, where it stands alone as an apophthegm. It seems more probable that the author of the play would have borrowed a line from one of the "sugared sonnets amongst private friends." The extreme fastidiousness required in the composition of the Sonnet, according to the poetical notions of that day, would not have warranted the adaptation of a line from a drama "sundry times played about the city of London," as the title-page tells us this was; but the play, without any injury to its poetical reputation, (to which, indeed in the matter of plays, little respect was paid,) might take a line from the Sonnet. Our reasoning may be defective, but our impression of the matter is very strong. The play was *published* in 1596, after being "sundry times played" in different theatres. William Herbert must have begun his career of licentiousness unusually early, and have had time to make a friend and abuse his confidence before he was fifteen — if the line is *original* in the Sonnet.

The Passionate Pilgrim contains a Sonnet, not in the larger collection — not forming, it would be said, any part of that continuous poem: —

"If music and sweet poetry agree,
As they must needs, the sister and the brother,
Then must the love be great 'twixt thee and me,
Because thou lov'st the one, and I the other.
Dowland to thee is dear, whose heavenly touch
Upon the lute doth ravish human sense;
Spenser to me, whose deep conceit is such
As, passing all conceit, needs no defence.
Thou lov'st to hear the sweet, melodious sound
That Phœbus' lute, the queen of music, makes;
And I in deep delight am chiefly drowned,
Whenas himself to singing he betakes.
One god is god of both, as poets feign;
One knight loves both, and both in thee remain."

Now, poor Spenser died, heart-broken, in January, 1599. The first three books of the "Fairy Queen," to which the words "deep conceit" are supposed to allude, were printed in 1590, the three other books in 1596. Spenser, pressed down by public duties and misfortunes, published nothing after. The Sonnet speaks of a living composer, Dowland, who was in repute as early as 1590; and it was probably written during the first burst of the glory which a living poet derived from his greatest work. The getter-up of The Passionate Pilgrim found it, as he found others, circulating amongst Shakspeare's "private friends." But how did it part company with many in the larger collection which resembles it in tone? Why was it not transferred to the larger collection, as two other Sonnets were transferred? Because, in 1598, it was published in a collection of poems written by Richard Barnfield, and the "getter-up" of the Sonnets knew not whether to assign it to Shakspeare or not. That it bears the mark of Shakspeare's hand we think is unquestionable. And this leads us to the last point to which we shall very briefly draw the reader's attention — the doubt which has been stated whether the hundred and fifty-four Sonnets published in 1609 were the same as Meres mentioned, in 1598, as amongst the compositions of Shakspeare, and familiar to his "private friends." Mr. Hallam thinks they are not the same, "both on account of the date, and from the peculiarly personal allusions they contain." One of the strongest of the personal allusions is contained in the 144th, originally printed in The Passionate Pilgrim. Where could the printer of the Passionate Pilgrim have obtained that Sonnet, except from some one of Shakspeare's "private friends"? If he so obtained it, why might not the collector of the volume of 1609 have obtained others of a similar character from a similar source? Would such productions have been circulated at all if they had been held to contain "peculiarly personal allusions"? If these are not the Sonnets which circulated amongst Shakspeare's "private friends," where are those Sonnets? Would Meres have spoken of them as calling to mind the sweetness of Ovid if only those published in The Passionate Pilgrim had existed, many of which were "Verses to Music," afterwards printed as such? Why should those Sonnets only have been printed which contain, or are supposed to contain, "peculiarly personal allusion"? The title-page of the collection of 1609 is "Shake-speare's Sonnets." We can only reconcile these matters with our belief that in 1609 were printed, without the cognizance of the author, all the Sonnets which could be found attributed to Shakspeare; that some of these formed a group of continuous poems; that some were detached; that no exact order could be preserved; and that accident has arranged them in the form in which they first were handed down to us.

If we have succeeded in producing satisfactory evidence that many of the Sonnets are not presented in a natural and proper order in the original edition, — if we have shown that there is occasionally not only a digression from the prevailing train of thought, by the introduction of an isolated Sonnet amongst a group, but a jarring and unmeaning interruption to that train of thought, — we have established a case that the original arrangement is no part of the poet's work, because that arrangement violates the principles of art, which Shakspeare clings to with such marvellous judgment in all his other productions. The inference, therefore, is, that the author of the Sonnets did not sanction their publication — certainly did not superintend it. This, we think, may be proved by another course of argument. The edition of 1609, although, taken as a whole, not very inaccurate, is full of those typographical errors which invariably occur when a manuscript is put into the hands of a printer to deal with it as he pleases, without reference to the author, or to any competent editor, upon any doubtful points. Malone, in a note upon the 77th Sonnet, very truly says, " *This*, *their*, and *thy* are so often confounded in these Sonnets, that it is only by attending to the context that we can discover which was the author's word." He is speaking of the original edition. It is evident, therefore, that in the progress of the book through the press there was no one capable of deciphering the obscurity of the manuscript by a regard to the context. The manuscript, in all probability, was made up of a copy of copies; so that the printer even was not responsible for those errors which so clearly show the absence of a presiding mind in the conduct of the printing. Malone has suggested that these constantly recurring mistakes in the use of *this*, *their*, *thy*, and *thine*, probably originated in the words being abbreviated in the manuscript, according to the custom of the time. But this species of mistake is by no means uniform. For example: from the 43d to the 48th Sonnet these errors occur with remarkable frequency: in one Sonnet, the 46th, this species of mistake happens four times. But we read on, and presently find that we may trust to the printed copy, which does not now violate the context. What can we infer from this, but that the separate poems were printed from different manuscripts, in which various systems of writing were employed, some using abbreviations, some rejecting them? If the *one* poem, as the first hundred and twenty-six Sonnets are called, had been printed either from the author's manuscript, or from a uniform copy of the author's manuscript, such differences of systematic error in some places, and of systematic correctness in others, would have been very unlikely to have occurred. If the poem had been printed under the author's eye, their existence would have been impossible.

The theory that the first hundred and twenty-six Sonnets were a continuous poem, or poems, addressed to one person, and that a very young man — and that the greater portion of the remaining twenty-eight Sonnets had reference to a female, with whom there was an illicit attachment on the part of the poet and the young man — involves some higher difficulties, if it is assumed that the publication was authorized by the author, or by *the* person to whom they are held to be addressed. Could Shakspeare, in 1609, authorize or sanction their publication? He was then living at Stratford, in the enjoyment of wealth; he was forty-five years of age; he was naturally desirous to associate with himself all those circumstances which constitute respectability of character. If the Sonnets had regard to actual circumstances connected with his previous career, would he, a husband, a father of two daughters, have authorized a publication so calculated to degrade him in the eyes of his family and his associates, if the verses could bear the construction now put upon them? We think not. On the other hand, did the one person to whom they are held to be addressed sanction their publication? Would Lord Pembroke have suffered himself to be styled "W. H., the only begetter of these ensuing Sonnets" — plain Mr. W. H. — he, a nobleman, with all the pride of birth and rank about him — and represented in these poems as a man of licentious habits, and treacherous in his licentiousness? The Earl of Pembroke, in 1609, had attained great honors in his political and learned relations. In the 1st year of James I. he was made a Knight of the Garter; in 1605, upon a visit of James to Oxford, he received the degree of Master of Arts; in 1607 he was appointed Governor of Portsmouth; and, more than all these honors, he was placed in the highest station by public opinion; he was, as Clarendon describes, "the most universally beloved and esteemed of any man of that age." Was this the man, in his mature years, distinctly to sanction a publication which it was understood recorded his profligacy? He was of "excellent parts, and a graceful speaker upon any subject, having a good proportion of learning, and a ready wit to apply to it," says Clarendon. Is there in the Sonnets the slightest allusion to the talents of the one person to whom they are held to be addressed? If, then, the publication was *not* authorized, in either of the modes assumed, we have no warrant whatever for having regard to the original order of the Sonnets, and in assuming a continuity *because* of that order. What, then, is the alternative? That the Sonnets were a collection of "Sibylline leaves" rescued from the perishableness of their written state by some person who had access to the high and brilliant circle in which Shakspeare was esteemed; and that this person's scrap-book, necessarily imperfect, and pretending to no order, found its way to the hands of a bookseller, who was too happy to give to that age what its most distinguished man had written at various periods, for his own amusement, and for the gratification of his "private friends."

We subjoin, for the more ready information of those who may be disposed to examine for themselves the question of the order of Shakspeare's Sonnets, (and it really is a question of great interest and rational curiosity,) the results of the two opposite theories — of their exhibiting almost perfect continuity, on the one hand; and of their being a mere collection of fragments, on the other. The one theory is illustrated with much ingenuity by Mr. Brown; the other was capriciously adopted by the editor of the collection of 1640.

Mr. Brown's Division into Six Poems.

First Poem. — Stanzas i. to xxvi. To his Friend, persuading him to Marry.

Second Poem. — Stanzas xxvii. to lv. To his Friend, who had robbed him of his Mistress — forgiving him.

Third Poem. — Stanzas lvi. to lxxvii. To his Friend, complaining of his Coldness, and warning him of Life's Decay.

Fourth Poem. — Stanzas lxxviii. to ci. To his Friend, complaining that he prefers another Poet's Praises, and reproving him for faults that may injure his character.

Fifth Poem. — Stanzas cii. to cxxvi. To his Friend, excusing himself for having been some time silent, and disclaiming the charge of Inconstancy.

Sixth Poem. — Stanzas cxxvii. to clii. To his Mistress, on her Infidelity.

Arrangement of the Edition of 1640.

In this arrangement the greater part of the Poems of the Passionate Pilgrim are blended, and are here marked P. P. In this collection the following Sonnets are not found: — 18, 19, 43, 56, 75, 76, 96, 126.

The Glory of Beauty. [67, 68, 69.]
Injurious Time. [60, 63, 64, 65, 66.]
True Admiration. [53, 54.]
The Force of Love. [57, 58.]
The Beauty of Nature. [59.]
Love's Cruelty. [1, 2, 3.]
Youthful Glory. [13, 14, 15.]
Good Admonition. [16, 17.]
Quick Prevention. [7.]
Magazine of Beauty. [4, 5, 6.]
An Invitation to Marriage. [8, 9, 10, 11, 12.]
False Belief. [138.]
A Temptation. [144.]
Fast and Loose. [P. P. 1.]
True Content. [21.]
A bashful Lover. [23.]
Strong Conceit. [22.]
A sweet Provocation. [P. P. 11.]
A constant Vow. [P. P. 3.]
The Exchange. [20.]
A Disconsolation. [27, 28, 29.]
Cruel Deceit. [P. P. 4.]
The Unconstant Lover. [P. P. 5.]
The Benefit of Friendship. [30, 31, 32.]
Friendly Concord. [P. P. 6.]
Inhumanity. [P. P. 7.]
A Congratulation. [38, 39, 40.]
Loss and Gain. [41, 42.]
Foolish Disdain. [P. P. 9.]
Ancient Antipathy. [P. P. 10.]
Beauty's Valuation. [P. P. 11.]
Melancholy Thoughts. [44, 45.]
Love's Loss. [P. P. 8.]

Love's Relief. [33, 34, 35.]
Unanimity. [36, 37.]
Loath to Depart. [P. P. 12, 13.]
A Masterpiece. [24.]
Happiness in Content. [25.]
A Dutiful Message. [26.]
Go and come quickly. [50, 51.]
Two faithful Friends. [46, 47.]
Careless Neglect. [48.]
Stout Resolution. [49.]
A Duel. [P. P. 14.]
Love-sick. [P. P. 15.]
Love's Labor Lost. [P. P. 16.]
Wholesome Counsel. [P. P. 17.]
Sat fuisse. [62.]
A living Monument. [55.]
Familiarity breeds Contempt. [52.]
Patiens Armatus. [61.]
A Valediction. [71, 72, 74.]
Nil magnis Invidia. [70.]
Love-sick. [80, 81.]
The Picture of true Love. [116.]
In Praise of his Love. [82, 83, 84, 85.]
A Resignation. [86, 87.]
Sympathizing Love. [P. P. 18.]
A Request to his Scornful Love. [88, 89, 90, 91.]
A Lover's Affection, though his Love prove Unconstant. [92, 93, 94, 95.]
Complaint for his Lover's Absence. [97, 98, 99.]
An Invocation to his Muse. [100, 101.]
Constant Affection. [104, 105, 106.]
Amazement. [102, 103.]
A Lover's Excuse for his long Absence. [109, 110.]
A Complaint. [111, 112.]
Self-flattery of her Beauty. [113, 114, 115.]
A Trial of Love's Constancy. [117, 118, 119.]
A good Construction of his Love's Unkindness. [120.]
Error in Opinion. [121.]
Upon the Receipt of a Table-Book from his Mistress. [122.]
A Vow. [123.]
Love's Safety. [124.]
An Entreaty for her Acceptance. [125.]

Upon her playing upon the Virginals. [128.]
Immoderate Lust. [129.]
In praise of her Beauty, though Black. [127, 130, 131, 132.]
Unkind Abuse. [133, 134.]
Love-suit. [135, 136.]
His Heart wounded by her Eye. [137, 139, 140.]
A Protestation. [141, 142.]
An Allusion. [143.]
Life and Death. [145.]
A Consideration of Death. [146.]
Immoderate Passion. [147.]
Love's powerful Subtlety. [148, 149, 150.]
Retaliation. [78, 79.]
Sunset. [73, 77.]
A Monument to Fame. [107, 108.]
Perjury. [151, 152.]
Cupid's Treachery. [153, 154.]

A LOVER'S COMPLAINT.

A LOVER'S COMPLAINT.

From off a hill whose concave womb re-worded[1]
A painful story from a sistering vale,
My spirits to attend this double voice accorded,
And down I laid[2] to list the sad-tuned tale:
Ere long espied a fickle maid full pale,
Tearing of papers, breaking rings a-twain,
Storming her world with sorrow's wind and rain.

Upon her head a platted hive of straw,
Which fortified her visage from the sun,
Whereon the thought might think sometime it saw
The carcass of a beauty spent and done.
Time had not scythed all that youth begun,
Nor youth all quit; but, spite of Heaven's fell
rage,
Some beauty peeped through lattice of seared age.

[1] *Re-worded*, echoed.

[2] *Laid.* So the original. But it is usually more correctly printed *lay*. The idiomatic grammar of Shakspeare's age ought not to be removed.

Oft did she heave her napkin [1] to her eyne,
Which on it had conceited characters,[2]
Laund'ring [3] the silken figures in the brine
That seasoned woe had pelleted [4] in tears,
And often reading what contents it bears;
As often shrieking undistinguished woe,
In clamors of all size, both high and low.

Sometimes her levelled eyes their carriage ride,
As they did battery to the spheres intend; [5]
Sometime diverted their poor balls are tied
To th' orbéd [6] earth: sometimes they do extend
Their view right on; anon their gazes lend
To every place at once, and nowhere fixed,
The mind and sight distractedly commixed.

Her hair, nor loose, nor tied in formal plat,
Proclaimed in her a careless hand of pride;
For some, untucked, descended her sheaved [7] hat,
Hanging her pale and pinéd cheek beside;
Some in her threaden fillet still did bide,
And, true to bondage, would not break from thence,
Though slackly braided in loose negligence.

1 *Napkin*, handkerchief. Iago says, of Desdemona's fatal handkerchief,—

"I am glad I have found this napkin."

2 *Conceited characters*, fanciful figures worked on the handkerchief.
3 *Laund'ring*, washing.
4 *Pelleted*, formed into pellets, or small balls.
5 Shakspeare often employs the metaphor of a piece of ordnance; but what in his plays is generally a slight allusion here becomes a somewhat quaint conceit.
6 *Th' orbéd.* We retain *orbéd* as a dissyllable, according to the original. Mr. Dyce has *the orbed.*
7 *Sheaved*, made of straw, collected from sheaves.

A thousand favors from a maund[1] she drew
Of amber, crystal, and of bedded jet,[2]
Which one by one she in a river threw,
Upon whose weeping margent she was set;
Like usury, applying wet to wet,
Or monarch's hands, that let not bounty fall
Where want cries "some," but where excess begs all.

Of folded schedules had she many a one,
Which she perused, sighed, tore, and gave the flood;
Cracked many a ring of posied gold and bone,
Bidding them find their sepulchres in mud;
Found yet mo[3] letters sadly penned in blood
With sleided silk[4] feat and affectedly
Enswathed, and sealed to curious secresy.

[1] *Maund*, a basket. The word is used in the old translation of the Bible.

[2] *Bedded.* So the original, the word probably meaning *jet imbedded*, or set, in some other substance. Steevens has *beaded jet*, —jet formed into beads; which Mr. Dyce adopts.

[3] *Mo*, more. This word is now invaribly printed *more.* It occurs in subsequent stanzas. Why should we destroy this little archaic beauty by a rage for modernizing?

[4] *Sleided silk.* The commentators explain this as "untwisted silk." In the chorus to the fourth act of Pericles, Marina is pictured, —

"When she weaved the sleided silk
With fingers long, small, white as milk."

Percy, in a note on this passage, says, "untwisted silk, prepared to be used in the weaver's sley." The first part of this description is certainly not correct. The silk is not untwisted, for it must be spun before it is woven; and a strong twisted silk is exactly what was required when letters were to be sealed "feat" (neatly) "to curious secresy." In Mr. Ramsay's introduction to his valuable edition of the Paston Letters, the old mode of sealing a letter is clearly described: "It was carefully folded, and fastened at the end by a sort of paper strap, upon which the seal was affixed; and under the seal a string, a silk thread, or even a straw, was frequently placed running around the letter."

These often bathed she in her fluxive eyes,
And often kissed, and often gave [1] to tear;
Cried, "O false blood! thou register of lies,
What unapprovéd witness dost thou bear!
Ink would have seemed more black and damnéd here!"
This said, in top of rage the lines she rents,
Big discontent so breaking their contents.

A reverend man that grazed his cattle nigh,
Sometime a blusterer, that the ruffle knew
Of court, of city, and had let go by
The swiftest hours, observéd as they flew,[2]
Towards this afflicted fancy [3] fastly drew;
And, privileged by age, desires to know,
In brief, the grounds and motives of her woe.

So slides he down upon his grainéd bat,[4]
And comely-distant sits he by her side;

[1] *Gave.* So the original. Malone changes the word to *'gan.* This appears to us, although it has the sanction of Mr. Dyce's adoption, an unnecessary change; *gave* is here used in the sense of gave the mind to, contemplated, made a movement towards, inclined to. Shakspeare has several times "my mind gave me;" and the word may, therefore, we think, stand alone here as expressing inclination.

[2] Malone, by making the sentence parenthetical which begins at "sometime a blusterer," and ends at "swiftest hours," causes the reverend man's attention to be drawn to the scattered fragments of letters as they flew—a very snow-storm of letters. Surely this is nonsense!

"The swiftest hours, observéd as they flew,"

clearly show that the reverend man, although he had been engaged in the ruffle, in the turmoil, of the court and city, had not suffered the swiftest hours to pass unobserved. He was a man of experience, and was thus qualified to give advice.

[3] *Fancy* is often used by Shakspeare in the sense of *love;* but here it means one that is possessed by fancy.

[4] *Bat,* club.

When he again desires her, being sat,
Her grievance with his hearing to divide:
If that from him there may be aught applied
Which may her suffering ecstasy assuage,
'Tis promised in the charity of age.

"Father," she says, "though in me you behold
The injury of many a blasting hour,
Let it not tell your judgment I am old;
Not age, but sorrow, over me hath power:
I might as yet have been a spreading flower,
Fresh to myself, if I had self-applied
Love to myself, and to no love beside.

"But woe is me! too early I attended
A youthful suit (it was to gain my grace)
Of one[1] by nature's outwards so commended,
That maiden's eyes stuck over all his face:
Love lacked a dwelling, and made him her place:
And when in his fair parts she did abide,
She was new lodged, and newly deified.

"His browny locks did hang in crooked curls;
And every light occasion of the wind
Upon his lips their silken parcels hurls.
What 's sweet to do, to do will aptly find:
Each eye that saw him did enchant the mind;
For on his visage was in little drawn,
What largeness thinks in paradise was sawn.[2]

"Small show of man was yet upon his chin;
His phœnix down began but to appear,

[1] *Of one*, the original reads *O one*.

[2] *Sawn*. Malone explains this as *seen;* but Boswell says that the word means *sown*, and that it is still so pronounced in Scotland.

Like unshorn velvet, on that termless skin,
Whose bear outbragged the web it seemed to wear;
Yet showed his visage [1] by that cost more [2] dear;
And nice affections wavering stood in doubt
If best 't were as it was, or best without.

"His qualities were beauteous as his form,
For maiden-tongued he was, and thereof free;
Yet, if men moved him, was he such a storm
As oft 'twixt May and April is to see,
When winds breathe sweet, unruly though they be.
His rudeness so with his authórized youth
Did livery falseness in a pride of truth.

"Well could he ride, and often men would say
That horse his mettle from his rider takes:
Proud of subjection, noble by the sway,
What rounds, what bounds, what course, what stop he makes!
And controversy hence a question takes,
Whether the horse by him became his deed,
Or he his manage by the well-doing steed.

"But quickly on this side the verdict went;
His real habitude gave life and grace
To appertainings and to ornament,
Accomplished in himself, not in his case: [3]
All aids, themselves made fairer by their place,
Can [4] for additions; yet their purposed trim
Pieced not his grace, but were all graced by him.

1 *Visage* is the inverted nominative case to *showed.*

2 *More.* So the original: in all the modern editions we have *most.*

3 *Case*, outward show.

4 *Can* is the original reading; but Malone changed it to *came*, and he justifies the change by a passage in Macbeth, Act I. Sc.

"So on the tip of his subduing tongue
All kind of arguments and question deep,
All replication prompt, and reason strong,
For his advantage still did wake and sleep:
To make the weeper laugh, the laugher weep,
He had the dialect and different skill,
Catching all passions in his craft of will;

"That he did in the general bosom reign
Of young, of old; and sexes both enchanted,
To dwell with him in thoughts, or to remain
In personal duty, following where he haunted:
Consents bewitched, ere he desire, have granted;
And dialogued for him what he would say,
Asked their own wills, and made their wills obey.

"Many there were that did his picture get,
To serve their eyes, and in it put their mind;
Like fools that in the imagination set
The goodly objects which abroad they find
Of lands and mansions, theirs in thought assigned;
And laboring in mo pleasures to bestow them,
Than the true gouty landlord which doth owe them:[1]

"So many have, that never touched his hand,
Sweetly supposed them mistress of his heart.

III., where he supposes the same mistake occurred. In that passage we did not receive the proposed correction; nor do we think it necessary to receive it here. *Can* is constantly used by the old writers, especially by Spenser, in the sense of *began;* and that sense, *began for additions*, is as intelligible as *came for additions*. *For* is used in the sense of *as*.

[1] There is a similar sarcastic thought in Timon, where the misanthrope, addressing himself to the gold he had found, says,—

"Thou 'lt go, strong thief,
When gouty keepers of thee cannot stand."

My woful self, that did in freedom stand,
And was my own fee-simple, (not in part,)
What with his art in youth, and youth in art,
Threw my affections in this charméd power,
Reserved the stalk, and gave him all my flower.

"Yet did I not, as some my equals did,
Demand of him, nor being desiréd yielded;
Finding myself in honor so forbid,
With safest distance I mine honor shielded:
Experience for me and many bulwarks builded
Of proofs new-bleeding, which remained the foil
Of this false jewel, and his amorous spoil.

"But ah! who ever shunned by precedent
The destined ill she must herself assay?
Or forced examples, 'gainst her own content,
To put the by-passed perils in her way?
Counsel may stop a while what will not stay;
For when we rage, advice is often seen
By blunting us to make our wits more keen.

"Nor gives it satisfaction to our blood,
That we must curb it upon others' proof,
To be forbid the sweets that seem so good,
For fear of harms that preach in our behoof.
O, appetite, from judgment stand aloof!
The one a palate hath that needs will taste,
Though reason weep, and cry, It is thy last.

'For further I could say, This man's untrue,
And knew the patterns of his foul beguiling;
Heard where his plants in others' orchards grew,
Saw how deceits were gilded in his smiling;
Knew vows were ever brokers to defiling;

Thought[1] characters and words, merely but art,
And bastards of his foul adulterous heart.

"And long upon these terms I held my city,
Till thus he 'gan besiege me: Gentle maid,
Have of my suffering youth some feeling pity,
And be not of my holy vows afraid:
That 's to you sworn, to none was ever said;
For feasts of love I have been called unto,
Till now did ne'er invite, nor never vow.

"All my offences that abroad you see
Are errors of the blood, none of the mind;
Love made them not; with acture[2] may they be,
Where neither party is nor true nor kind:
They sought their shame that so their shame did find;
And so much less of shame in me remains,
By how much of me their reproach contains.

"Among the many that mine eyes have seen,
Not one whose flame my heart so much as warmed,
Or my affection put to the smallest teen,[3]
Or any of my leisures ever charmed:
Harm have I done to them, but ne'er was harmed,
Kept hearts in liveries, but mine own was free,
And reigned, commanding in his monarchy.

[1] Malone — and he is followed in all modern editions — puts a comma after *thought*, and says, "It is here, I believe, a substantive." Surely *thought* is a verb. We have a regular sequence of verbs — heard — saw — knew — thought. How can thought be art? the art is in the expression of the thoughts by "characters and words." He who said "words were given us to conceal our thoughts" is a better commentator upon the passage than Malone.

[2] *Acture* is explained as synonymous with *action*.

[3] *Teen*, grief.

" Look here what tributes wounded fancies sent me,
Of paléd pearls, and rubies red as blood;
Figuring that they their passions likewise lent me
Of grief and blushes, aptly understood
In bloodless white and the encrimsoned mood;
Effects of terror and dear modesty,
Encamped in hearts, but fighting outwardly.

" And lo! behold these talents[1] of their hair,
With twisted metal amorously impleached,[2]
I have received from many a several fair,
(Their kind acceptance weepingly beseeched,)
With the annexions of fair gems enriched,
And deep-brained sonnets that did amplify
Each stone's dear nature, worth, and quality.

" The diamond, why 't was beautiful and hard,
Whereto his invised[3] properties did tend;
The deep-green emerald, in whose fresh regard
Weak sights their sickly radiance do amend;
The heaven-hued sapphire and the opal blend
With objects manifold; each several stone,
With wit well blazoned, smiled or made some moan.

" Lo! all these trophies of affections hot,
Of pensived and subdued desires the tender,
Nature hath charged me that I hoard them not,
But yield them up where I myself must render,
That is, to you, my origin and ender:
For these, of force, must your oblations be,
Since I their altar, you enpatron me.

[1] *Talents* is here used in the sense of something precious.
[2] *Impleached*, interwoven.
[3] *Invised*, invisible

"O then advance of yours that phraseless hand,
Whose white weighs down the airy scale of praise;
Take all these similes to your own command,
Hallowed with sighs that burning lungs did raise;
What me your minister, for you obeys,
Works under you; and to your audit comes
Their distract parcels in combinéd sums.

"Lo! this device was sent me from a nun,
Or sister sanctified of holiest note;
Which late her noble suit[1] in court did shun,
Whose rarest havings[2] made the blossoms[3] dote;
For she was sought by spirits of richest coat,[4]
But kept cold distance, and did thence remove,
To spend her living in eternal love.

"But O, my sweet, what labor is 't to leave
The thing we have not, mastering what not strives?
Paling[5] the place which did no form receive,
Playing patient sports in unconstrainéd gyves:
She that her fame so to herself contrives,
The scars of battle 'scapeth by the flight,
And makes her absence valiant, not her might.

"O pardon me, in that my boast is true;
The accident which brought me to her eye,

1 *Suit.* "The noble suit in court" is, we think, the suit made to her in court. Mr. Dyce says *suitors.*

2 *Havings.* Malone receives this as *accomplishments;* Mr. Dyce as *fortune.*

3 *Blossoms*, young men; the flower of the nobility.

4 *Of richest coat*, of highest descent.

5 *Paling.* In the old copy, *playing.* Malone's emendation of *paling* is sensible as well as ingenious.

Upon the moment did her force subdue,
And now she would the cagéd cloister fly:
Religious love put out religion's eye:
Not to be tempted, would she be immured,
And now, to tempt all, liberty procured.

"How mighty then you are, O, hear me tell!
The broken bosoms that to me belong
Have emptied all their fountains in my well,
And mine I pour your ocean all among:
I strong o'er them, and you o'er me being strong,
Must for your victory us all congest,
As compound love to physic your cold breast.

"My parts had power to charm a sacred sun,
Who, disciplined and dieted[1] in grace,
Believed her eyes when they to assail begun,
All vows and consecrations giving place.
O most potential love! vow, bond, nor space,
In thee hath neither sting, knot, nor confine,
For thou art all, and all things else are thine.

"When thou impressest, what are precepts worth
Of stale example? When thou wilt inflame,
How coldly those impediments stand forth
Of wealth, of filial fear, law, kindred, fame!
Love's arms are peace, 'gainst rule, 'gainst sense, 'gainst shame,
And sweetens in the suffering pangs it bears,
The aloes of all forces, shocks, and fears.

"Now all these hearts that do on mine depend,
Feeling it break, with bleeding groans they pine,

[1] *And dieted.* The old copy reads *I died.* A correspondent suggested the change to Malone.

And supplicant their sighs to you extend,
To leave the battery that you make 'gainst mine,
Lending soft audience to my sweet design,
And credent soul to that strong bonded oath,
That shall prefer and undertake my troth.

"This said, his watery eyes he did dismount,
Whose sights till then were levelled on my face;
Each cheek a river running from a fount
With brinish current downward flowed apace:
O, how the channel to the stream gave grace!
Who, glazed with crystal, gate[1] the glowing roses
That flame through water which their hue encloses.

"O father, what a hell of witchcraft lies
In the small orb of one particular tear!
But with the inundation of the eyes
What rocky heart to water will not wear?
What breast so cold that is not warmèd here?
O cleft effect![2] cold modesty, hot wrath,
Both fire from hence and chill extincture hath!

"For lo! his passion, but an art of craft,
Even there resolved my reason into tears;
There my white stole of chastity I daffed,
Shook off my sober guards, and civil[3] fears;
Appear to him, as he to me appears,
All melting; though our drops this difference bore,
His poisoned me, and mine did him restore.

[1] *Gate*, got, procured.
[2] *O cleft effect.* The reading of the original is *Or, cleft effect.* Malone substituted "*O cleft effect.*"
[3] *Civil*, decorous.

"In him a plenitude of subtle matter,
Applied to cautels,[1] all strange forms receives,
Of burning blushes, or of weeping water,
Or swooning paleness; and he takes and leaves,
In either's aptness, as it best deceives,
To blush at speeches rank, to weep at woes,
Or to turn white and swoon at tragic shows;

"That not a heart which in his level came
Could 'scape the hail of his all-hurting aim,
Showing fair nature is both kind and tame;
And, veiled in them, did win whom he would maim:
Against the thing he sought he would exclaim;
When he most burned in heart-wished luxury,
He preached pure maid, and praised cold chastity.

"Thus merely with the garment of a Grace
The naked and concealéd fiend he covered,
That the unexperienced gave the tempter place,
Which, like a cherubim, above them hovered.
Who, young and simple, would not be so lovered?
Ah me! I fell: and yet do question make
What I should do again for such a sake.

"O, that infected moisture of his eye,
O, that false fire which in his cheek so glowed,
O, that forced thunder from his heart did fly,
O, that sad breath his spongy lungs bestowed,
O, all that borrowed motion, seeming owed,[2]
Would yet again betray the fore-betrayed,
And new pervert a reconciléd maid!"

[1] *Cautels*, deceitful purposes.
[2] *Owed*, owned; his own.

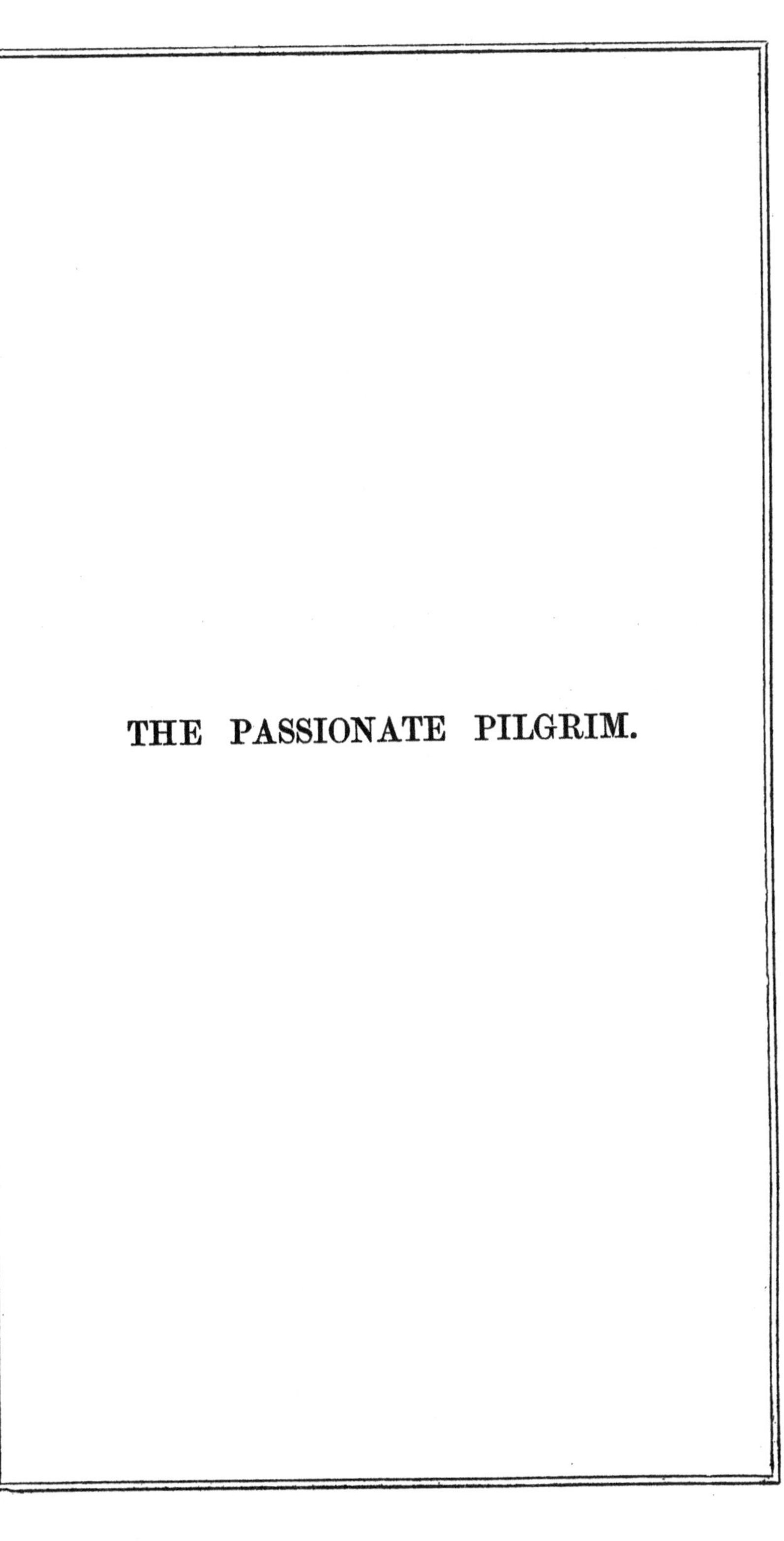

THE PASSIONATE PILGRIM.

THE PASSIONATE PILGRIM.

Did not the heavenly rhetoric of thine eye,
'Gainst whom the world could not hold argument,
Persuade my heart to this false perjury?
Vows for thee broke deserve not punishment.
A woman I forswore; but I will prove,
Thou being a goddess, I forswore not thee:
My vow was earthly, thou a heavenly love;
Thy grace being gained cures all disgrace in me.
My vow was breath, and breath a vapor is:
Then, thou fair sun, that on this earth doth shine,
Exhale this vapor vow; in thee it is:
If broken, then it is no fault of mine.
  If by me broke, what fool is not so wise
  To lose an oath to win a paradise?[1]

[1] The foregoing Sonnet appears, with some variations, in Love's Labor 's Lost, the first edition of which was printed in 1598. We give the lines in which the variations occur: —

> "'Gainst whom the world *cannot* hold argument."
> "*Vows are but breath*, and breath a vapor is;
> Then thou fair sun, *which* on *my* earth *dost* shine,
> *Exhal'st* this vapor vow; in thee it is."

The text of the play is evidently superior to that in The Passionate Pilgrim.

II.

Sweet Cytherea, sitting by a brook,
With young Adonis, lovely, fresh, and green,
Did court the lad with many a lovely look,
Such looks as none could look but beauty's queen.
She told him stories to delight his ear;
She showed him favors to allure his eye;
To win his heart, she touched him here and there:
Touches so soft still conquer chastity.
But whether unripe years did want conceit,
Or he refused to take her figured proffer,
The tender nibbler would not touch the bait,
But smile and jest at every gentle offer:
  Then fell she on her back, fair queen, and toward;
  He rose and ran away; ah, fool, too froward!

III.

If love make me forsworn, how shall I swear to love?
O, never faith could hold, if not to beauty vowed:
Though to myself forsworn, to thee I'll constant prove;
Those thoughts, to me like oaks, to thee like osiers bowed.
Study his bias leaves, and makes his book thine eyes,
Where all those pleasures live that art can comprehend.
If knowledge be the mark, to know thee shall suffice;
Well learnèd is that tongue that well can thee commend;
All ignorant that soul that sees thee without wonder;
Which is to me some praise, that I thy parts admire:
Thine eye Jove's lightning seems, thy voice his dreadful thunder.
Which (not to anger bent) is music and sweet fire.

Celestial as thou art, O, do not love that wrong,
To sing the heavens' praise with such an earthly tongue.[1]

IV.

Scarce had the sun dried up the dewy morn,
And scarce the herd gone to the hedge for shade,
When Cytherea, all in love forlorn,
A longing tarriance for Adonis made,
Under an osier growing by a brook,
A brook where Adon used to cool his spleen.
Hot was the day, she hotter that did look
For his approach, that often there had been.
Anon he comes, and throws his mantle by,
And stood stark naked on the brook's green brim:
The sun looked on the world with glorious eye,
Yet not so wistly as this queen on him:
He, spying her, bounced in, whereas he stood;
O Jove, quoth she, why was not I a flood?

V.

Fair is my love, but not so fair as fickle;
Mild as a dove, but neither true nor trusty:
Brighter than glass, and yet, as glass is, brittle;
Softer than wax, and yet, as iron, rusty:
A lily pale, with damask die to grace her,
None fairer, nor none falser to deface her.

[1] This Sonnet also occurs in Love's Labor's Lost, in which copy there are variations in several lines. In the second we read, "*Ah*, never faith;" in the third, "*faithful* prove;" in the fourth, "*were* oaks;" in the sixth, "*would* comprehend;" in the eleventh, "lightning *bears*." The concluding lines are as follows:—

"Celestial as thou art, O *pardon*, love, *this* wrong,
That sings heaven's praise with such an earthly tongue."

Her lips to mine how often hath she joined,
Between each kiss her oaths of true love swearing!
How many tales to please me hath she coined,
Dreading my love, the loss thereof still fearing!
  Yet in the midst of all her pure protestings,
  Her faith, her oaths, her tears, and all were jestings.

She burned with love, as straw with fire flameth,
She burned out love, as soon as straw outburneth;
She framed the love, and yet she foiled the framing,
She bade love last, and yet she fell a turning.
  Was this a lover, or a lecher whether?
  Bad in the best, though excellent in neither.

VI.

If music and sweet poetry agree,
As they must needs, the sister and the brother,
Then must the love be great 'twixt thee and me,
Because thou lov'st the one, and I the other.
Dowland to thee is dear, whose heavenly touch
Upon the lute doth ravish human sense;
Spenser to me, whose deep conceit is such,
As, passing all conceit, needs no defence.
Thou lov'st to hear the sweet melodious sound
That Phœbus' lute, the queen of music, makes;
And I in deep delight am chiefly drowned,
Whenas himself to singing he betakes.
  One god is god of both, as poets feign;
  One knight loves both, and both in thee remain.

VII.

Fair was the morn, when the fair queen of love,[1]
*   *   *   *   *   *   *   *
Paler for sorrow than her milk-white dove,
For Adon's sake, a youngster proud and wild;
Her stand she takes upon a steep-up hill;
Anon Adonis comes with horn and hounds;
She, silly queen, with more than love's good will,
Forbade the boy he should not pass those grounds;
Once, quoth she, did I see a fair, sweet youth
Here in these brakes deep-wounded with a boar,
Deep in the thigh, a spectacle of ruth!
See in my thigh, quoth she, here was the sore:
  She showed hers; he saw more wounds than one,
  And blushing fled, and left her all alone.

VIII.

Sweet rose, fair flower, untimely plucked, soon vaded,[2]
Plucked in the bud, and vaded in the spring!
Bright orient pearl, alack! too timely shaded!
Fair creature, killed too soon by death's sharp sting!
  Like a green plum that hangs upon a tree,
  And falls, through wind, before the fall should be.

I weep for thee, and yet no cause I have;
For why? thou left'st me nothing in thy will.
And yet thou left'st me more than I did crave;
For why? I cravéd nothing of thee still:
  O yes, dear friend, I pardon crave of thee;
  Thy discontent thou didst bequeath to me.

1 The second line is lost.

2 *Vaded*, faded. This form of the word often occurs in Shakspeare, and has been too frequently changed in reprints.

IX.

Venus, with Adonis[1] sitting by her,
Under a myrtle shade began to woo him:
She told the youngling how god Mars did try her,
And as he fell to her, she fell to him.
Even thus, quoth she, the warlike god embraced
me;
And then she clipped Adonis in her arms:
Even thus, quoth she, the warlike god unlaced me;
As if the boy should use like loving charms.
Even thus, quoth she, he seizéd on my lips,
And with her lips on his did act the seizure;
And as she fetchéd breath, away he skips,
And would not take her meaning nor her pleasure.
Ah! that I had my lady at this bay,
To kiss and clip me till I run away!

X.

Crabbéd age and youth
Cannot live together;
Youth is full of pleasance,
Age is full of care:
Youth like summer morn,
Age like winter weather;
Youth like summer brave,
Age like winter bare.

[1] This Sonnet is found in "Fidessa," by B. Griffin, 1596. There are great variations in that copy, for which see Illustrations. Amongst others we have the epithet *young* before Adonis. If we make a pause after Venus, the epithet is not necessary to the metre. The fourth line is given more metrically in "Fidessa:"—

"And as he fell to her, *so* she fell to him."

Youth is full of sport,
Age's breath is short,
  Youth is nimble, age is lame;
Youth is hot and bold,
Age is weak and cold;
  Youth is wild, and age is tame.
Age, I do abhor thee,
Youth, I do adore thee;
  O, my love, my love is young!
Age, I do defy thee;
O sweet shepherd, hie thee,
  For methinks thou stay'st too long.

XI.

Beauty is but a vain and doubtful good,
A shining gloss, that vadeth suddenly;
A flower that dies, when first it 'gins to bud;
A brittle glass, that 's broken presently:
  A doubtful good, a gloss, a glass, a flower,
  Lost, vaded, broken, dead within an hour.

And as goods lost are seld or never found,
As vaded gloss no rubbing will refresh,
As flowers dead lie withered on the ground,
As broken glass no cement can redress,[1]
  So beauty, blemished once, for ever 's lost,
  In spite of physic, painting, pain, and cost.

[1] In the twenty-ninth volume of the "Gentleman's Magazine" a copy of this poem is given, as from an ancient manuscript, in which there are the following variations: —

"And as goods lost are seld or never found,
As faded gloss no rubbing will *excite*,
As flowers dead lie withered on the ground,
As broken glass no cement can *unite*."

XII.

Good night, good rest. Ah! neither be my share:
She bade good night, that kept my rest away;
And daffed me to a cabin hanged with care,
To descant on the doubts of my decay.
Farewell, quoth she, and come again to-morrow;
Fare well I could not, for I supped with sorrow.

Yet at my parting sweetly did she smile,
In scorn or friendship, nill I construe whether:
'T may be, she joyed to jest at my exile,
'T may be, again to make me wander thither:
Wander, a word for shadows like myself,
As take the pain, but cannot pluck the pelf.

XIII.

Lord, how mine eyes throw gazes to the east!
My heart doth charge the watch; the morning rise
Doth cite each moving sense from idle rest.
Not daring trust the office of mine eyes,
While Philomela sits and sings, I sit and mark;
And wish her lays were tunéd like the lark;

For she doth welcome daylight with her ditty,
And drives away dark, dismal-dreaming night:
The night so packed, I post unto my pretty;
Heart hath his hope, and eyes their wishéd sight;
Sorrow changed to solace, solace mixed with sorrow;
For why? she sighed, and bade me come to-morrow.

Were I with her, the night would post too soon:
But now are minutes added to the hours;

To spite me now, each minute seems a moon;[1]
Yet not for me, shine sun to succor flowers!
Pack night, peep day; good day, of night now borrow;
Short, night, to-night, and length thyself to-morrow.

SONNETS

SUNDRY NOTES OF MUSIC.

XIV.

It was a lordling's daughter, the fairest one of three,
That likéd of her master as well as well might be,
Till looking on an Englishman, the fairest that eye could see,
Her fancy fell a turning.
Long was the combat doubtful, that love with love did fight,
To leave master loveless, or kill the gallant knight:
To put in practice either, alas it was a spite
Unto the silly damsel.

[1] *A moon.* The original has *an hour* — evidently a misprint. The emendation of *moon*, in the sense of *month*, is by Steevens, and it ought to atone for some faults of the commentator.

But one must be refuséd, more mickle was the pain,
That nothing could be uséd, to turn them both to gain,
For of the two the trusty knight was wounded with disdain:
Alas, she could not help it!
Thus art, with arms contending, was victor of the day,
Which by a gift of learning did bear the maid away;
Then lullaby, the learnéd man hath got the lady gay;
For now my song is ended.

XV.

On a day, (alack the day!)
Love, whose month was ever May,
Spied a blossom passing fair,
Playing in the wanton air:
Through the velvet leaves the wind,
All unseen, 'gan passage find;
That the lover, sick to death,
Wished himself the heaven's breath.
Air, quoth he, thy cheeks may blow;
Air, would I might triumph so!
But, alas, my hand hath sworn
Ne'er to pluck thee from thy thorn:
Vow, alack, for youth unmeet,
Youth, so apt to pluck a sweet.
Thou for whom Jove would swear
Juno but an Ethiope were;
And deny himself for Jove,
Turning mortal for thy love.[1]

[1] This beautiful little poem also occurs in Love's Labor's Lost. In that copy, in the second line, we find "*is every* May;" *every*

XVI.

My flocks feed not,
My ewes breed not,
My rams speed not,
All is amiss:
Love is dying,
Faith 's defying,
Heart 's denying,
Causer of this,[1]
All my merry jigs are quite forgot,
All my lady's love is lost, God wot:
Where her faith was firmly fixed in love,
There a nay is placed without remove.
One silly cross
Wrought all my loss;
O frowning Fortune, cursèd, fickle dame.
For now I see,
Inconstancy
More in women than in men remain.

which is repeated in the folio of 1623, is clearly a mistake. In the eleventh line we have, —

"But, *alack*, my hand *is* sworn."

In the play there is a couplet not found in The Passionate Pilgrim: —

"Do not call it sin in me,
That I am forsworn for thee."

These lines precede "Thou for whom."

1 We have two other ancient copies of this poem — one in "England's Helicon," 1600; the other in a collection of Madrigals by Thomas Weelkes, 1597. In "England's Helicon" these lines are thus given: —

"Love is denying, Faith is defying;
Hearts renging, (renying,) causer of this."

In black mourn I,
All fears scorn I,
Love hath forlorn me,
  Living in thrall:
Heart is bleeding,
All help needing,
(O, cruel speeding!)
  Fraughted with gall.
My shepherd's pipe can sound no deal,[1]
My wether's bell rings doleful knell;
My curtail dog, that wont to have played,
Plays not at all, but seems afraid;
With sighs so deep,
Procures[2] to weep,
  In howling-wise, to see my doleful plight.
How sighs resound
Through heartless ground,
  Like a thousand vanquished men in bloody fight!

Clear wells spring not,
Sweet birds sing not,
Green plants bring not
  Forth; they die;[3]
Herds stand weeping,
Flocks all sleeping,
Nymphs back peeping,
  Fearfully.
All our pleasure known to us poor swains,
All our merry meetings on the plains,

[1] *No deal*, in no degree: *some deal* and *no deal* were common expressions.

[2] *Procures*. The curtail dog is the nominative case to this verb.

[3] The reading in Weelkes's Madrigals is an improvement of this passage:—

"Loud bells ring not
Cheerfully."

All our evening sport from us is fled,
All our love is lost, for Love is dead.
Farewell, sweet lass,[1]
Thy like ne'er was
For a sweet content, the cause of all my moan:[2]
Poor Coridon
Must live alone,
Other help for him I see that there is none.

XVII.

Whenas thine eye hath chose the dame,
And stalled the deer that thou should'st strike,[3]
Let reason rule things worthy blame,
As well as fancy, partial might;[4]
Take counsel of some wiser head,
Neither too young, nor yet unwed.

And when thou com'st thy tale to tell,
Smooth not thy tongue with filéd talk,
Lest she some subtle practice smell;
(A cripple soon can find a halt:)
But plainly say thou lov'st her well,
And set her person forth to sell.[5]

1 *Lass.* This is the reading of Weelkes. The Passionate Pilgrim has *love.*

2 *Moan.* This is the reading in "England's Helicon." The Passionate Pilgrim has *woe.*

3 *Strike.* So the original. Mr. Dyce, who seldom indulges in conjectural emendation, alters the word to *smite*, "for the sake of the rhyme." This we think is scarcely allowable; for there are many examples of loose rhymes in these little poems. In the seventh stanza of this poem we have *nought* to rhyme with *oft.*

4 *Fancy* is here used as *love*, and *might* as *power*. Steevens, mischievously, we should imagine, changed *partial might* to *partial tike;* and Malone adopts this reading, which makes Cupid a bull-dog.

5 *Sell.* The reading of The Passionate Pilgrim is *sale.* A manuscript in the possession of Mr. Lysons gives us *sell.*

What though her frowning brows be bent,
Her cloudy looks will calm[1] ere night;
And then too late she will repent,
That thus dissembled her delight;
  And twice desire, ere it be day,
  That which with scorn she put away.

What though she strive to try her strength
And ban and brawl, and say thee nay,
Her feeble force will yield at length,
When craft hath taught her thus to say:
  "Had women been so strong as men,
  In faith you had not had it then."

And to her will frame all thy ways;
Spare not to spend, — and chiefly there
Where thy desert may merit praise,
By ringing in thy lady's ear:
  The strongest castle, tower, and town,
  The golden bullet beats it down.

Serve always with assuréd trust,
And in thy suit be humble, true;
Unless thy lady prove unjust,
Press never thou to choose anew:
  When time shall serve, be thou not slack
  To proffer, though she put thee back.

The wiles and guiles that women work,
Dissembled with an outward show,
The tricks and toys that in them lurk,
The cock that treads them shall not know.

[1] *Calm* is the reading of the Passionate Pilgrim; the manuscript just mentioned has *clear*.

Have you not heard it said full oft,
A woman's nay doth stand for nought?

Think women still to strive with men,
To sin, and never for to saint:
There is no heaven, by holy then,
When time with age shall them attaint.[1]
Were kisses all the joys in bed,
One woman would another wed.

But soft; enough, — too much I fear,
Lest that my mistress hear my song;
She 'll not stick to round me i' th' ear,
To teach my tongue to be so long:
Yet will she blush, here be it said,
To hear her secrets so bewrayed.

XVIII.

Live with me, and be my love,
And we will all the pleasures prove
That hills and valleys, dales and fields,
And all the craggy mountains yields.

There will we sit upon the rocks,
And see the shepherds feed their flocks,
By shallow rivers, by whose falls
Melodious birds sing madrigals.

1 These four lines are thus given in Mr. Lysons's manuscript: —

"Think, women love to match with men,
And not to live so like a saint:
Here is no heaven; they holy then
Begin, when age doth them attaint."

The one copy is somewhat more intelligible than the other.

There will I make thee a bed of roses,
With a thousand fragrant posies,
A cap of flowers, and a kirtle
Embroidered all with leaves of myrtle.

A belt of straw and ivy buds,
With coral clasps and amber studs;
And if these pleasures may thee move,
Then live with me, and be my love.

LOVE'S ANSWER.

If that the world and love were young,
And truth in every shepherd's tongue,
These pretty pleasures might me move
To live with thee and be thy love.[1]

XIX.

As it fell upon a day,
In the merry month of May,
Sitting in a pleasant shade
Which a grove[2] of myrtles made,
Beasts did leap, and birds did sing,
Trees did grow, and plants did spring:
Every thing did banish moan
Save the nightingale alone:

[1] We insert this poem in the order in which it appears in The Passionate Pilgrim. The variations of other copies will be found in our Illustrations.

[2] This poem is also incompletely printed in "England's Helicon;" where it bears the signature *Ignoto*. There are some variations in the twenty-eight lines there given, as in the case before us, of *grove* in The Passionate Pilgrim, which in "England's Helicon" is *group*.

She, poor bird, as all forlorn,
Leaned her breast up-till[1] a thorn,
And there sung the dolefull'st ditty,
That to hear it was great pity:
Fie, fie, fie, now would she cry,
Teru, Teru, by and by:
That to hear her so complain,
Scarce I could from tears refrain;
For her griefs so lively shown,
Made me think upon mine own.
Ah! thought I, thou mourn'st in vain;
None take pity on thy pain:
Senseless trees, they cannot hear thee;
Ruthless bears,[2] they will not cheer thee.
King Pandion, he is dead;
All thy friends are lapped in lead:
All thy fellow-birds do sing,
Careless of thy sorrowing.
[Even so, poor bird, like thee,
None alive will pity me.[3]]
Whilst as fickle Fortune smiled,
Thou and I were both beguiled.
Every one that flatters thee
Is no friend in misery.
Words are easy like the wind;
Faithful friends are hard to find.
Every man will be thy friend,
Whilst thou hast wherewith to spend;
But if store of crowns be scant,
No man will supply thy want.

1 *Up-till.* This is given *against* in "England's Helicon."
2 *Bears.* In "England's Helicon" *beasts.*
3 The poem in "England's Helicon" here ends; but the two lines with which it concludes are wanting in The Passionate Pilgrim.

If that one be prodigal,
Bountiful they will him call:
And with such-like flattering,
"Pity but he were a king."
If he be addict to vice,
Quickly him they will entice;
If to women he be bent,
They have him at commandement;
But if fortune once do frown,
Then farewell his great renown;
They that fawned on him before,
Use his company no more.
He that is thy friend indeed,
He will help thee in thy need;
If thou sorrow, he will weep;
If thou wake, he cannot sleep:
Thus of every grief in heart
He with thee doth bear a part.
These are certain signs to know
Faithful friend from flattering foe.

SONG.

Take, O, take those lips away,
 That so sweetly were forsworn,
And those eyes, the break of day,
 Lights that do mislead the morn:
But my kisses bring again,
Seals of love, but sealed in vain.

Hide, O, hide those hills of snow,
  Which thy frozen bosom bears,
On whose tops the pinks that grow
  Are of those that April wears.
But first set my poor heart free,
Bound in those icy chains by thee.[1]

[1] The collection entitled The Passionate Pilgrim, &c., ends with the Sonnet to Sundry Notes of Music which we have numbered XIX. Malone adds to the collection this exquisite song, of which we find the first verse in Measure for Measure. (See Illustrations.)

VERSES

AMONG THE

ADDITIONAL POEMS TO CHESTER'S LOVE'S MARTYR, 1601.

LET the bird of loudest lay,
On the sole Arabian tree,[1]
Herald sad and trumpet be,
To whose sound chaste wings obey.

But thou, shrieking harbinger,
Foul pre-currer of the fiend,
Augur of the fever's end,
To this troop come thou not near

[1] There is a curious coincidence in a passage in The Tempest:—

" Now I will believe
That there are unicorns; that in Arabia
There is one tree, the phœnix throne."

From this session interdict
Every fowl of tyrant wing,
Save the eagle, feathered king:
Keep the obsequy so strict.

Let the priest in surplice white,
That defunctive music can,[1]
Be the death-divining swan,
Lest the requiem lack his right.

And thou, treble-dated crow,
That thy sable gender mak'st
With the breath thou giv'st and tak'st,
'Mongst our mourners shalt thou go.

Here the anthem doth commence:
Love and constancy is dead;
Phœnix and the turtle fled
In a mutual flame from hence.

So they loved, as love in twain
Had the essence but in one;
Two distincts, division none;
Number there in love was slain.

Hearts remote, yet not asunder;
Distance, and no space was seen
'Twixt the turtle and his queen;
But in them it were a wonder.

So between them love did shine,
That the turtle saw his right
Flaming in the phœnix' sight:
Either was the other's mine.

[1] *Can*, knows.

Property was thus appalled,
That the self was not the same;
Single nature's double name
Neither two nor one was called.

Reason, in itself confounded,
Saw division grow together;
To themselves yet either-neither,
Simple were so well compounded:

That it cried how true a twain
Seemeth this concordant one!
Love hath reason, reason none,
If what parts can so remain.

Whereupon it made this threne[1]
To the phœnix and the dove,
Co-supremes and stars of love;
As chorus to their tragic scene.

Threnos.

Beauty, truth, and rarity,
Grace in all simplicity,
Here enclosed in cinders lie

Death is now the phœnix' nest;
And the turtle's loyal breast
To eternity doth rest,

Leaving no posterity:—
'Twas not their infirmity
It was married chastity.

[1] *Threne*, funereal song.

Truth may seem, but cannot be ;
Beauty brag, but 'tis not she ;
Truth and beauty buried be.

To this urn let those repair
That are either true or fair ;
For these dead birds sigh a prayer.

ILLUSTRATIONS

OF

A LOVER'S COMPLAINT, THE PASSIONATE PILGRIM, &c.

A LOVER'S COMPLAINT was first printed with the Sonnets in 1609. It was reprinted in 1640, in that collection called Shakspeare's Poems, in which the original order of the Sonnets was entirely disregarded, some were omitted, and this poem was thrust in amidst translations from Ovid which had been previously claimed by another writer. Of these we shall have presently to speak. There can be no doubt of the genuineness of A Lover's Complaint. It is distinguished by that condensation of thought and outpouring of imagery which are the characteristics of Shakspeare's poems. The effect consequent upon these qualities is, that the language is sometimes obscure, and the metaphors occasionally appear strange and forced. It is very different from any production of Shakspeare's contemporaries. As in the case of the Venus and Adonis, and the Lucrece, we feel that the power of the writer is in perfect subjection to his art. He is never carried away by the force of his own conceptions. We mention these attributes merely with reference to the undoubted character of the poem as belonging to the Shakspearian system: we shall have occasion to notice it again.

The PASSIONATE PILGRIM was originally published in 1599, by William Jaggard, with the name of Shakspeare on the title-page. A reprint, with some additions and alterations of arrangement, appeared in 1612, bearing the following title: "The Passionate Pilgrime, or certaine amorous Sonnets, betweene Venus and Adonis, newly corrected and augmented. By W. Shakspeare. The third Edition. Whereunto is newly added two Love-Epistles, the first from Paris to Hellen, and Hellen's Answere backe again to Paris. Printed by W. Jaggard, 1612." The second edition was in all probability, a mere reprint of the first edition; but in the third edition there are, as the title-page implies, important alterations. There is one alteration which is not expressed in the title page. A distinction is established in the character of the poems by classifying six of them under a second title-page, "Sonnets to Sundry Notes of Musick." This distinction we have preserved. There can be no doubt, we apprehend, that the "newly added two Love-Epistles, the first from Paris to Hellen, and Hellen's Answere backe again to Paris," were not written by Shakspeare. There is the best evidence that they were written by Thomas Heywood. In 1609 that writer published a folio volume of considerable pretension, entitled "Troia Britanica, or Great Britaine's Troy." In this volume appear the two translations from Ovid which William Jaggard published as Shakspeare's in 1612. Heywood in that year published a treatise entitled "An Apology for Actors;" to which is prefixed an epistle to his bookseller, Nicholas Okes. The letter is a curious morsel in literary history: —

"To my approved good friend, Mr. Nicholas Okes.

"The infinite faults escaped in my book of Britain's Troy, by the negligence of the printer, as the misquotations, mistaking of syllables, misplacing half-lines, coining of strange and never-heard-of words: these being without number, when I would have taken a particular account of the errata, the printer answered me, he would not publish his own disworkmanship, but rather let his own fault lie upon the neck of the author: and being fearful that others of his quality had been of the same nature and condition, and finding you, on the contrary, so careful and industrious, so serious and laborious, to do the author all the rights of the press, I could not choose but gratulate your honest endeavors with this short remembrance. Here, likewise, I must necessarily insert a manifest injury done me in that work, by taking the two Epistles of Paris to Helen, and Helen to Paris, and printing them in a less volume, under the name of another, which may put the world in opinion I might steal them from him, and he, to do himself right, hath since published them in his own name: but as I must acknowledge my lines not worthy his patronage under whom he hath published them, so the author I know much offended with M. Jaggard that (altogether unknown to him) presumed to make so bold with his name. These, and the like dishonesties, I know you to be clear of; and I could wish but to be the happy author of so worthy a work as I could willingly commit to your care and workmanship.

"Yours ever,

"THOMAS HEYWOOD."

Jaggard, upon the publication of this, appears to have been compelled to do some sort of justice to Heywood, however imperfect. He cancelled the title-page of the edition of The Passionate Pilgrim of 1612, removing the name of Shakspeare, and printing the collection without any author's name. Malone had a copy of the book with both title-pages. This transaction naturally throws great discredit on the honesty of the publisher; and might lead us to suspect that Heywood's was not the only case in which Shakspeare was "much offended with M. Jaggard, that (altogether unknown to him) presumed to make so bold with his name." There are other pieces in The Passionate Pilgrim that have been attributed on reasonable grounds to other authors than Shakspeare. It may be well, therefore, that we should run through the whole collection, offering a few brief observations on the authenticity of these poems.

The two first Sonnets in Jaggard's edition of The Passionate Pilgrim are those which, with some alterations, appear as the 138th and the 144th in the collection of Sonnets published in 1609. The variations of those Sonnets, as they appeared in The Passionate Pilgrim, are given in our foot-notes at pages 216 and 219. The third Sonnet in the collection (the first in our reprint) is found in Love's Labor 's Lost. The fourth is one of the four Sonnets on the subject of Venus and Adonis. In Malone's first edition of these poems (1780) he followed the order of the original, as we now do; but in his posthumous edition, by Boswell, that order is changed, and the four Sonnets on the subject of Venus and Adonis are placed together, the first in the series. Malone's opinion, which he did not subsequently alter, was, that "several of the Sonnets in this collection seem to have been essays of the author when he first conceived the notion of writing a poem on the subject of Venus and Adonis, and before the scheme of his work was completely adjusted." Boswell justly says that some doubt is thrown upon Malone's conjecture by the circumstance that one of these four Sonnets, with some variations, is found in a volume of poems published before The Passionate Pilgrim, namely, "Fidessa more Chaste than Kinde," by B. Griffin, 1596. In Griffin's little volume, which has been reprinted, the Sonnet stands as follows: —

"Venus, with young Adonis sitting by her,
Under a myrtle shade began to woo him;
She told the youngling how god Mars did try her,
And as he fell to her, so fell she to him.
Even thus, quoth she, the wanton god embraced me;
And thus she clasped Adonis in her arms:
Even thus, quoth she, the warlike god unlaced me,
As if the boy should use like loving charms.
But he, a wayward boy, refused her offer,
And ran away, the beauteous queen neglecting;
Showing both folly to abuse her proffer,
And all his sex of cowardice detecting.
O, that I had my mistress at that bay,
To kiss and clip me till I ran away!"

The variations between this Sonnet and that printed in the Passionate Pilgrim are very remarkable; but there can be no doubt, we should think, that the authorship belongs to Griffin. This volume was not published anonymously; and it is dedicated "to Mr. Wm. Essex, of Lambourne, Berks, and to the Gentlemen of the Inns of Court." It is not likely that he would have adopted a Sonnet by Shakspeare floating about in society, and made it his own by these changes.

The fifth poem in Jaggard's collection is Biron's Sonnet in Love's Labor 's Lost. The seventh, "Fair is my love," stands as Shakspeare's, without any rival to impugn Jaggard's authority. The eighth is not so fortunate. It would be pleasant to believe that the Sonnet, commencing

"If music and sweet poetry agree,"

was written by Shakspeare.* It would be satisfactory that the

* We have previously expressed an opinion that it was written by Shakspeare: it has been generally attributed to him; and we had adopted the received opinion, looking chiefly at the character of the Sonnet. See page 319.

greatest dramatic poet of the world should pay his homage to that great contemporary from whose exhaustless wells of imagination every real lover of poetry has since drawn waters of "deep delight." But that Sonnet is claimed by another; and we believe that the claim must be admitted. There was another publisher of the name of Jaggard — John Jaggard; and he, in 1598, printed a volume bearing this title: "Encomion of Lady Pecunia; or, the Praise of Money: The Complaint of Poetrie for the Death of Liberalitie: *i. e.* The Combat betweene Conscience and Covetousness in the Minde of Man: with Poems in divers Humors." The volume bears the name, as author, of Richard Barnfield, graduate of Oxford, who had previously published a volume entitled "Cynthia." The volume of 1598 contains a Sonnet "addressed to his friend Master R. L., in praise of Music and Poetry." This is the Sonnet that a year after William Jaggard prints with the name of Shakspeare. But Barnfield's volume contains another poem, which the publisher of The Passionate Pilgrim also assigns to Shakspeare, amongst the "Sonnets to Sundry Notes of Music" — the last in the collection, —

"As it fell upon a day."

It is remarkable that, after the publication of Barnfield's volume in 1598, and The Passionate Pilgrim in 1599, a large portion of this poem was, in 1600, printed in "England's Helicon," with the signature of "Ignoto." It there follows the poem which is the 18th in The Passionate Pilgrim, —

"My flocks feed not."

That poem bears the title of "The Unknown Shepherd's Complaint," and is also signed, in "England's Helicon," "Ignoto." "As it fell upon a day" is entitled "Another of the same Shepherd's." Both the poems in "England's Helicon" immediately follow one bearing the signature of "W. Shakespeare," the beautiful Sonnet in Love's Labor 's Lost, —

"On a day, alack the day," —

which is given as one of the Sonnets to Music in The Passionate Pilgrim.

For the following poems in The Passionate Pilgrim no claim of authorship has appeared further to impugn the credibility of W. Jaggard: —

"Sweet rose, fair flower."
"Crabbed age and youth."
"Beauty is but a vain and doubtful good."
"Good night, good rest."
"Lord, how mine eyes."
"It was a lording's daughter."
"Whenas thine eye."

But there is a poem, imperfectly printed in The Passionate Pilgrim, (and which we have reprinted, that the reader may have before him what that work originally contained,) of a higher reputation than any poem in the collection.

"Live with me, and be my love"

is printed in "England's Helicon" with the signature of "Chr. Marlow," and the copy there given is as follows: —

THE PASSIONATE SHEPHERD TO HIS LOVE.

Come live with me, and be my love,
And we will all the pleasures prove
That valleys, groves, hills, and fields,
Woods, or steepy mountains yields.

And we will sit upon the rocks,
Seeing the shepherds feed their flocks,
By shallow rivers, to whose falls
Melodious birds sing madrigals.

And I will make thee beds of roses,
And a thousand fragrant posies,
A cap of flowers, and a kirtle
Embroidered all with leaves of myrtle.

A gown made of the finest wool,
Which from our pretty lambs we pull;
Fair linèd slippers for the cold,
With buckles of the purest gold:

A belt of straw, and ivy buds
With coral clasps and amber studs.
And if these pleasures may thee move,
Come live with me, and be my love.

The shepherd swains shall dance and sing
For thy delights each May-morning;
If these delights thy mind may move,
Then live with me, and be my love.

CHR. MARLOW.

In that collection it is immediately succeeded by another poem, almost equally celebrated, bearing the signature of "Ignoto:"—

THE NYMPH'S REPLY TO THE SHEPHERD.

If all the world and love were young,
And truth in every shepherd's tongue,
These pretty pleasures might me move
To live with thee, and be thy love.

Time drives the flocks from field to fold,
When rivers rage, and rocks grow cold;
And Philomel becometh dumb;
The rest complains of cares to come.

The flowers do fade, and wanton fields
To wayward winter reckoning yields;
A honey tongue, a heart of gall,
Is fancy's spring, but sorrow's fall.

Thy gowns, thy shoes, thy beds of roses,
Thy cap, thy kirtle, and thy posies,
Soon break, soon wither, soon forgotten,
In folly ripe, in reason rotten.

Thy belt of straw, and ivy buds,
Thy coral clasps, and amber studs,
All these in me no means can move
To come to thee, and be thy love.

But could youth last, and love still breed,
Had joys no date, nor age no need,
Then these delights my mind might move
To live with thee, and be thy love.

IGNOTO.

lustrations of The Merry Wives of Windsor, Act III., we have already noticed the probable authorship of these poems. Warburton, upon the authority of The Passionate Pilgrim, assigns "Come live with me" to Shakspeare. But we fear that Mr. William Jaggard's authority is not quite so much to be relied upon as that of "England's Helicon;" and, moreover, there was an honest witness living some fifty years after, whose traditionary evidence must go far to settle the point. We cannot resist the pleasure of transcribing dear Izaak Walton's testimony: "Look! under that broad beech-tree I sat down when I was last this way a-fishing. And the birds in the adjoining grove seemed to have a friendly contention with an echo, whose dead voice seemed to live in a hollow tree near to the brow of that primrose-hill. There I sat viewing the silver streams glide silently towards their centre, the tempestuous sea; but sometimes opposed by rugged roots and pebble-stones, which broke their waves, and turned them into foam. And sometimes I beguiled time by viewing the harmless lambs — some leaping securely in the cool shade, whilst others sported themselves in the cheerful sun; and saw others craving comfort from the swollen udders of their bleating dams. As thus I sat, these and other sights had so fully possessed my soul with content that I thought, as the poet has happily expressed it, —

'I was for that time lifted above earth,
And possessed joys not promised in my birth.'

As I left this place, and entered into the next field, a second pleasure entertained me: 'twas a handsome milkmaid, that had not yet attained so much age and wisdom as to load her mind with any fears of many things that will never be, as too many men too often do; but she cast away all care, and sung like a nightingale: her voice was good, and the ditty fitted for it; it was that smooth song which was made by Kit Marlow, now at least fifty years ago. And the milkmaid's mother sung an answer to it, which was made by Sir Walter Raleigh in his younger days.

"They were old-fashioned poetry, but choicely good; I think much better than the strong lines that are now in fashion in this critical age. Look yonder! on my word, yonder they both be a-milking again. I will give her the chub, and persuade them to sing those two songs to us."

We have now gone through all the poems of The Passionate Pilgrim; and, taking away the five poems which are undoubtedly Shakspeare's, but which are to be found in the Sonnets and Love's Labor 's Lost, and considering at least as apocryphal those which have been assigned to other authors, there is not a great deal left that posterity may thank Mr. William Jaggard for having rescued from oblivion.

There are two other poems that usually follow The Passionate Pilgrim, though they form no part of that collection. The first is the celebrated song of

"Take, O take those lips away."

Our readers are aware that the first stanza is found in Measure for Measure, as sung by a boy to Mariana, who says, "Break off thy song." The two stanzas are in the tragedy, ascribed to Fletcher of "Rollo, Duke of Normandy." There is no possibility, we apprehend, of deciding the authorship of the second stanza, (see Illustrations of Measure for Measure, Act IV.) The other poem, beginning, —

"Let the bird of loudest lay," —

is found with Shakspeare's name in a book printed in 1601, the greater part of which consists of a poem translated from the Italian by Robert Chester, entitled "Love's Martyr; or, Rosalin's Complaint: allegorically shadowing the Truth of Love, in the constant Fate of the Phœnix and Turtle." There is a second title to this volume prefixed to some supplementary verses: "Hereafter follow diverse Poetical Essaies on the former Subject, viz., the Turtle and Phœnix. Done by the best and chiefest of our modern Writers, with their Names subscribed to their particular Works. Never before extant." The name "Wm. Shake-speare" is subscribed to this poem, in the same way that the names of Ben Jonson, Marston, and Chapman are subscribed to other poems.

SUPPLEMENTARY NOTICE

TO THE

POEMS.

"If the first heir of my invention prove deformed, I shall be sorry it had so noble a godfather." These are the words which, in relation to the Venus and Adonis, Shakspeare addressed, in 1593, to the Earl of Southampton. Are we to accept them literally? Was the Venus and Adonis the first production of Shakspeare's imagination? Or did he put out of his view those dramatic performances which he had then unquestionably produced, in deference to the critical opinions which regarded plays as works not belonging to "invention"? We think that he used the words in a literal sense. We regard the Venus and Adonis as the production of a very young man, improved, perhaps, considerably in the interval between its first composition and its publication, but distinguished by peculiarities which belong to the wild luxuriance of youthful power, — such power, however, as few besides Shakspeare have ever possessed.

A deep thinker and eloquent writer, Julius Charles Hare, thus describes "the spirit of self-sacrifice," as applied to poetry: —

"The might of the imagination is manifested by its launching forth from the petty creek, where the accidents of birth moored it, into the wide ocean of being, — by its going abroad into the world around, passing into whatever it meets with, animating it, and becoming one with it. This complete union and identification of the poet with his poem, — this suppression of his own individual insulated consciousness, with its narrowness of thought and pettiness of feeling, — is what we admire in the great masters of that which for this reason we justly call classical poetry, as representing that which is symbolical and universal, not that which is merely occasional and peculiar. This gives them that majestic calmness which still breathes upon us from the statues of their gods. This invests their works with that lucid, transparent atmosphere wherein every form stands out in perfect definiteness and distinctness, only beautified by the distance which idealizes it. This has delivered those works from the casualties of time and space, and has lifted them up like stars into the pure firmament of thought, so that they do not shine on one spot alone, nor fade like earthly flowers, but journey on from clime to clime, shedding the light of beauty on generation after generation. The same quality, amounting to a total extinction of his own selfish being, so that his spirit became a mighty organ through which Nature gave utterance to the full diapason of her notes, is what we wonder at in our own great dramatist, and is the groundwork of all his other powers; for it is only when purged of selfishness that the intellect becomes fitted for receiving the inspirations of genius." *

What Mr. Hare so justly considers as the great moving principle of "classical poetry," — what he further notes as the preëminent characteristic of "our own great dramatist," — is abundantly found in that great dramatist's earliest work. Coleridge was the first to point out this pervading quality in the Venus and Adonis: and he has done this

* The Victory of Faith; and other Sermons." By Julius Charles Hare, M. A. 1840. P. 277.

so admirably, that it would be profanation were we to attempt to elucidate the point in any other than his own words: —

"It is throughout as if a superior spirit, more intuitive, more intimately conscious, even than the characters themselves, not only of every outward look and act, but of the flux and reflux of the mind in all its subtlest thoughts and feelings, were placing the whole before our view; himself meanwhile unparticipating in the passions, and actuated only by that pleasurable excitement which had resulted from the energetic fervor of his own spirit in so vividly exhibiting what it had so accurately and profoundly contemplated. I think I should have conjectured from these poems, that even then the great instinct which impelled the poet to the drama was secretly working in him, prompting him by a series and never-broken chain of imagery, always vivid, and, because unbroken, often minute, — by the highest effort of the picturesque in words of which words are capable, higher, perhaps, than was ever realized by any other poet, even Dante not excepted, — to provide a substitute for that visual language, that constant intervention and running comment by tone, look, and gesture, which in his dramatic works he was entitled to expect from the players. His Venus and Adonis seem at once the characters themselves, and the whole representation of those characters by the most consummate actors. You seem to be *told* nothing, but to see and hear every thing. Hence it is, that, from the perpetual activity of attention required on the part of the reader, — from the rapid flow, the quick change, and the playful nature of the thoughts and images, — and, above all, from the alienation, and, if I may hazard such an expression, the utter *aloofness* of the poet's own feelings from those of which he is at once the painter and the analyst, — that though the very subject cannot but detract from the pleasure of a delicate mind, yet never was poem less dangerous on a moral account." *

Coleridge, in the preceding chapter of his "Literary Life," says, "During the first year that Mr. Wordsworth and

* "Biographia Litoraria," 1817, vol. ii. p. 15.

I were neighbors, our conversations turned frequently on the two cardinal points of poetry — the power of exciting the sympathy of the reader by a faithful adherence to the truth of nature, and the power of giving the interest of novelty by the modifying colors of imagination." In Coleridge's "Literary Remains," the Venus and Adonis is cited as furnishing a signal example of "that affectionate love of nature and natural objects, without which no man could have observed so steadily, or painted so truly and passionately, the very minutest beauties of the external world." The description of the hare-hunt is there given at length as a specimen of this power. A remarkable proof of the completeness as well as accuracy of Shakspeare's description lately presented itself to our mind, in running through a little volume, full of talent, published in 1825, "Essays and Sketches of Character, by the late Richard Ayton, Esq." There is a paper on hunting, and especially on hare-hunting. He says, "I am not one of the perfect fox-hunters of these realms; but having been in the way, of late, of seeing a good deal of various modes of hunting, I would, for the benefit of the uninitiated, set down the results of my observations." In this matter he writes with a perfect unconsciousness that he is describing what any one has described before. But as accurate an observer *had* been before him: —

"She (the hare) generally returns to the seat from which she was put up, running, as all the world knows, in a circle, or something sometimes like it, we had better say, that we may keep on good terms with the mathematical. At starting, she tears away at her utmost speed for a mile or more, and distances the dogs half-way: she then returns, diverging a little to the right or left, that she may not run into the mouths of her enemies — a necessity which accounts for what we call the circularity of her course. Her flight from home is direct and precipitate; but on her way back, when she has gained a little time for consideration and stratagem, she describes a curious labyrinth of short turnings and windings, as if to perplex the dogs by the intricacy of her track."

Compare this with Shakspeare: —

"And when thou hast on foot the purblind hare,
Mark the poor wretch to overshoot his troubles,

How he outruns the wind, and with what care
He cranks and crosses, with a thousand doubles:
The many musits through the which he goes
Are like a labyrinth to amaze his foes."

Mr. Ayton thus goes on: —

"The hounds, whom we left in full cry, continue their music without remission as long as they are faithful to the scent; as a summons, it should seem, like the seaman's cry, to pull together, or keep together, and it is a certain proof to themselves and their followers that they are in the right way. On the instant that they are "at fault," or lose the scent, they are silent. * * * * * * The weather, in its impression on the scent, is the great father of "faults," but they may arise from other accidents, even when the day is in every respect favorable. The intervention of ploughed land, on which the scent soon cools or evaporates, is at least perilous; but sheep-stains, recently left by a flock, are fatal: they cut off the scent irrecoverably — making a gap, as it were, in the clew, in which the dogs have not even a hint for their guidance."

Compare Shakspeare again:—

"Sometime he runs among a flock of sheep,
To make the cunning hounds mistake their smell,
And sometime where earth-delving conies keep,
To stop the loud pursuers in their yell;
And sometime sorteth with a herd of deer;
Danger deviseth shifts; wit waits on fear:

"For there his smell with others being mingled,
The hot scent-snuffing hounds are driven to doubt,
Ceasing their clamorous cry till they have singled
With much ado the cold fault cleanly out;
Then do they spend their mouths: Echo replies,
As if another chase were in the skies.'

One more extract from Mr. Ayton: —

"Suppose, then, after the usual rounds, that you see the hare at last (a sorry mark for so many foes) sorely beleaguered — looking dark and draggled — limping heavily along; then stopping to listen — again tottering on a little — and again stopping; and at every step, and every pause, hearing the death-cry grow nearer and louder."

One more comparison, and we have exhausted Shakspeare's description: —

"By this poor Wat, far off upon a hill,
Stands on his hinder legs with listening ear,

To harken if his foes pursue him still;
Anon their loud alarums he doth hear;
And now his grief may be comparèd well
To one sore sick that hears the passing bell.

"Then shalt thou see the dew-bedabbled wretch
Turn and return, indenting with the way;
Each envious briar his weary legs doth scratch,
Each shadow makes him stop, each murmur stay:
For misery is trodden on by many,
And being low, never relieved by any."

Here, then, be it observed, are not only the same objects, the same accidents, the same movement, in each description, but the very words employed to convey the scene to the mind are often the same in each. It would be easy to say that Mr. Ayton copied Shakspeare. We believe he did not. There is a sturdy ingenuousness about his writings which would have led him to notice the Venus and Adonis if he had had it in his mind. Shakspeare and he had each looked minutely and practically upon the same scene; and the wonder is, not that Shakspeare was an accurate describer, but that in him the accurate is so thoroughly fused with the poetical, that it is one and the same life.

The celebrated description of the courser in the Venus and Adonis is another remarkable instance of the accuracy of the young Shakspeare's observation. Not the most experienced dealer ever new the *points* of a horse better. The whole poem, indeed, is full of evidence that the circumstances by which the writer was surrounded, in a country district, had entered deeply into his mind, and were reproduced in the poetical form. The bird "tangled in a net" — the "di-dapper peering through a wave" — the "blue-veined violets" — the

"Red morn, that ever yet betokened
Wreck to the seaman, tempest to the field" —

the fisher that forbears the "ungrown fry" — the sheep "gone to fold" — the caterpillars feeding on "the tender leaves" — and, not to weary with examples, that exquisite image, —

"Look how a bright star shooteth from the sky,
So glides he in the night from Venus' eye," —

all these bespeak a poet who had formed himself upon nature, and not upon books. To understand the value, as well as the rarity of this quality in Shakspeare, we should open any contemporary poem. Take Marlowe's "Hero and Leander" for example. We read line after line, beautiful, gorgeous, running over with a satiating luxuriousness; but we look in vain for a single familiar image. Shakspeare describes what he has seen, throwing over the real the delicious tint of his own imagination. Marlowe looks at Nature herself very rarely; but he knows all the conventional images by which the real is supposed to be elevated into the poetical. His most beautiful things are thus but copies of copies. The mode in which each poet describes the morning will illustrate our meaning : —

"Lo! here the gentle lark, weary of rest,
From his moist cabinet mounts up on high,
And wakes the morning, from whose silver breast
The sun ariseth in his majesty;
Who doth the world so gloriously behold,
The cedar-tops and hills seem burnished gold."

We feel that *this* is true. Compare —

"By this Apollo's golden harp began
To sound forth music to the ocean;
Which watchful Hesperus no sooner heard
But he the day bright-bearing car prepared,
And ran before, as harbinger of light,
And with his flaring beams mocked ugly Night,
Till she, o'ercome with anguish, shame, and rage,
Danged down to hell her loathsome carriage."

We are taught that *this* is classical.

Coleridge has observed that, "in the Venus and Adonis, the first and most obvious excellence is the perfect sweetness of the versification; its adaptation to the subject; and the power displayed in varying the march of the words without passing into a loftier and more majestic rhythm than was demanded by the thoughts, or permitted by the propriety of preserving a sense of melody predominant." * This self-controlling power of "varying the march of the words without passing into a loftier and more majestic rhythm" is, perhaps, one of the most signal instances of Shakspeare's consummate mastery of his art, even as a very young man. He who, at the proper season, knew how to strike the grandest music within the compass of our own powerful and sonorous language, in his early productions breathes out his thoughts

"To the Dorian mood
Of flutes and soft recorder."

The sustained sweetness of the versification is never cloying; and yet there are no violent contrasts, no sudden elevations: all is equable in its infinite variety. The early comedies are full of the same rare beauty. In Love's Labor 's Lost — The Comedy of Errors — A Midsummer Night's Dream — we have verses of alternate rhymes formed upon the same model as those of the Venus and Adonis, and producing the same feeling of placid delight by their exquisite harmony. The same principles on which he built the versification of the Venus and Adonis exhibited to him the grace which these elegiac harmonies would impart to the scenes of repose in the progress of a dramatic action.

We proceed to the Lucrece. Of that poem the date of the composition is fixed as accurately as we can desire. In the dedication to the Venus and Adonis the poet says, "If your honor seem but pleased, I account myself highly praised, and vow to take advantage of all idle hours, till I have honored you with some graver labor." In 1594, a year after the Venus and Adonis, Lucrece was published, and was dedicated to Lord Southampton. This, then, was undoubtedly the "graver labor;" this was the pro-

* "Biographia Literaria," vol. ii. p. 14.

duce of the "idle hours" of 1593. Shakspeare was then nearly thirty years of age — the period at which it is held by some he first began to produce any thing original for the stage. The poet unquestionably intended the "graver labor" for a higher effort than had produced the "first heir" of his invention. He describes the Venus and Adonis as "unpolished lines" — lines thrown off with youthful luxuriousness and rapidity. The verses of the Lucrece are "untutored lines" — lines formed upon no established model. There is to our mind the difference of eight or even ten years in the aspect of these poems — a difference as manifest as that which exists between Love's Labor 's Lost, and Romeo and Juliet. Coleridge has marked the great distinction between the one poem and the other : —

"The Venus and Adonis did not perhaps allow the display of the deeper passions. But the story of Lucretia seems to favor, and even demand, their intensest workings. And yet we find in *Shakspeare's* management of the tale neither pathos nor any other *dramatic* quality. There is the same minute and faithful imagery as in the former poem, in the same vivid colors, inspirited by the same impetuous vigor of thought, and diverging and contracting with the same activity of the assimilative and of the modifying faculties; and with a yet larger display, a yet wider range of knowledge and reflection: and, lastly, with the same perfect dominion, often *domination*, over the whole world of language." *

It is in this paragraph that Coleridge has marked the difference — which a critic of the very highest order could alone have pointed out — between the power which Shakspeare's mind possessed of going out of itself in a narrative poem, and the dramatic power. The same mighty, and to most unattainable, power, of utterly subduing the self-conscious to the universal, was essential to the highest excellence of both species of composition, — the poem and

* "Biographia Literaria," vol. ii. p. 21.

the drama. But the exercise of that power was essentially different in each. Coleridge, in another place, says, "In his very first production he projected his mind out of his own particular being, and felt, and made others feel, on subjects no way connected with himself except by force of contemplation, and that sublime faculty by which a great mind becomes that on which it meditates."* But this "sublime faculty" went greatly farther when it became dramatic. In the narrative poems of an ordinary man we perpetually see the narrator. Coleridge, in a passage previously quoted, has shown the essential superiority of Shakspeare's narrative poems, where the whole is placed before our view, the poet unparticipating in the passions. There is a remarkable example of how strictly Shakspeare adhered to this principle in his beautiful poem of a Lover's Complaint. There the poet is actually present to the scene:—

> "From off a hill whose concave womb re-worded
> A plaintful story from a sistering vale,
> My spirits to attend this double voice accorded,
> And down I laid to list the sad-tuned tale."

But not one word of comment does he offer upon the revelations of the "fickle maid full pale." The dramatic power, however, as we have said, is many steps beyond this. It dispenses with narrative altogether. It renders a complicated story, or stories, *one* in the action. It makes the characters reveal *themselves*, sometimes by a word. It trusts for every thing to the capacity of an audience to appreciate the greatest subtilties, and the nicest shades of passion, *through* the action. It is the very reverse of the oratorical power, which repeats and explains. And how is it able to effect this prodigious mastery over the senses and the understanding? By raising the mind of the spectator, or reader, into such a state of poetical excitement as corresponds in some degree to the excitement of the poet, and

* "Literary Remains," vol. ii. p. 54.

thus clears away the mists of our ordinary vision, and irradiates the whole complex moral world in which we for a time live, and move, and have our being, with the brightness of his own intellectual sunlight. Now it appears to us that, although the Venus and Adonis, and the Lucrece, do not pretend to be the creations of this wonderful power — their forms did not demand its complete exercise — they could not have been produced by a man who did not possess the power, and had assiduously cultivated it in his own proper field. In the second poem, more especially, do we think the power has reached a higher development, indicating itself in "a yet wider range of knowledge and reflection."

Malone says, "I have observed that Painter has inserted the story of Lucrece in the first volume of his 'Palace of Pleasure,' 1567, on which I make no doubt our author formed his poem." Be it so. The story of Lucrece in Painter's novel occupies four pages. The first page describes the circumstances that preceded the unholy visit of Tarquin to Lucrece; nearly the whole of the two last pages detail the events that followed the death of Lucrece. A page and a half at most is given to the tragedy. This is proper enough in a narrative, whose business it is to make all the circumstances intelligible. But the narrative poet, who was also thoroughly master of the dramatic power, concentrates all the interest upon the main circumstances of the story. He places the scene of those circumstances before our eyes at the very opening: —

> "From the besieged Ardea all in post,
> Borne by the trustless wings of false desire,
> Lust-breathèd Tarquin leaves the Roman host,
> And to Collatium bears," &c.

The preceding circumstances which impel this journey are then rapidly told. Again, after the crowning action of the tragedy, the poet has done. He tells the consequences of it with a brevity and simplicity indicating the most consummate art: —

"When they had sworn to this advisèd doom,
They did conclude to bear dead Lucrece thence;
To show her bleeding body thorough Rome,
And so to publish Tarquin's foul offence:
Which being done with speedy diligence,
The Romans plausibly did give consent
To Tarquin's everlasting banishment."

He has thus cleared away all the encumbrances to the progress of the main action. He would have done the same had he made Lucrece the subject of a drama. But he has to tell his painful story, and to tell it all: not to exhibit a portion of it, as he would have done had he chosen the subject for a tragedy. The consummate delicacy with which he has accomplished this is beyond all praise, perhaps above all imitation. He puts forth his strength on the accessaries of the main incident. He delights to make the chief actors analyse their own thoughts,— reflect, explain, expostulate. All this is essentially undramatic, and he meant it to be so. But then, what pictures does he paint of the progress of the action, which none but a great dramatic poet, who had visions of future Macbeths and Othellos before him, could have painted! Look, for example, at that magnificent scene, when

"No comfortable star did lend his light,"

of Tarquin leaping from his bed, and softly smiting his falchion on a flint, lighting a torch

"Which must be loadstar to his lustful eye."

Look, again, at the exquisite domestic incident which tells of the quiet and gentle occupation of his devoted victim:—

"By the light he spies
Lucretia's glove, wherein her needle sticks;
He takes it from the rushes where it lies."

The hand to which that glove belongs is described in the very perfection of poetry: —

> "Without the bed her other fair hand was,
> On the green coverlet; whose perfect white
> Showed like an April daisy on the grass."

In the chamber of innocence Tarquin is painted with terrific grandeur, which is overpowering by the force of contrast: —

> "This said, he shakes aloft his Roman blade,
> Which, like a falcon towering in the skies,
> Coucheth the fowl below with his wings' shade."

The complaint of Lucrece after Tarquin has departed was meant to be undramatic. The action advances not. The character develops not itself in the action. But the poet makes his heroine bewail her fate in every variety of lament that his boundless command of imagery could furnish. The letter to Collatine is written — a letter of the most touching simplicity: —

> "Thou worthy lord
> Of that unworthy wife that greeteth thee,
> Health to thy person! Next vouchsafe to afford
> (If ever, love, thy Lucrece thou wilt see)
> Some present speed to come and visit me:
> So I commend me from our house in grief;
> My woes are tedious, though my words are brief."

Again the action languishes, and again Lucrece surrenders herself to her grief. The

> "Skilful painting, made for Priam's Troy,"

is one of the most elaborate passages of the poem, essentially cast in an undramatic mould. But this is but a prelude to the catastrophe, where, if we mistake not, a strength of passion is put forth which is worthy him who drew the terrible agonies of Lear: —

"Here with a sigh, as if her heart would break,
She throws forth Tarquin's name : 'He, he,' she says,
But more than 'he' her poor tongue could not speak;
Till after many accents and delays,
Untimely breathings, sick and short assays,
She utters this : 'He, he, fair lords, 'tis he,
That guides this hand to give this wound to me.'"

Malone, in his concluding remarks upon the Venus and Adonis, and Lucrece, says, "We should do Shakspeare injustice were we to try them by a comparison with more modern and polished productions, or with our present idea of poetical excellence." This was written in the year 1780 — the period which rejoiced in the "polished productions" of Hayley and Miss Seward, and founded its "idea of poetical excellence" on some standard which, secure in its conventional forms, might depart as far as possible from simplicity and nature, to give us words without thought, arranged in verses without music. It would be injustice indeed to Shakspeare to try the Venus and Adonis, and Lucrece, by such a standard of "poetical excellence." But we have outlived that period. By way of apology for Shakspeare, Malone adds, "that few authors rise much above the age in which they live." He further says "The poems of Venus and Adonis, and the Rape of Lucrece, whatever opinion may be now entertained of them, were certainly much admired in Shakspeare's lifetime." This is consolatory. In Shakspeare's lifetime there were a few men that the world has since thought somewhat qualified to establish an idea of poetical excellence" — Spenser, Drayton, Jonson, Fletcher, Chapman, for example. These were not much valued in Malone's golden age of "more modern and polished productions;" — but let that pass. We are coming back to the opinions of this obsolete school; and we venture to think the majority of readers now will not require us to make an apology for Shakspeare's poems.

If Malone thought it necessary to solicit indulgence for the Venus and Adonis, and Lucrece, he drew even a more timid breath when he ventured to speak of the Sonnets. "I do not feel any great propensity to stand forth as the champion of these compositions. However, as it appears to me that they have been somewhat underrated, I think it incumbent on me to do them that justice to which they seem entitled." No wonder he speaks timidly. The great poetical lawgiver of his time — the greater than Shakspeare, for he undertook to mend him, and refine him and make him fit to be tolerated by the super-elegant intellects of the days of George III. — had pronounced that the Sonnets were too bad even for his genius to make tolerable. He, Steevens, who would take up a play of Shakspeare's in the condescending spirit with which a clever tutor takes up a smart boy's verses, — altering a word here, piecing out a line there, commending this thought, shaking his head at this false prosody, and acknowledging upon the whole that the thing is pretty well, seeing how much the lad has yet to learn, — he sent forth his decree that nothing less than an act of parliament could compel the reading of Shakspeare's Sonnets. For a long time mankind bowed before the oracle; and the Sonnets were not read. Wordsworth has told us something about this: —

"There is extant a small volume of miscellaneous poems, in which Shakspeare expresses his feelings in his own person. It is not difficult to conceive that the editor, George Steevens, should have been insensible to the beauties of one portion of that volume, the Sonnets; though there is not a part of the writings of this poet where is found, in an equal compass, a greater number of exquisite feelings felicitously expressed. But, from regard to the critic's own credit, he would not have ventured to talk of an act of parliament not being strong enough to compel the perusal of these, or any production of Shakspeare, if he had not known that the people of England were ignorant of the treasures contained in those little pieces." *

That ignorance has been removed; and no one has contributed more to its removal, by creating a school of poetry

* Preface to Poetical Works.

founded upou Truth and Nature, than Wordsworth himself. The critics of the last century have passed away: —

"Peor and Baälim
Forsake their temples dim."

By the operation of what great sustaining principle is it that we have come back to the just appreciation of "the treasures contained in those little pieces"? The poet-critic will answer: —

"There never has been a period, and perhaps never will be, in which vicious poetry, of some kind or other, has not excited more zealous admiration, and been far more generally read, than good; but this advantage attends the good, that the *individual*, as well as the species, survives from age to age: whereas, of the depraved, though the species be immortal, the individual quickly *perishes:* the object of present admiration vanishes, being supplanted by some other as easily produced, which, though no better, brings with it at least the irritation of novelty, — with adaptation, more or less skilful, to the changing humors of the majority of those who are most at leisure to regard poetical works when they first solicit their attention. Is it the result of the whole, that, in the opinion of the writer, the judgment of the people is not to be respected? The thought is most injurious; and could the charge be brought against him, he would repel it with indignation. The people have already been justified, and their eulogium pronounced by implication, when it is said, above — that, of *good* poetry, the *individual,* as well as the species, *survives.* And how does it survive but through the people? What preserves it but their intellect and their wisdom?

'Past and future are the wings
On whose support, harmoniously conjoined,
Moves the great spirit of human knowledge.' — MS.

The voice that issues from this spirit is that *vox populi* which the deity inspires. Foolish must he be who can mistake for this a local acclamation, or a transitory outcry

— transitory though it be for years, local though from a nation! Still more lamentable is his error who can believe that there is any thing of divine infallibility in the clamor of that small, though loud portion of the community, ever governed by factitious influence, which, under the name of the PUBLIC, passes itself, upon the unthinking, for the PEOPLE."*

It is this perpetual mistake of the public for the people that has led to the belief that there was a period when Shakspeare was neglected. He was *always* in the heart of the people. There, in that deep, rich soil, have the Sonnets rested during two centuries; and here and there in remote places have the seeds put forth leaves and flowers. All young imaginative minds now rejoice in their hues and their fragrance. But this preference of the fresh and beautiful of poetical life to the *pot-pourri* of the last age must be a regulated love. Those who, seeing the admiration which now prevails for these outpourings of "exquisite feelings felicitously expressed," talk of the Sonnets as equal, if not superior, to the greatest of the poet's mighty dramas, compare things that admit of no comparison. Who would speak in the same breath of the gem of Cupid and Psyche, and the Parthenon? In the Sonnets, exquisite as they are, the poet goes not out of himself, (at least in the *form* of the composition,) and he walks, therefore, in a narrow circle of art. In the Venus and Adonis, and the Lucrece, the circle widens. But in the Dramas, the centre is the Human Soul, the circumference the Universe.

* Preface to Poetical Works

SUPPLEMENTARY NOTICE

TO THE

ROMAN PLAYS.

The German critic, Horn, concludes some remarks upon Shakspeare's King John with a passage that may startle those who believe that the truth of history, and the truth of our great dramatic teacher of history, are altogether different things:—

"The hero of this piece stands not in the list of personages, and could not stand with them; for the idea should be clear without personification. The hero is England.

"What the poet chose to express of his view of the dignity and worth of his native land he has confided to the Bastard to embody in words:—

> 'This England never did, nor never shall,
> Lie at the proud foot of a conqueror,
> But when it first did help to wound itself.'

But Shakspeare is immeasurably more than Falconbridge, and he would have the reader and the spectator more also. These lines are not intended to be fixed upon England at the beginning of the fourteenth century alone; they are not even confined to England generally. They are for the elevation of the views of a state — of a people. Happy for England that she possesses a poet who so many years since has spoken to her people as the highest and most splendid teacher! The full consequences of his teaching have not yet been sufficiently revealed; they may perhaps never wholly be exhibited. We, however, know that in England a praiseworthy zeal for their country's history prevails amongst the people. But who first gave true life to that history?"

In the three great dramas that are before us, the idea, not personified, but full of a life that animates and forms every scene, is ROME. Some one said that Chantrey's bust of a great living poet was more like than the poet himself. Shakspeare's Rome, we venture to think, is more like than the Rome of the Romans. It is the idealized Rome, true indeed to her every-day features, but embodying that expression of character which belongs to the universal rather than the accidental. And yet how varied is the idea of Rome which the poet presents to us in these three great mirrors of her history! In the young Rome of Coriolanus we see the terrible energy of her rising ambition checked and overpowered by the factious violence of her contending *classes*. We know that the prayer of Coriolanus is a vain prayer: —

"The honored gods
Keep Rome in safety, and the chairs of justice
Supplied with worthy men! plant love among us!
Throng our large temples with the shows of peace,
And not our streets with war!"

In the matured Rome of Julius Cæsar we see her riches and her glories about to be swallowed up in a domestic conflict of *principles*: —

"Rome, thou hast lost the breed of noble bloods!
When went there by an age, since the great flood,
But it was famed with more than with one man?
When could they say, till now, that talked of Rome,
That her wide walks encompassed but one man?"

In the slightly older Rome of Antony, her power, her magnificence, are ready to perish in the selfishness of *individuals :* —

> "Let Rome in Tiber melt ! and the wide arch
> Of the ranged empire fall ! "

Rome was saved from anarchy by the supremacy of one. Shakspeare did not live to make the Cæsars more immortal.

Schlegel has observed that "these plays are the very thing itself ; and under the apparent artlessness of adhering closely to history as he [Shakspeare] found it, an uncommon degree of art is concealed." In our edition of these plays we have given, with great fulness, the passages from Plutarch, as translated by North, which the poet followed — sometimes even to the literal adoption of the biographer's words. This is the "apparent artlessness." But Schlegel has also shown us the principles of the "uncommon art : " "Of every historical transaction Shakspeare knows how to seize the true poetical point of view, and to give unity and rounding to a series of events detached from the immeasurable extent of history, without in any degree changing them." But he adopts the literal only when it enters into "the true poetical point of view ; " and is, therefore, in harmony with the general poetical truth, which in many subordinate particulars necessarily discards all pretension of "adhering closely to history." Jonson has left us two Roman plays produced essentially upon a different principle. In his "Sejanus" there is scarcely a speech or an incident that is not derived from the ancient authorities ; and Jonson's own edition of the play is crowded with references as minute as would have been required from any modern annalist. In his Address to the Readers he says, "Lest in some nice nostril the quotations might savor affected, I do let you know that I abhor nothing more ; and I have only done it to show my integrity in the story." The character of the dramatist's mind, as well as the abundance of his learning, determined this mode of proceeding; but it is evident that he worked upon a false principle of art. His characters are, therefore, puppets carved and stuffed according to the descriptions, and made to speak according to the very words, of Tacitus and Suetonius; — but they are not living men. It is the same in his "Catiline." Cicero is the great actor in that play; and he moves as Sallust, corrected by other authorities, made him move; and speaks as he spoke himself in his own orations. Jonson gives the whole of Cicero's first oration against Catiline, in a translation amounting to some three hundred lines. It may be asked, what can we have that may better present Cicero to us than the descriptions of the Roman historians, and Cicero's own words? We answer, six lines of Shakspeare, not found in the books: —

> "The angry spot doth glow on Cæsar's brow,
> And all the rest look like a chidden train.
> Calphurnia's cheek is pale; and Cicero
> Looks with such ferret and such fiery eyes,
> As we have seen him in the Capitol,
> Being crossed in conference with some senators."

Gifford, speaking of Jonson's two Roman tragedies, says, "He has apparently succeeded in his principal object, which was to exhibit the characters of the drama to the spectators of his days precisely as they appeared to those of their own. The plan was scholastic, but it was not judicious. The difference between the *dramatis personæ* and the spectators was too wide; and the very accuracy to which he aspired would seem to take away much of the power of pleasing. Had he drawn men instead of Romans, his success might have been more assured."* We presume to think that there is here a slight confusion of terms. If Jonson had succeeded in his principal object, and *had* exhibited his characters precisely as they *appeared*

* Memoirs of Jonson, p. ccxx. — Works, 9 vols.

in their own days, his representation would have been the truth. But he has drawn, according to this intelligent critic, Romans instead of men, and therefore his success was not perfectly assured. Not drawing *men*, he did not draw his characters as they appeared in their own days; but as he pieced out their supposed appearance from incidental descriptions or formal characterizations — from party historians or prejudiced rhetoricians. If he had drawn *Romans* as they were, he would have drawn *men* as they were. They were not the less men because they were Romans. He failed to draw the men, principally on account of the limited range of his imaginative power; he copied instead of created. He repeated, says Gifford, "the ideas, the language, the allusions," which "could only be readily caught by the contemporaries of Augustus and Tiberius." He gave us, partly on this account, also, shadows of life, instead of the "living features of an age so distant from our own," as his biographer yet thinks he gave. Shakspeare worked upon different principles, and certainly with a different success.

The leading idea of Coriolanus — the pivot upon which all the action turns — the key to the bitterness of factious hatred which runs through the whole drama — is the contest for power between the patricians and plebeians. This is a broad principle, assuming various modifications in various states of society, but very slightly varied in its foundations and its results. He that truly works out the exhibition of this principle must paint *men*, let the scene be the Rome of the first Tribunes, or the Venice of the last Doges. With the very slightest changes of accessaries, the principle stands for the contests between aristocracy and democracy, in any country or in any age — under a republic or a monarchy — in England under Queen Victoria, in the United States under President Tyler. The historical truth, and the philosophical principle, which Shakspeare has embodied in Coriolanus are universal. But suppose he had possessed the means of treating the subject with what some would call historical accuracy; had learnt that Plutarch, in the story of Coriolanus, was probably dealing only with a legend; that, if the story is to be received as true, it belongs to a later period; that in this later period there were very nice shades of difference between the classes composing the population of Rome; that the balance of power was a much more complex thing than he found in the narrative of Plutarch: further suppose that, proud of this learning, he had made the universal principle of the plebeian and patrician hostility subsidiary to an exact display of it, according to the conjectures which modern industry and acuteness have brought to bear on the subject. It is evident, we think, that he would have been betrayed into a false principle of art; and would necessarily have drawn Roman shadows, instead of vital and enduring men. As it is, he has drawn men so vividly — under such permanent relations to each other — with such universal manifestations of character, that some persons of strong political feelings have been ready to complain, according to their several creeds, either that his plebeians are too brutal, or his patricians too haughty. A polite democracy, a humane oligarchy, would be better. Johnson somewhat rejoices in the amusing exhibition of "plebeian malignity and tribunitian insolence." Hazlitt, who is more than half angry on the other side of the question, says, "The *whole* dramatic moral of Coriolanus is, that those who have little shall have less, and that those who have much shall take all that others have left." Let us see.

With his accustomed consummate judgment in his opening scenes, Shakspeare throws us at once into the centre of the contending classes of early Rome. We have no description of the nature of the factions; we behold them: —

"1 *Cit.* You are all resolved rather to die than to famish.
Cit. Resolved, resolved!

1 *Cit.* First, you know, Caius Marcius is chief enemy to the people.

Cit. We know't, we know't.

1 *Cit.* Let us kill him, and we'll have corn at our own price.

Cit. No more talking on't: let it be done."

The foundation of the violence is misery; — its great stimulant is ignorance. The people are famishing for want of corn; — they will kill one man, and that will give them corn at their own price: the murder will turn scarcity into plenty. Hazlitt says that Shakspeare "spared no occasion of baiting the rabble." If to show that misery acting upon ignorance produces the same effects in all ages be "baiting the rabble," he has baited them. But he has not painted the "mutinous citizens" with an undiscriminating contempt. One that displays a higher power than his fellows of reasoning or remonstrance, and yet is zealous enough to resist what he thinks injustice, says of Caius Marcius, —

"Consider you what services he has done for his country."

The people are sometimes ungrateful; but Shakspeare chose to show that some amongst them could be just. The people have their favorites. "Worthy Menenius Agrippa" has the good word of the mutinous citizens. Shakspeare gave them no unworthy favorite. His rough humor, his true kindliness, his noble constancy, form a character that the people have always loved, even whilst they are rebuked and chastened. But if the poet has exhibited the democratic ignorance in pretty strong colors, has he shrunk from presenting us a full-length portrait of patrician haughtiness? Caius Marcius in the first scene claims no sympathies: —

"Would the nobility lay aside their ruth,
And let me use my sword, I'd make a quarry
With thousands of these quartered slaves, as high
As I could pick my lance."

Till Caius Marcius has become Coriolanus, and we see that the popular violence is under the direction of demagogues — the same never-varying result of the same circumstances — we feel no love for him. It is under oppression and ingratitude that his pride becomes sublime. But he has previously deserved our homage, and in some sort our affection. The poet gradually wins us to an admiration of the hero by the most skilful management. First, through his mother. What a glorious picture of an antique matron, from whom her son equally derived his pride and his heroism, is presented in the exquisite scene where Volumnia and Valeria talk of him they loved, according to their several natures! Who but Shakspeare could have seized upon the spirit of a Roman woman of the highest courage and mental power bursting out in words such as these? —

"*Vol.* His bloody brow
With his mailed hand then wiping, forth he goes;
Like to a harvest-man, that 's tasked to mow
Or all, or lose his hire.
Vir. His bloody brow! O, Jupiter, no blood!
Vol. Away, you fool! it more becomes a man
Than gilt his trophy. The breasts of Hecuba,
When she did suckle Hector, looked not lovelier
Than Hector's forehead, when it spit forth blood
At Grecian swords' contending."

This is a noble preparation for the scenic exhibition of the deeds of Caius Marcius. Amidst the physical strength, and the mental energy, that make the triumphant warrior, the poet, by a few of his magical touches, has shown us the ever-present loftiness of mind that denotes qualities far beyond those which belong to mere animal courage. His contempt of the Romans who are "beaten back," and the "Romans with spoils," is equally withering. It is not sufficient for him to win one battle. The force of character through which he thinks that nothing is done whilst any thing remains to do, shows that Shakspeare understood the stuff of which a great general is made. His remonstrance to Cominius —

> "Where is the enemy? Are you lords o' the field?
> If not, why cease you till you are so?" —

is not in Plutarch. It is supplied to us by a higher authority, — by the instinct by which Shakspeare knew the great secret of success in every enterprise, — the determination to be successful. One example more of the skill with which Shakspeare makes Caius Marcius gradually obtain the uncontrolled homage of our hearts. The proud conqueror who rejects all gifts and honors, who has said, —

> "I have some wounds upon me, and they smart
> To hear themselves remembered," —

asks a gift of his superior officer: —

> "*Cor.* I sometime lay, here in Corioli,
> At a poor man's house; he used me kindly:
> He cried to me; I saw him prisoner;
> But then Aufidius was within my view,
> And wrath o'erwhelmed my pity: I request you
> To give my poor host freedom."

We now see only the true hero. He realizes the noble description of the "Happy Warrior" which the great poet of our own days has drawn with so masterly a hand: —

> "Who, doomed to go in company with Pain,
> And Fear, and Bloodshed, miserable train!
> Turns his necessity to glorious gain;
> In face of these doth exercise a power
> Which is our human nature's highest dower;
> Controls them and subdues, transmutes, bereaves
> Of their bad influence, and their good receives,
> By objects, which might force the soul to abate
> Her feeling, rendered more compassionate."

We have forgotten the fierce patrician who would make a quarry of the Roman populace.

And this, we suppose, is what Hazlitt objects to in Shakspeare's conduct of this play. The character of Coriolanus rises upon us. The sufferings and complaints of his enemies are merged in their factious hatred. "Poetry," says the critic, "is right royal. It puts the individual for the species, the one above the infinite many, might before right." Now we apprehend that Shakspeare has not treated the subject of Coriolanus after this right royal fashion of poetry. He has dealt fairly with the vices as well as the virtues of his hero. The scene in the second act, in which Coriolanus stands for the consulship, is amongst the most remarkable examples of Shakspeare's insight into character. In Plutarch he found a simple fact related without any comment: "Now, Marcius, following this custom, showed many wounds and cuts upon his body, which he had received in seventeen years' service at the wars and in many sundry battles, being ever the foremost man that did set out feet to fight; so that there was not a man among the people but was ashamed of himself to refuse so valiant a man; and one of them said to another, We must needs choose him consul; there is no remedy." But in his representation of this fact Shakspeare had to create a character, and to make that character act and re-act upon the character of the people. Coriolanus was essentially and necessarily proud. His education, his social position, his individual supremacy made him so. He lives in a city of factions, and he dislikes, of course, the faction opposed to his order. The people represent the opinions that he dislikes, and he therefore dislikes the people. That he has pity and love for humanity, however humble, we have already seen. Coming into contact with the Roman populace for their suffrages, his uppermost thought is, "bid them wash their faces and keep their teeth clean." He outwardly despises that vanity of the people which will not reward desert unless it go hand in hand with solicitation. He betrays his contempt for the canvassed, even whilst he is canvassing: —

> "I will, sir, flatter my sworn brother, the people, to earn a dearer estimation of them; 'tis a condition they account gentle: and since the wisdom of their choice is rather to have my hat than my heart, I will practice the insinuating nod, and be off to them most counterfeitly: that is, sir, I will counterfeit the bewitchment of some popular man, and give it bountifully to the desirers. Therefore, beseech you, I may be consul."

The satire is not obsolete. The desperation with which he at last roars out his demand for their voices, as if he were a chorus mocking himself and the people with the most bitter irony, is the climax of this wonderful exhibition: —

> "Your voices: for your voices I have fought;
> Watched for your voices; for your voices, bear
> Of wounds two dozen odd; battles thrice six
> I have seen and heard of; for your voices
> Have done many things, some less, some more: your
> voices:
> Indeed, I would be consul."

The people have justice enough to elect the man for his deeds; but they have not strength enough to abide by their own election. When they are told by the Tribunes that they have been treated scornfully, they can bear to be rebuked by their demagogues — to have their "ignorant election" revoked — to suffer falsehoods to be put in their mouth — to be the mere tools of their weak though crafty leaders. It is Shakspeare's praise, in his representation of this plebeian and patrician conflict, that he, for the most part, shows the people as they always are, — just, generous, up to a certain point. But put that thing called a demagogue amongst them, — that cold, grovelling, selfish thing, without sympathies for the people, the real despiser of the people, because he uses them as tools, — and then there is no limit to their unjust violence. In the subsequent scenes we see not the people at all in the exercise of their own wills. We see only Brutus and Sicinius speaking the voice, not of the people, but of their individual selfishness. In the first scene of the third act the Tribunes insult Coriolanus; and from that moment the lion lashes himself up into a fury which will be deadly. The catastrophe is only deferred when the popular clamor for the Tarpeian Rock subsides into the demand that he should answer to them once again in the market-place. The mother of Coriolanus abates something of her high nature when she counsels her son to a dissembling submission: —

> "*Vol.* Because that now it lies you on to speak
> To the people; not by your own instruction,
> Nor by the matter which your heart prompts you,
> But with such words as are but roted in
> Your tongue, though but bastards, and syllables
> Of no allowance, to your bosom's truth."

This is the prudence even of an heroic woman; but she fears for her son. She is somewhat lowered by the instruction. But the poet knew that a real contempt for the people, allied to a strong desire for the honors which the people have to bestow, must produce this lip-service. Coriolanus does not heed the instructions of his mother. He approaches temperately to his questioners; he puts up vows for the safety of Rome from the depths of his full heart; he is in earnest to smother his pride and his resentment, but the coarse Tribune calls him "traitor." There can be but one issue; he is banished.

Some of the historians say that, although Coriolanus joined the enemies of his country, he provoked no jealousies amongst the native leaders of those enemies; that he died honored and rewarded; that his memory was even reverenced at Rome. Shakspeare probably knew not this version of the legend of Coriolanus. If he had known it, he would not have adopted it. He had to show the false step which Coriolanus took. He had to teach that his proud resentment hurried him upon a course which brought evils worse than the Tarpeian Rock. And yet we are compelled to admire him; we can scarcely blame him. It has not been our good fortune to see John Kemble in this his greatest character: if we had, we probably should have received into our minds an embodied image of the moral grandeur of that scene when Coriolanus stands upon the hearth of Tullus Aufidius, and says, —

> "My name is Caius Marcius, who hath done
> To thee particularly, and to all the Volces,
> Great hurt and mischief."

The words are almost literally copied from Plutarch; but the wondrous art of the poet is shown in the perfect agreement of these words with the minutest traits of the man's character which had preceded them. The answer of Aufidius is not in Plutarch; and here Shakspeare invests the rival of Coriolanus with a majesty of language which has for its main object to call us back to the real greatness of the banished man: —

> "Know thou first,
> I loved the maid I married: never man
> Sighed truer breath; but that I see thee here,
> Thou noble thing! more dances my rapt heart
> Than when I first my wedded mistress saw
> Bestride my threshold."

Brief and rapid is their agreement to make war upon Rome. In the great city herself, "Coriolanus is not much missed but with his friends," according to the Tribune; no harm can come to Rome; the popular authority will whip the slave that speaks of evil news. Shakspeare again "baits the rabble," according to Hazlitt; though he reluctantly adds, "what he says of them is very true:" —

> "*Cit.* Faith, we hear fearful news.
> 1 *Cit.* For mine own part,
> When I said banish him, I said 't was pity.

> 2 *Cit.* And so did I.
> 3 *Cit.* And so did I; and to say the truth, so did very many of us. That we did we did for the best; and though we willingly consented to his banishment, yet it was against our will."

When Shakspeare made Coriolanus ask the freedom of the poor man that had used him kindly, he showed the tenderness that was at the bottom of that proud heart. When Rome is beleagured, Cominius reports thus of his unsuccessful mission to her banished son: —

> "*Com.* I offered to awaken his regard
> For his private friends. His answer to me was,
> He could not stay to pick them in a pile
> Of noisome, musty chaff. He said, 't was folly
> For one poor grain or two to leave unburnt,
> And still to nose the offence."

His old general and companion in arms touched nothing but his pride. Menenius, his "beloved in Rome," undertakes a similar mission. The answer of Coriolanus is, —

> "Wife, mother, child, I know not. My affairs
> Are servanted to others."

But the moment that Coriolanus has declared to Aufidius

> "Fresh embassies
> Nor from the state, nor private friends, hereafter
> Will I lend ear to,"

his mother, his wife, his child appear. But he will stand

> "As if a man were author of himself,
> And knew no other kin."

What a scene follows! The warrior is externally calm, as if he were a god, above all passions and affections. The wondrous poetry in which he speaks seems in its full harmony as if it held the man's inmost soul in a profound consistency. But the passion is coming. "I have sat too long" is the prelude to

"O, mother, mother,
What have you done? Behold, the heavens do ope,
The gods look down, and this unnatural scene
They laugh at. O, my mother, mother! O!
You have won a happy victory to Rome:
But, for your son, — believe it, O, believe it,
Most dangerously you have with him prevailed,
If not most mortal to him."

Volumnia speaks no other word. The mother and the son, the wife and the husband, the child and the father, have parted forever. The death of Coriolanus in the "goodly city" of Antium is inevitable: —

"*Cor.* Cut me to pieces, Volces; men and lads,
Stain all your edges on me. — Boy! False hound!
If you have writ your annals true, 't is there,
That, like an eagle in a dove-cot, I
Fluttered your Volcians in Corioli:
Alone I did it. — Boy!
Auf. Why, noble lords,
Will you be put in mind of his blind fortune,
Which was your shame, by this unholy braggart,
'Fore your own eyes and ears?
Con. Let him die for 't."

The struggle for power amongst the Classes of young Rome ends in the death of the proud patrician by the swords of those whom he had conquered. He had presented his throat to Tullus Aufidius, —

"Which not to cut, would show thee but a fool."

But Aufidius would first use him who said he would fight

"Against my cankered country with the spleen
Of all the under fiends."

The retribution is a fearful one. Hazlitt observes, "What Shakspeare says of them [the rabble] is very true; what he says of their betters is also very true; *though he dwells less upon it.*" Shakspeare teaches by action as well as by words. The silly rabble escape with a terrible fright: Coriolanus loses his home, his glory, his life, for his pride and his revenge.

Years, perhaps centuries, had rolled on. Rome had seen a constitution which had reconciled the differences of the patricians and the plebeians. The two orders had built a temple to Concord. Her power had increased; her territory had extended. In compounding their differences, the patricians and the plebeians had appropriated to themselves all the wealth and honors of the state. There was a neglected class that the social system appeared to reject, as well as to despise. The aristocratic party was again brought into a more terrible conflict with the impoverished and the destitute. Civil war was the natural result. Sulla established a short-lived constitution. The dissolution of the Republic was at hand: the struggle was henceforth to be not between classes, but individuals. The death of Julius Cæsar was soon followed by the final termination of the contest between the republican and the monarchical *principle.* Shakspeare saw the grandeur of the crisis; and he seized upon it for one of his lofty expositions of political philosophy. He has treated it as no other poet would have treated it, because he saw the exact relations of the contending principle to the future great history of mankind. The death of Cæsar was not his catastrophe: it was the death of the Roman Republic at Philippi.

Shakspeare, in the opening scene of his Julius Cæsar, has marked very distinctly the difference between the citizens of this period, and the former period of Coriolanus. In the first play, they are a turbulent body, without regular occupation. They are in some respects a military body. They would revenge with their pikes: the wars would eat them up. In Julius Cæsar, on the contrary, they are "mechanical"—the carpenter or the cobbler. They "make holiday to see Cæsar, and to rejoice in his triumph." The speech of Marullus, the Tribune, brings the Rome of the hour vividly before us. It is the Rome of mighty conquests and terrible factions. Pompey has had his triumphs; and now the men of Rome

> "Strew flowers in his way
> That comes in triumph over Pompey's blood."

But the triumphant man himself appears. When he speaks, the music and the shouts are silent. When he speaks not, the air is again filled with sounds of greeting. There is a voice in the crowd, "shriller than the music." The Soothsayer cries, "Beware the Ides of March;" but "he is a dreamer." The procession passes on; two men remain who are to make the dream a reality. Of all Shakspeare's characters, none require to be studied with more patient attention than those of Brutus and Cassius, that we may understand the resemblances and the differences of each. The leading distinctions between these two remarkable men, as drawn by Shakspeare, appear to us to be these: Brutus acts wholly upon principle; Cassius partly upon impulse. Brutus acts only when he has reconciled the contemplation of action with his speculative opinions; Cassius allows the necessity of *some* action to run before and govern his opinions. Brutus is a philosopher; Cassius is a partisan. Brutus, therefore, deliberates and spares; Cassius precipitates and denounces. Brutus is the nobler instructor; Cassius the better politician. Shakspeare, in the first great scene between them, brings out these distinctions of character upon which future events so mainly depend. Cassius does not, like a merely crafty man, use only the arguments to conspiracy which will most touch Brutus; but he mixes with them, in his zeal and vehemence, those which have presented themselves most strongly to his own mind. He had a personal dislike of Cæsar, as Cæsar had of him. Cassius begins artfully: he would first move Brutus through his affection, and next through his self-love. He is opening a set discourse on his own sincerity, when the shouting of the people makes Brutus express his fear that they "choose Cæsar for their king." Cassius at once leaves his prepared speeches, and assumes that because Brutus fears it he would not have it so: —

"I would not, Cassius; yet I love him well."

Cassius sees that the love which Brutus bears to Cæsar will be an obstacle; and he goes on to disparage Cæsar. He could not buffet the waves with Cassius: when he had a fever in Spain, —

"Alas! *it* cried, 'Give me some drink, Titinius.'"

Brutus answers not; but marks "another general shout." Cassius then strikes a different note: —

"Brutus and Cæsar: What should be in that Cæsar?
Why should that name be sounded more than yours?

At last Cassius hits upon a *principle:* —

"O! you and I have heard our fathers say,
There was a Brutus once that would have brooked
The eternal devil to keep his state in Rome
As easily as a king."

The Stoic is at last moved: —

"Brutus had rather be a villager,
Than to repute himself a son of Rome
Under these hard conditions, as this time
Is like to lay upon us."

In the next scene, when Cæsar is returning from the games, the great dictator describes Cassius — the Cassius with "a lean and hungry look," the "great observer" — as one whom he could fear, if he could fear any thing. In the subsequent dialogue with Casca, where the narrative of what passed at the games is conducted with a truth that puts the very scene before us, Cassius again strikes in with the thought that is uppermost in his mind. Brutus says that Cæsar "hath the falling sickness:" the reply of Cassius is most characteristic: —

> "No, Cæsar hath it not; but you, and I,
> And honest Casca, we have the falling sickness."

Brutus goes home to meditate. The energy of Cassius is never weary. In the storm he is still the conspirator. The "impatience of the heavens" furnishes him an argument against the man

> "Prodigious grown,
> And fearful, as these strange irruptions are."

The plot is maturing. Brutus especially is to be won.

Coleridge, who, when he doubts of a meaning in Shakspeare, — or, what is rarer, suggests that there is some inconsistency in the conduct of the scene, or the development of character, — has the highest claim upon our deferential regard, gives the soliloquy of Brutus in the beginning of the second act with the following observations: "This speech is singular; — at least, I do not at present see into Shakspeare's motive, his *rationale,* or in what point of view he meant Brutus's character to appear. For surely — (this I mean is what I say to myself, with my present *quantum* of insight, only modified by my experience in how many instances I had ripened into a perception of beauties, where I had before descried faults) — surely, nothing can seem more discordant with our historical preconceptions of Brutus, or more lowering to the intellect of the Stoico-Platonic tyrannicide, than the tenets here attributed to him — to him, the stern Roman republican; namely, — that he would have no objection to a king, or to Cæsar, a monarch in Rome, would Cæsar but be as good a monarch as he now seems disposed to be! How, too, could Brutus say that he found no personal cause — none — in Cæsar's past conduct as a man? Had he not passed the Rubicon? Had he not entered Rome as a conqueror? Had he not placed his Gauls in the Senate? Shakspeare, it may be said, has not brought these things forward. True; — and this is just the ground of my perplexity. What character did Shakspeare mean his Brutus to be?"* To this question we venture to reply according to our imperfect conception of the character of Brutus. Shakspeare meant him not for a conspirator. He has a terror of conspiracy: —

> "Where wilt thou find a cavern dark enough
> To mask thy monstrous visage?"

He has been "with himself at war," speculating, we doubt not, upon the strides of Cæsar towards absolute power, but unprepared to resist them. Of Cæsar he has said, "I love him well;" he now says, —

> "I know no personal cause to spurn at him."

We are by no means sure of the correct punctuation of this passage as it is usually given. Brutus has come to a conclusion in the watches of the night: —

> "It must be by his death."

He disavows, however, any personal hatred to Cæsar: —

* Literary Remains, vol. ii. p. 139.

"And for my part,
I know no *personal* cause to spurn at him."

He then adds, —

"But for the *general* — he would be crowned:
How that might change his nature, there's the question."

He goes from the personal cause to the general cause: "He would be crowned." As a triumvir, a dictator, Brutus had no personal cause against Cæsar; but the name of king, which Cassius poured into his ear, rouses all his speculative republicanism. His experience of Cæsar calls from him the acknowledgment that Cæsar's affections sway not more than his reason; but crown him, and his nature might be changed. We must bear in mind that Brutus is not yet committed to the conspiracy. The character that Shakspeare meant his Brutus to be is not yet fully developed. He is yet irresolute; and his reasonings are, therefore, to a certain extent, inconsequential: —

"Since Cassius first did whet me against Cæsar,
I have not slept.
Between the acting of a dreadful thing
And the first motion, all the interim is
Like a phantasma, or a hideous dream."

He is instigated from without; the principles associated with the name of Brutus stir him from within: —

"My ancestors did from the streets of Rome
The Tarquin drive when he was called a king."

The "faction" come. Cassius and Brutus speak together apart. Let us turn aside for a moment to see how Shakspeare fills up this terrible pause. Other poets would have made the inferior men exchange oaths, and cross hands, and whisper, and ejaculate. He makes every thing depend upon the determination of Brutus and Cassius; and the others, knowing it so depends, speak thus: —

"*Dec.* Here lies the east: doth not the day break here?
Casca. No.
Cin. O, pardon, sir, it doth; and yon gray lines
That fret the clouds are messengers of day.
Casca. You shall confess that you are both deceived.
Here, as I point my sword, the sun arises;
Which is a great way growing on the south,
Weighing the youthful season of the year.
Some two months hence, up higher toward the north
He first presents his fire; and the high east
Stands, as the Capitol, directly here."

Is this nature? The truest and most profound nature. The minds of all men thus disencumber themselves, in the moments of the most anxious suspense, from the pressure of an overwhelming thought. There is a real relief, if some accidental circumstance, like

"The gray lines that fret the clouds,"

can produce this disposition of the mind to go out of itself for an instant or two of forgetfulness.

But Brutus is changed. We have no doubt *now* of his character. He is the leader, Cassius the subordinate. He is decided in his course: he will not "break with" Cicero; he will not destroy Antony. We recognize the gentleness of his nature even while he is preparing for assassination: -

"O, that we then could come by Cæsar's spirit,
And not dismember Cæsar!"

In the exquisite scene with Portia which follows, our love for the man is completed; we learn what he has suffered before he has taken his resolution. There is something more than commonly touching in these words: —

> "You are my true and honorable wife;
> As dear to me as are the ruddy drops
> That visit my sad heart."

The pathos in some degree depends upon our knowledge of the situation of the speaker, which Portia does not know.

The scenes which we have now run over bring us to the end of the second act. Nothing can be more interesting, we think, than to follow Shakspeare with Plutarch in hand; and we have furnished the ready means of doing so in our Illustrations. The poet adheres to the facts of history with a remarkable fidelity. A few hard figures are painted upon a canvas; the outlines are distinct, the colors are strong; but there is no art in the composition, no grouping, no light and shadow. This is the historian's picture. We turn to the poet. We recognize the same figures, but they appear to live; they are in harmony with the entire scene in which they move; we have at once the reality of nature, and the ideal of art, which is a higher nature. Compare the dialogue in the first act between Cassius and Brutus, and the same dialogue as reported by Plutarch, for an example of the power by which the poet elevates all he touches, without destroying its identity. When we arrive at the stirring scenes of the third act, this power is still more manifest. The assassination scene is as literal as may be; but it offers an example apt enough of Shakspeare's mode of dramatizing a fact. When Metellus Cimber makes suit for his brother, and the conspirators appear as intercessors, the historian says, "Cæsar at the first simply refused their kindness and entreaties; but afterwards, perceiving they still pressed on him, he violently thrust them from him." The poet enters into the mind of Cæsar, and clothes this rejection of the suit in characteristic words. Hazlitt, after noticing the profound knowledge of character displayed by Shakspeare in this play, says, "If there is any exception to this remark, it is in the hero of the piece himself. We do not much admire the representation here given of Julius Cæsar, nor do we think it answers the portrait given of him in his 'Commentaries.' He makes several vaporing and rather pedantic speeches, and does nothing. Indeed, he has nothing to do. So far, the fault of the character is the fault of the plot." The echoes of this opinion are many; and the small critics wax bold upon the occasion. Boswell says, "There cannot be a stronger proof of Shakspeare's deficiency in classical knowledge than the boastful language he has put in the mouth of the most accomplished man of all antiquity, who was not more admirable for his achievements than for the dignified simplicity with which he has recorded them." Courtenay had hazarded, in his notice of Henry VIII., the somewhat bold assertion, "that Shakspeare used very little artifice, and, in truth, had very little design, in the construction of the greater number of his historical characters." Upon the character of Julius Cæsar he says that Plutarch having been supposed to pass over this character somewhat slightly, is "a corroboration of my remark upon the slight attention which Shakspeare paid to his historical characters. The conversation with Antony about fat men, and with Calphurnia about her dreams, came conveniently into his plan; and some lofty expressions could hardly be avoided in portraying one who was known to the whole world as a great conqueror. Beyond this, our poet gave himself no trouble." This is certainly an easy way of disposing of a complicated question. Did Shakspeare give himself no trouble about the characterization of Brutus and Cassius? In them did he indicate no points of character but what he found in Plutarch? Is not his characterization of Cæsar himself a considerable expansion of what he found set down by the historian? At *the exact period of the action of this drama,*

Cæsar, possessing the reality of power, was haunted by the weakness of passionately desiring the title of king. Plutarch says, "The chiefest cause that made him mortally hated was the covetous desire he had to be called king." This is the pivot upon which the whole action of Shakspeare's tragedy turns. There might have been another mode of treating the subject. The death of Julius Cæsar might have been the catastrophe. The republican and the monarchical principles might have been exhibited in conflict. The republican principle would have triumphed in the fall of Cæsar; and the poet would have previously held the balance between the two principles, or have claimed, indeed, our largest sympathies for the principles of Cæsar and his friends, by a true exhibition of Cæsar's greatness and Cæsar's virtues. The poet chose another course. And are we then to talk, with ready flippancy, of ignorance and carelessness — that he wanted classical knowledge — that he gave himself no trouble? "The fault of the character is the fault of the plot," says Hazlitt. It would have been nearer the truth had he said, — the character is determined by the plot. While Cæsar is upon the scene, it was for the poet, largely interpreting the historian, to show the inward workings of "the covetous desire he had to be called king;" and most admirably, according to our notions of characterization, has he shown them. Cæsar is "in all but name a king." He is surrounded by all the external attributes of power; yet he is not satisfied: —

> "The angry spot doth glow on Cæsar's brow."

He is suspicious — he fears. But he has acquired the policy of greatness — to seem what it is not. To his intimate friend he is an actor: —

> "I rather tell thee what is to be feared
> Than what I fear: for always I am Cæsar."

When Calphurnia has recounted the terrible portents of the night — when the augurers would not that Cæsar should stir forth — he exclaims, —

> "The gods do this in shame of cowardice :
> Cæsar should be a beast without a heart,
> If he should stay at home to-day for fear.
> No, Cæsar shall not. Danger knows full well
> That Cæsar is more dangerous than he.
> We were two lions littered in one day,
> And I the elder and more terrible ;
> And Cæsar shall go forth."

But to whom does he utter this, the "boastful language,' which so offends Boswell? To the servant who has brought the message from the augurers; before *him* he could show no fear. But the very inflation of his language shows that he did fear; and an instant after, when the servant no doubt is intended to have left the scene, he says to his wife, —

> "Mark Antony shall say I am not well,
> And for thy humor I will stay at home."

Read Plutarch's account of the scene between Decius and Cæsar, when Decius prevails against Calphurnia, and Cæsar decides to go. In the historian we have not a hint of the splendid characterization of Cæsar struggling between his fear and his pride. Wherever Shakspeare found a minute touch in the historian that could harmonize with his general plan, he embodied it in his character of Cæsar. Who does not remember the magnificent lines which the poet puts into the mouth of Cæsar? —

> "Cowards die many times before their deaths ;
> The valiant never taste of death but once.
> Of all the wonders that I yet have heard,
> It seems to me most strange that men should fear ;
> Seeing that death, a necessary end,
> Will come when it will come."

A very slight passage in Plutarch, with reference to other circumstances of Cæsar's life, suggested this: "When some of his friends did counsel him to have a guard for the safety of his person, and some also did offer themselves to serve him, he would never consent to it, but said it was better to die once than always to be afraid of death." We have already noticed the skill with which Shakspeare, upon a very bald narrative, has dramatized the last sad scene in which Cæsar was an actor. The tone of his last speech is indeed boastful: —

> "I do know but one
> That unassailable holds on his rank,
> Unshaked of motion: and, that I am he,
> Let me a little show it."

That Cæsar knew his power, and made others know it, who can doubt? He was not one who, in his desire to be king, would put on the robe of humility. Altogether, then, we profess to receive Shakspeare's characterization of Cæsar with a perfect confidence that he produced that character upon fixed principles of art. It is not the prominent character of the play; and it was not meant to be so. It is true to the narrative upon which Shakspeare founded it; but, what is of more importance, it is true to every natural conception of what Cæsar must have been at the exact moment of his fall.

We have seen the stoic Brutus — in reality a man of strong passions and deep feelings — gradually warm up to the great enterprise of asserting his principles by one terrible blow, for triumph or for extinction. The blow is given. The excitement which succeeds is wondrously painted by the poet, without a hint from the historian. The calm of the gentle Brutus is lifted up, for the moment, into an attitude of terrible sublimity. It is he who says, —

"Stoop, Romans, stoop,
And let us bathe our hands in Cæsar's blood
Up to the elbows, and besmear our swords:
Then walk we forth, even to the market-place;
And, waving our red weapons o'er our heads,
Let 's all cry, Peace, Freedom, and Liberty!"

From that moment, the character flags; the calmness returns; something also of the irresolution comes back. Brutus is too high minded for his position. Another comes upon the scene; another of different temperament, of different powers. He is not one that, like Brutus, will change "offence" to "virtue and to worthiness" by the force of character. He is one that "revels long o' nights." But he possesses courage, eloquence, high talent, and, what renders him most dangerous, he is sufficiently unprincipled. Cassius knew him, and would have killed him. Brutus does not know him, and he suffers him "to bury Cæsar." The conditions upon which Brutus permits Antony to speak are Shakspeare's own; and they show his wonderful penetration into the depths of character: —

"You shall not in your funeral speech blame us,
But speak all good you can devise of Cæsar;
And say you do 't by our permission;
Else shall you not have any hand at all
About his funeral. And you shall speak,
In the same pulpit whereto I am going,
After my speech is ended."

The opportunity is not lost by Antony. Hazlitt, acute enough in general, appears to us singularly superficial in his remarks on this play: "Mark Antony's speech over the dead body of Cæsar has been justly admired for the mixture of pathos and art in it: that of Brutus certainly is not so good." In what way is it not so good? As a specimen of eloquence, put by the side of Antony's, who can doubt that it is tame, passionless, severe, and therefore ineffective. But as an example of Shakspeare's wonderful power of characterization, it is beyond all praise. It was the consummate artifice of Antony that made him say, —

> "I am no orator, as Brutus is."

Brutus was *not* an orator. Under great excitement he is twice betrayed into oratory: when he addresses the conspirators, "No, not an oath;" and after the assassination, "Stoop, Romans, stoop." He is a man of just intentions, of calm understanding, of settled purpose, when his principles are to become actions. But his notion of oratory is this: —

> "I will myself into the pulpit first,
> And show the reason of our Cæsar's death."

And he does show the *reason*. The critics have made amusing work with this speech. Warburton says, "This speech of Brutus is wrote in imitation of his famed laconic brevity, and is very fine in its kind; but no more like that brevity than his times were like Brutus's." To this Mr. Monck Mason rejoins, "I cannot agree with Warburton that this speech is very fine in its kind. I can see no degree of excellence in it, but think it a very paltry speech, for so great a man, on so great an occasion." The commentators have not a word of approbation for the speech of Antony to counterbalance this. There was a man, however, of their times, Martin Sherlock, who wrote "A Fragment on Shakspeare," in a style sufficiently hyperbolical, but who, nevertheless, was amongst the few who then ventured to think that "the barbarian," Shakspeare, possessed art and judgment. Of Antony's speech he thus expresses his opinion: "Every line of this speech deserves an eulogium; and, when you have examined it attentively you will allow it, and will say, with me, that neither Demosthenes, nor Cicero, nor their glorious rival, the immortal Chatham, ever made a better." There may be exaggerations in both styles of criticism: the speech of Antony may not be equal to Demosthenes, and the speech of Brutus may not be a very paltry speech. But, each being written by the same man, we have a right to accept each with a conviction that the writer was capable of making a good speech for Brutus as well as for Antony; and that, if he did not do so, he had very abundant reasons. It requires no great refinement to understand his reasons. The excitement of the great assertion of republican principles, which was to be acted over, —

"In states unborn, and accents yet unknown," —

had been succeeded by a momentary calm. In the very hour of the assassination, Brutus had become its apologist to Antony: —

"Our reasons are so full of good regard,
That were you, Antony, the son of Cæsar,
You should be satisfied."

He is already preparing in mind for "the pulpit." He will present, calmly and dispassionately, the "reason of our Cæsar's death." He expects that Antony will speak with equal moderation — all good of Cæsar — no blame of Cæsar's murderers; and he thinks it an advantage to speak *before* Antony. He knew not what *oratory* really is. But Shakspeare knew, and he painted Antony. Another great poet made the portrait a description: —

"He seemed
For dignity composed and high exploit:
But all was false and hollow; though his tongue
Dropped manna, and could make the worse appear
The better reason, to perplex and dash
Maturest counsels: for his thoughts were low;
To vice industrious, but to nobler deeds
Timorous and slothful: yet he pleased the ear."

The end of Antony's oratory is perfect success : —

> "Now let it work ! Mischief, thou art afoot ;
> Take thou what course thou wilt ! "

The rhetoric has done its work : the conflict of principles is coming to a close ; the conflict of individuals is about to begin ; it is no longer a question of republican Rome, or monarchical Rome. The question is, whether it shall be the Rome of Antony, or the Rome of Octavius ; for Lepidus there is no chance : —

> "This is a slight, unmeritable man."

But even he is ready to do his work. He can proscribe ; he can even consent to the death of his brother, "upon conditions." He requires that "Publius shall not live." Antony has no scruples to save his "sister's son : " —

> "He shall not live : look, with a spot I damn him."

Such an intense representation of selfishness was never before given in a dozen lines. What power have Brutus and Cassius to oppose to this worldly wisdom ? Is it the virtue of Brutus ? Of him who

> "Condemned and noted Lucius Pella,
> For taking bribes here of the Sardians."

Of him who

> "Had rather be a dog and bay the moon"

than

> "Contaminate his fingers."

Of him who says, —

> "I had rather coin my heart,
> And drop my blood for drachmas, than to wring
> From the hard hands of peasants their vile trash
> By any indirection!"

No; the man of principles must fall before the man of expediency. He can conquer Cassius by his high-mindedness; for Cassius, though somewhat politic, has nobility enough in him to bow before the majesty of virtue. Coleridge says, "I know no part of Shakspeare that more impresses on me the belief of his genius being superhuman than this scene between Brutus and Cassius." This language has been called idolatry: some critic, we believe, says "blasphemous;" yet let any one with common human powers try to produce such a scene. The wonderful thing in it, and that which — in a subsequent sentence, which we scarcely dare quote — Coleridge points out, is the complete preservation of character. All dramatic poets have tried to imitate this scene. Dryden preferred his imitation, in the famous dialogue between Antony and Ventidius, to any thing which he had written "in this kind." It is full of high rhetoric, no doubt; but its rhetoric is that of generalizations. The plain, rough soldier, the luxurious chief, reproach and weep, are angry and cool again, shake hands, and end in "hugging," as the stage direction has it. They say all that people would say under such circumstances, and they say it well. But the matchless art of Shakspeare consists as much in what he holds back as in what he puts forward. Brutus subdues Cassius by the force of his moral strength, without the slighest attempt to command the feelings of a sensitive man. When Cassius *is* subdued, he owns that he has been hasty. They are friends again, hand and heart. Is not the knowledge of character something above the ordinary reach of human sagacity when the following words come in as if by accident? —

> "*Bru.* Lucius, a bowl of wine.
> *Cass.* I did not think you could have been so angry.

Bru. O, Cassius, I am sick of many griefs.
Cass. Of your philosophy you make no use,
If you give place to accidental evils.
Bru. No man bears sorrow better: Portia is dead.
Cass. Ha! Portia?
Bru. She is dead.
Cass. How 'scaped I killing when I crossed you so!"

This is not in Plutarch.

The shade of Cæsar has summoned Brutus to meet him at Philippi. The conversation of the republican chiefs before the battle is well to be noted: —

"*Cass.* Now, most noble Brutus,
The gods to-day stand friendly; that we may,
Lovers in peace, lead on our days to age!
But, since the affairs of men rest still uncertain,
Let's reason with the worst that may befall.
If we do lose this battle, then is this
The very last time we shall speak together:
What are you then determined to do?
Bru. Even by the rule of that philosophy
By which I did blame Cato for the death
Which he did give himself: — I know not how,
But I do find it cowardly and vile,
For fear of what might fall, so to prevent
The time of life: — arming myself with patience,
To stay the providence of some high powers
That govern us below.
Cass. Then, if we lose this battle,
You are contented to be led in triumph
Through the streets of Rome?
Bru. No, Cassius, no: think not, thou noble Roman,
That ever Brutus will go bound to Rome;
He bears too great a mind."

The parallel passage in Plutarch is as follows: —

"Then Cassius began to speak first, and said, The gods grant us, O Brutus, that this day we may win the field, and ever after to live all the rest of our life quietly, one with another. But sith the gods have so ordained it that the greatest and chiefest things amongst men are most uncertain, and that, if the battle fall out otherwise to-day than we wish or look for, we shall hardly meet again, what art thou then determined to do — to fly, or die? Brutus answered him, Being yet but a young man, and not over-greatly experienced in the world, I *trust* (I know not how) a certain rule of philosophy, by the which I did greatly blame and reprove Cato for killing of himself, as being no lawful nor godly act touching the gods, nor concerning men valiant, not to give place and yield to Divine Providence, and not constantly and patiently to take whatsoever it pleaseth him to send us, but to draw back and fly: but being now in the midst of the danger, I am of a contrary mind; for if it be not the will of God that this battle fall out fortunate for us, I will look no more for hope, neither seek to make any new supply of war again, but will rid me of this miserable world, and content me with my fortune."

The critics say that Shakspeare makes Brutus express himself inconsistently. He will await the determination of Providence, but he will not go bound to Rome. Mr. Courtenay explains how "the inconsistency arises from Shakspeare's misreading of the first speech; for Brutus, according to North, referred to his opinion against suicide as one that he had entertained in his youth, but had now abandoned." This writer in a note also explains that the perplexity consists in North saying *I trust*, instead of using the past tense. He then adds, "Shakspeare's adoption of a version contradicted not only by a passage immediately following, but by the event which he presently portrays, is a striking instance of his careless use of his authorities." * Very triumphant, no doubt. Most literal critics, why have you not rather confided in Shakspeare than in yourselves? When he deserts Plutarch, he is true to something higher than Plutarch. In Brutus he has drawn a man of speculation; one who is moved to kill the man he loves upon no personal motive, but upon a theory; one who fights his last battle upon somewhat speculative principles; one, however, who, from his gentleness, his constancy, his fortitude, has subdued men of more active minds to the admiration of his temper and to the adoption of his opinions. Cassius never reasons about suicide: it is his instant rem-

* Commentaries on the Historical Plays, vol. ii. p. 255.

edy; a remedy which he rashly adopts, and ruins, therefore, his own cause. Brutus reasons against it; and he does not revoke his speculative opinions even when the consequences to which they lead are pointed out to him. Is not this nature? and must we be told that this nicety of characterization resulted from Shakspeare carelessly using his authorities: trusting to the false tense of a verb, regardless of the context? "But he contradicts himself," says the critic, "by the event which he presently portrays." Most wonderfully has Shakspeare redeemed his own consistency. It is when the mind of the speculative man is not only utterly subdued by adverse circumstances, but bowed down before the pressure of supernatural warnings, that he deliberately approaches his last fatal resolve. What is the work of an instant with Cassius is with Brutus a tentative process. Clitus, Dardanius, Volumnius, Strato, are each tried. The irresistible pressure upon his mind, which leads him not to fly with his friends, is the *destiny* which hovers over him:—

"*Bru.* Come hither, good Volumnius: list a word.
Vol. What says my lord?
Bru. Why, this, Volumnius:
The ghost of Cæsar hath appeared to me
Two several times by night: at Sardis, once;
And, this last night, here in Philippi fields.
I know my hour is come."

The exclamation of Brutus over the body of Cassius is,—

"The last of all the Romans, fare thee well!"

Brutus himself is the last assertor of the old Roman *principles*:—

"This was the noblest Roman of them all:
All the conspirators, save only he,
Did that they did in envy of great Cæsar;
He only, in a general honest thought,
And common good to all, made one of them."

The scene is changed. The boldest, perhaps the noblest, of the Roman triumvirs, has almost forgotten Rome, and governs the Asiatic world with a magnificence equalled only by the voluptuousness into which he is plunged. In Rome, Octavius Cæsar is almost supreme. It is upon the cards which shall govern the *entire* world. The history of *individuals* is henceforth the history of Rome.

"Of all Shakspeare's historical plays," says Coleridge, "Antony and Cleopatra is by far the most wonderful." He again says, assigning it a place even higher than that of being the most wonderful of the *historical* plays, "The highest praise, or, rather, form of praise, of this play, which I can offer in my own mind, is the doubt which the perusal always occasions in me, whether the Antony and Cleopatra is not, in all exhibitions of a giant power in its strength and vigor of maturity, a formidable rival of Macbeth, Lear, Hamlet, and Othello." * The epithet "wonderful" is unquestionably the right one to apply to this drama. It is too vast, too gorgeous, to be approached without some prostration of the understanding. It pours such a flood of noonday splendor upon our senses, that we cannot gaze upon it steadily. We have read it again and again; and the impression which it leaves again and again is that of wonder. We can comprehend it, reduce its power to some standard, only by the analysis of *a part.* Mrs. Jameson has adopted this course in one of her most brilliant "Characteristics of Women." Treading in her steps timidly, we may venture to attempt a companion sketch to her portrait of "Cleopatra." It is in the spirit of the play itself, as the last of the Roman series, that we shall endeavor to follow it, by confining ourselves as much as may be to an *individual.* We use the word in the sense in which Mr. Hare uses it, after some good-natured ridicule of the newspaper "individuals:" a man "is an individual, so far as he is an integral whole, different and distinct from

* Literary Remains, vol. ii. p. 142.

other men; and that which makes him what he is, that in which he differs and is distinguished from other men, is his individuality, and individualizes him." *

The Antony of this play is, of course, the Antony of Julius Cæsar; not merely the historical Antony, but the dramatic Antony, drawn by the same hand. He is the orator that showed dead Cæsar's mantle to the Roman people; he is the soldier that after his triumph over Brutus said, "This was a man." We have seen something of his character; we have learnt a little of his voluptuousness; we have heard of the "masker and the reveller;" we have beheld the unscrupulous politician. But we cannot think meanly of him. He is one great, either for good or for evil. Since he fought at Philippi he has passed through various fortunes: Cæsar thus apostrophizes him:—

"When thou once
Was beaten from Modena, where thou slew'st
Hirtius and Pansa, consuls, at thy heel
Did Famine follow; whom thou fought'st against,
Though daintily brought up, with patience more
Than savages could suffer."

There came an after-time when, at Alexandria,—

"Our courteous Antony,
Whom ne'er the word of 'No' woman heard speak,
Being barbered ten times o'er, goes to the feast;
And, for his ordinary, pays his heart."

This is the Antony that Shakspeare, in the play before us, brings upon the scene. Rome is to him nothing. He will hear not its ambassadors:—

"There 's not a minute of our lives should stretch
Without some pleasure now."

* Guesses at Truth, p. 139.

But "a Roman thought hath struck him." He does hear the messenger. Labienus has overrun Asia. He winces at the thought of his own inertness, but he will know the truth: —

> "Speak to me home: mince not the general tongue."

Another messenger comes. Brief is his news: —

> "Fulvia, thy wife, is dead;"

and brief is the question which follows: —

> "Where died she?"

The comment shows the man: —

> "There's a great spirit gone: *thus did I desire it.*"

We learn why he did desire it, in the scene with Cleopatra, in which he announces his departure. Often has he heard, from the same lips, the bitter irony of

> "What says *the married woman?*"

He has been bound to Cleopatra not only by her "infinite variety," but by her caprice and her force of ridicule. His moral power is as weak as his physical courage is strong. Cleopatra paints the magnificent soldier and the infatuated lover in a few words: —

> "The demi-Atlas of this earth, the arm
> And burgonet of men. He's speaking now,
> Or murmuring 'Where's my serpent of old Nile?'
> *For so he calls me.*"

He has fled from Cleopatra, but he sends her his messenger: —

> "All the east,
> Say thou, shall call her mistress."

In this temper he meets Cæsar, and he marries Octavia.

The interview between Antony and Cæsar is most masterly. The constrained courtesy on each side — the coldness of Cæsar — the frank apologies of Antony — the suggestion of Agrippa, so opportune, and yet apparently so unpremeditated — the ready assent of Antony — all this — matter for rhetorical flourishes of at least five hundred lines in the hands of an ordinary dramatist — may be read without a start or an elevation of the voice. It is solid business throughout. Antony, we might think, was a changed man. Enobarbus, who knows him, is of a different opinion. Wonderfully has he described Cleopatra; and when Mecænas says, —

> "Now Antony must leave her utterly," —

the answer is prophetic: —

> "Never; he will not:
> Age cannot wither her, nor custom stale
> Her infinite variety."

Against this power Enobarbus knows that the "beauty, wisdom, modesty" of Octavia will be a fragile bond. And Antony knows this himself. He knows this while he protests, —

> "I have not kept my square; but that to come
> Shall all be done by the rule."

And yet he is not wholly a dissembler. Shakspeare has most skilfully introduced the soothsayer, at the moment when Antony's moral weakness appears to have put on some show of strength. He found the incident in Plutarch; but he has made his own application of it: —

"Be it art, or hap,
He hath spoken true. The very dice obey him:
And in our sports my better cunning faints
Under his chance: if we draw lots, he speeds:
His cocks do win the battle still of mine,
When it is all to nought; and his quails ever
Beat mine, inhooped, at odds."

Therefore, —

"I will to Egypt."

To establish an independent throne? — to entrench himself against the power of Augustus in an Asiatic empire? No.

"And though I make this marriage for my peace,
I' the east my pleasure lies."

The reckless, short-sighted voluptuary was never drawn more truly. His entire policy is shaped by his passion. The wonderful scene in which his marriage with Octavia is made known to Cleopatra assures us that in the extremest intemperance of self-will he will have his equal. Cleopatra would have Antony unmarried, —

"So half my Egypt were submerged, and made
A cistern for scaled snakes."

According to Enobarbus, the unmarrying will scarcely be necessary for her gratification: —

"*Eno.* Octavia is of a holy, cold, and still conversation.
Men. Who would not have his wife so?
Eno. Not he, that himself is not so; which is Mark Antony."

The drinking scene between the Triumvirs and Pompey is one of those creations which render Shakspeare so entirely above, and so utterly unlike, other poets. Every line is a trait of character. We here see the solemn, "unmeritable" Lepidus; the cautious Cæsar; the dashing, clever, genial Antony. His eye dances; his whole visage "doth cream and mantle;" the corners of his mouth are drawn down, as he hoaxes Lepidus with the most admirable fooling: —

> "*Lep.* What manner o' thing is your crocodile?
> *Ant.* It is shaped, sir, like itself; and it is as broad as it hath breadth: it is just so high as it is, and moves with its own organs," &c.
> "*Lep.* 'T is a sharp serpent."

The revelry grows louder and louder, till "the Egyptian bacchanals" close the scene. Who can doubt that Antony bears "the holding" the loudest of all? —

> "As loud
> As his strong sides can volley."

These are not the lords of the world of the French tragedy. Grimm, who, upon the whole, has a leaning to Shakspeare, says, "Il est assez ridicule sans doute de faire parler les valets comme les héros; mais il est beaucoup *plus ridicule encore* de faire parler aux héros le langage du peuple."* To make them drunk is worse even than the worst of the ridiculous. It is impossible to define such a sin. We think, with Dogberry, it is "flat burglary as ever was committed." Upton has a curious theory, which would partly make Shakspeare to belong to the French school. The hero of this play, according to this theory, does not speak "the language of the people." Upton says, "Mark Antony, as

* Correspondance Littéraire, Troisième Partie, tom. i. p. 129.

Plutarch informs us, affected the Asiatic manner of speaking, which much resembled his own temper, being ambitious, unequal, and very rhodomontade. . . . . This style our poet has very artfully and learnedly interspersed in Antony's speeches."* Unquestionably the language of Antony is more elevated than that of Enobarbus, for example. Antony was of the poetical temperament — a man of high genius — an orator, who could move the passions dramatically — a lover, that knew no limits to his devotion, because he loved imaginatively. When sorrow falls upon him, the poetical parts of his character are more and more developed; we forget the sensualist. But even before the touch of grief has somewhat exalted his nature, he takes the poetical view of poetical things. What can be more exquisite than his mention of Octavia's weeping at the parting with her brother? —

> "The April's in her eyes: it is love's spring,
> And these the showers to bring it on."

And, higher still: —

> "Her tongue will not obey her heart, nor can
> Her heart inform her tongue: the swan's down feather,
> That stands upon the swell at the full of tide,
> And neither way inclines."

This, we think, is not "the Asiatic manner of speaking."

Cold is Antony's parting with Octavia: —

> "Choose your own company, and command what cost
> Your heart has mind to."

Rapid is his meeting with Cleopatra. She "hath nodded

* Critical Observations, p. 100.

him to her." The voluptuary has put on his eastern magnificence: —

"I' the market-place, on a tribunal silvered,
Cleopatra and himself in chairs of gold
Were publicly enthroned."

He rejects all counsel: "I'll fight at sea." And so

"The greater cantle of the world is lost
With very ignorance."

Now comes the generosity of his character — of the same growth as his magnificence and his recklessness. He exhorts his friends to take his treasure and fly to Cæsar. His self-abasement is most profound: —

"I have offended reputation."

But he has not yet learnt wisdom. Cleopatra is present, and then, —

"Fall not a tear, I say; one of them rates
All that is won or lost. Give me a kiss;
Even this repays me."

He then becomes a braggart; he will challenge Cæsar, "sword against sword." Profound is the comment of Enobarbus: —

"I see, men's judgments are
A parcel of their fortunes; and things outward
Do draw the inward quality after them,
To suffer all alike."

Cæsar's ambassador comes to Cleopatra. He tempts her; — and it almost looks as if she yielded to the temptation. He kisses her hand, at the instant Antony enters: —

"Moon and stars!
Whip him."

This is partly jealousy; partly the last assertion of small power by one accustomed to unlimited command. Truly Enobarbus says, —

"'T is better playing with a lion's whelp,
Than with an old one dying."

Shakspeare makes this man the interpreter of his own wisdom: —

"I see still
A diminution in our captain's brain
Restores his heart. When valor preys on reason,
It eats the sword it fights with. I will seek
Some way to leave him."

Enobarbus *does* leave him. But he first witnesses

"One of those odd tricks which sorrow shoots
Out of the mind."

Antony puts forth the poetry of his nature in his touching words to his followers, ending in

"Let's to supper, come,
And drown consideration."

When he hears of the treachery of Enobarbus, he again tasks the generosity of his spirit to the utmost: —

"Go, Eros, send his treasure after; do it:
Detain no jot, I charge thee."

He has driven Cæsar "to his camp." All Cleopatra's trespass is forgotten in one burst of enthusiasm: —

"My nightingale,
We have beat them to their beds. What, girl? though gray
Do something mingle with our younger brown;
Yet ha' we a brain that nourishes our nerves,
And can get goal for goal of youth."

Another day comes, and it brings another note: —

"All is lost;
This foul Egyptian hath betrayed me."

Cleopatra says truly, —

"He is more mad
Than Telamon for his shield."

The scene which terminates with Antony falling on his sword is in the highest style of Shakspeare — and that is to give the highest praise. Hazlitt has eloquently said of its magnificent opening, "This is, without doubt, one of the finest pieces of poetry in Shakspeare. The splendor of the imagery, the semblance of reality, the lofty range of picturesque objects hanging over the world, their evanescent nature, the total uncertainty of what is left behind, are just like the mouldering schemes of human greatness." But, be it observed, the poetry is all in keeping with the character of the man. Let us once more repeat it: —

"*Ant.* Eros, thou yet behold'st me.
Eros. Ay, noble lord.
Ant. Sometime we see a cloud that's dragonish:
A vapor, sometime, like a bear, or lion,
A towered citadel, a pendent rock,
A forked mountain, or blue promontory
With trees upon't, that nod unto the world,
And mock our eyes with air: thou hast seen these signs;
They are black vesper's pageants.
Eros. Ay, my lord.
Ant. That which is now a horse, even with a thought
The rack dislimns; and makes it indistinct,
As water is in water.

Eros. It does, my lord.
Ant. My good knave, Eros, now thy captain is
Even such a body; here I am Antony,
Yet cannot hold this visible shape, my knave."

The images describe the Antony, melting into nothingness; but the splendor of the imagery is the reflection of Antony's mind, which, thus enshrined in poetry, can never become "indistinct,"—will always "hold this visible shape." Dryden has also tried to produce a poetical Antony, precisely under the same circumstances. We transcribe a passage:—

"*Ant.* My eyes
Are open to her falsehood: my whole life
Has been a golden dream, of Love and Friendship.
But, now I wake, I'm like a merchant, roused
From soft repose, to see his vessel sinking,
And all his wealth cast o'er. Ingrateful woman!
Who followed me, but as the swallow summer,
Hatching her young ones in my kindly beams,
Singing her flatteries to my morning wake;
But, now my winter comes, she spreads her wings,
And seeks the spring of Cæsar."

All for Love, Act V.

We hasten to the end. The magnificence of Antony's character breathes out of his parting spirit:—

"The miserable change now at my end,
Lament nor sorrow at: but please your thoughts,
In feeding them with those my former fortunes
Wherein I lived, the greatest prince o' the world,
The noblest: and do now not basely die,
Nor cowardly put off my helmet to
My countryman,—A ROMAN BY A ROMAN
VALIANTLY VANQUISHED."

www.ingramcontent.com/pod-product-compliance
Lightning Source LLC
LaVergne TN
LVHW021200120826
845150LV00011B/1036